The Black West

Revised Edition

FULCRUM

To Dr. Sara Jackson
dear friend, teacher, scholar

Library of Congress Cataloging-in-Publication Data

Katz, William Loren.
The Black West / by William Loren Katz.—1st ed.
p. cm.
Originally published: New York : Doubleday, 1971.
Includes bibliographical references and index.
1. African Americans—West (U.S.)—History.   2. African Americans—West (U.S.)—Biography.
3. African American pioneers—West (U.S.)—History.   4. Frontier and pioneer life—West (U.S.)
5. West (U.S.)—History   6. West (U.S.)—Biography.
I. Title.
E185.925.K37 2005
978'.00496073'00922—dc22   2003061218

ISBN 978-1-68275-226-5

First edition published in 1971.

Printed in the United States of America.
0 9 8 7 6 5 4 3 2 1

Fulcrum Publishing
4690 Table Mountain Drive, Suite 100
Golden, Colorado 80403
800-992-2908 • 303-277-1623
fulcrumbookstore.ipgbook.com

Revised Edition

The
Black
West

A Documentary and Pictorial History
of the African American Role in the
Westward Expansion of the United States

William Loren Katz
Foreword by Dr. Quintard Taylor

Other Books by William Loren Katz

The Cruel Years: American Voices at the Dawn of the 20th Century

Black Pioneers: An Untold Story

Black Legacy: A History of New York's African Americans

Black Indians: A Hidden Heritage

Flight from the Devils: Six Slave Narratives

The Lincoln Brigade: A Picture History

Black Women of the Old West

Proudly Red and Black

A History of Multicultural America, eight volumes

Exploration to the War of 1812, 1492–1814

The Westward Movement and Abolitionism, 1815–1850

The Civil War and the Last Frontier, 1850–1880

The Great Migrations, 1880–1912

The New Freedom to the New Deal, 1913–1939

World War II to the New Frontier, 1940–1963

The Great Society to the Reagan Era, 1964–1990

Minorities Today

Black People Who Made the Old West

Breaking the Chains: African American Slave Resistance

The Invisible Empire: The Ku Klux Klan's Impact on US History

An Album of Nazism

An Album of the Great Depression

Making Our Way: America at the Turn of the Century

Minorities in American History, six volumes

An Album of the Civil War

An Album of the Reconstruction

The Constitutional Amendments

A History of Black Americans

A Guide to Black Studies Resources

American Majorities and Minorities

Five Slave Narratives

Teachers' Guide to American Negro History

Eyewitness: A Living Documentary of the African American Contribution to US History

Contents

Foreword by Quintard Taylor .... *ix*

From the Author: Tribute to My Favorite Detectives .... *xi*

Introduction .... *xvii*

1. Indians and Africans in the Age of Exploration 1

2. Trappers, Guides, and Mountain Men 28

3. Going West 42

4. Slavery on the Frontier 68

5. The Crisis Years 89

6. The Civil War in the West 105

7. California 117

8. The Cowhands 145

9. Exodus to Kansas 178

10. The Buffalo Soldiers 200

11. Oklahoma 232

12. Black Women of the Last Frontier 249

13. Empire: Buffalo Soldiers Abroad 271

14. A Black West in White America 283

    Afterword 296

    Acknowledgments 299

    Bibliography 302

    Photo Credits 310

    Index 314

Foreword

In 1971 I began my professorial teaching career at Washington State University. At the time I assumed that my research and teaching interests would follow the work I had done in African American urban history in graduate school at the University of Minnesota. While I was lecturing in an African American history class that fall, an undergraduate student, Billy Ray Flowers, challenged me to understand that African American history was made in the West as well as the South and the North. I took up that challenge and begin my lifelong dedication to studying Black history in the West.

That same year William L. Katz's *The Black West: A Pictorial History* was released, and it provided a road map for my subsequent research. Then and now the book with its rare photos, succinct narrative, and newly uncovered documents, made clear the impossibility of continuing to overlook this history as so many had done up to that point.

A close look at the structure of my 1998 book, *In Search of the Racial Frontier: African Americans in the American West, 1528–1990*, reveals the guiding influence of *The Black West*. The explorers, fur traders, early settlers, cowboys, and buffalo soldiers quickened my interest and challenged me and many others across the nation, to take note of the people who heretofore had been excluded from definitive histories of the region, from textbooks at every level, and from what at the time shaped popular culture, the movies, and TV.

Three chapters were particularly important in shaping my vision of the West: "Slavery in the West," "California," and "Oklahoma." While *The Black West* was not the first book to cover these areas, it was my introduction to the people and events that shaped the African American experience west of the 98th meridian. *Slavery in the West*, for example, exposed me for the first time to the peculiar institution in the trans-Mississippi West. The chapter on California introduced me not only to African American participation in the Gold Rush, but just as importantly to the first significant urban settlements, which would become critical in understanding the contemporary Black West. The Oklahoma chapter made me aware for the first time of the complex and often contradictory relationship between two groups of color, African Americans and Native Americans.

This edition contains a new chapter on the Civil War in the West, exploring the challenges by Black and white westerners faced in responding to the Lincoln Administration's initial intent to wage war for the preservation of the Union without abolishing slavery where it existed. Black and white Western abolitionists refused to concede that point, and soon after the first shots were fired on Fort Sumter, Union officers in the West were incorporating Black soldiers into their ranks. Those accounts should put to rest the idea that the 54th Massachusetts Infantry Regiment included the first Black soldiers in the war. This chapter also complicates the usual Black-white binary in discussions of the Civil War by introducing the conflict in Indian Territory, which proved to be as deeply divided as the entire nation over slavery and seccession. Confederate Indians fought Union loyalists, who also incorporated some of the Black soldiers into their ranks, thus creating the first truly multicultural army in the Civil War.

I was too young and professionally inexperienced to have written the foreword for the first edition in 1971. I am flattered and humbled to be asked to write this now for the sixth edition. The fact that there is a sixth edition is powerful testimony to the continued strength and appeal of *The Black West*. I have absolutely no doubt that it will inspire others as it did a young assistant professor at Washington State University forty-seven years ago.

Quintard Taylor
Scott and Dorothy Bullitt Professor of American History (Emeritus)
University of Washington, Seattle

From the Author: Tribute to My Favorite Detectives

Last year, as I entered my nineties, I began preparing new editions of some of my forty books. As I worked, I again stared back at the many individuals who provided enormous help throughout my career.

Some had suggested people and events and organizations I had not stumbled on as research topics. Others confirmed areas I was exploring but pointed to neglected material and figures requiring attention. And still others handed me documents and pictures from their personal family collection with a (gentle) "Don't forget to use this!" command.

Like every other time I stopped to look at my many benefactors, beginning in my high school years, I was not surprised to find that so many were women. And, given the focus of my research for more than half a century, it is even less surprising that many of these helpers were women of color – those with and without scholarly credentials.

My earliest books had stirred artists from many fields to communicate their warmth and enthusiasm for the subject matter, often sending along their artistic responses – poems, biographical studies, drawings, paintings, religious novels, and so forth. Most striking was the response from a young creative writer who taught in the Mississippi Freedom Schools in 1967: Alice Walker. She sent along her warm regards, and later responded to the publisher of a new edition of *The Black West* with a statement of admiration for my research and what she believed was its greater meaning. She soon sent me her first book of poems, then her first novel, and soon I discovered she used my research on Black Indians as the foundation stone in her work, *Temple of My Familiar*. For a historian just launching his career, it was quite the starting gun.

What I am saying is that many people who responded to my work were beginners, but they were hardly minor figures in my research. They were determined explorers who made a significant contribution and difference for both my books, and for me personally as a researcher, fact assembler, and titled author. I diligently tried to capture their efforts in acknowledgment pages so my reading public could share my appreciation for their contributions.

Sadly, a few flickered in and out of my life so briefly they had little time to offer their names. Most prominent in my memory is the tall Black professor who recognized and stopped me on a stair landing during an African American history conference in New York City in the late 1960s. He thrust his photograph of a young Ida B. Wells into my hands and then hurried on without explaining who he was or how he came on the picture of young Wells at the outset of her antilynching crusade.

In this photo, Ida Wells's face shows her daring and enormous courage in her effort to end mob lynching by exposing its false claims of protecting white womanhood. (She was driven from her home, and her newspaper office was burned by a mob.)

Through her work, she showed how this false argument allowed its perpetrators – from Southern governors to local sheriffs to ordinary white citizens – to gain impunity and continue their scourge of illegal mass murders. Elected officials and the Southern press also encouraged these murders, which took about three lives a week from the late 19th to early 20th centuries.

By the time I put together *Black Women of the Old West*, seasoned historians and museum curators enthusiastically contributed research suggestions, advice, and pictures. Barbara Richardson of Tucson, Arizona, and I worked out a financial arrangement so her beautiful private picture collection would be fully represented among these Western women of color. Barbara also contributed a picture-essay on the subject for a subsequent edition of *The Black West*. Prominent white women historians, delighted the subject was being seriously explored, ensured that I was invited to scholarly conferences to display and discuss my pictures and research.

Needless to say, this outpouring of love and help by fellow historians was personally overwhelming, and made the coffee-table-size project a success among critics ranging from the Sunday *New York Times Book Review* to ordinary readers.

As I reminisce about the course of these wonderful relationships, I would be remiss in not mentioning one of the other friendships that grew from my life's work. Back in 1976, I was working away one afternoon when a man named George Tooks walked up the stairs to my apartment holding out what looked like a summons. We had never spoken or met, he came unannounced, and because he was so neatly dressed and thrusting that envelope, I assumed the bad news, "You've been served!"

The Tooks brothers – Lance, George, and Ed – with me in my home office around 1976.

Was I ever wrong! George and Ed Tooks, in connection with an Ossie Davis theater workshop, were seeking tales of Black pioneers. They grew up in Altoona, Pennsylvania, loved horses and tales of Black cowhands, and kept hearing rumors about Black and Indigenous ancestors. When they found my book, *The Black West*, they were on their way to becoming prize-winning musical directors. After reading my book, George had simply looked up my address and walked over to meet me.

During our afternoon together, he offered me a copy of his and his brother's cassette, "Black Son of the West," saying it was dedicated to me, and we listened to his take on the Black Western experience. Since prejudice against Indians was so blatant in Altoona, his Aunt Rosalind had brought up George's family hiding the family's Apache and Cherokee ancestry behind her African American roots. The brothers almost accidently discovered

PHIL POMPEY FIXICO

Phil Pompey Fixico was born into African and Native American families, and if the DNA and career of a single name today can symbolize the history of heroic Black Indian resistance to colonialism and slavery in North America, it is Phil Pompey Fixico.

In 2009, Fixico founded the Semiroon Historical Society, and three years later he recommended that the National Park Service ask me to deliver the Keynote Speech at their groundbreaking conference. The subject of my speech, "The Underground Railroad That Ran South (through Indian country)," was an increasingly forgotten chapter of history. Fixico's goal was to reveal this thrilling story of resistance.

Fixico introduced me as "the godfather of Black Indian studies," and we teamed up to bring this story to the wider public through media interviews and essays. Many pages in this revised edition of *The Black West* are based on his family's lifelong contribution.

Fixico, born in 1947, thought he was just another struggling Black child in Los Angeles. At age fifty-two, he learned from a Black Indian cousin that his family tree could be traced back to Renty Mcintosh Rentie, an ancestor born in French West Africa in 1800 and sold as a slave. He confirmed this fact with other descendants of Oklahoma's Seminole Maroon community.

Anthropologist Kevin Mulroy wrote a sixteen-thousand-word study of Fixico's family roots for the scholarly journal *Ethnohistory: African-Native American Lives in the Americas*. The Smithsonian featured a version of Mulroy's article in their publication, *Indivisible* (Washington D.C.: Smithsonian, 2009). Mulroy used the Fixico-Bruner-Rentie family tree to explore many kinds of African and Indigenous American connections in the Americas.

Mulroy's widely cited work explained how Fixico's ancestors led varied roles in resisting European colonialism and slavery, ranging from cagey diplomacy to guerilla warfare. Fixico's great-grandfather, Seminole Maroon band leader Caesar Bruner, had a child with a Mikasuki Seminole named Dinah Fixico. Their child was Pompey Bruner Fixico, Phil's paternal grandfather.

Phil's great-grandfather, Caesar Bruner, married Nancy Lincoln, the granddaughter of Prophet Abraham, the Seminole Maroon warrior of "Fort Negro" fame. They had eight children and a plethora of cousins through the generations. Beginning in 1816, Prophet Abraham and other Fixico ancestors battled the U.S. Army in Florida in three Seminole Wars, from 1816–1852. Abraham was among those who served as interpreters and negotiators when the United States seized and purchased Florida.

Fixico (center) and the 2019 delegation of Maroon descendants address the United Nations.

Fixico's Seminole kinfolk continued the long Black Indian resistance. Caesar Bruner (paternal grandfather), Pickett Rentie (great-great-grandfather), and Seminole Osa Eneha Fixico (another great-great-grandfather) all survived Chief Opothleyahola's terrifying 1861 "Trail of Blood on Ice" from Oklahoma to Kansas. In May 1862, all three men joined the First Indian Home Guard in the first African American Civil War unit. In September 1862, the three were among General Blount's Kansas Army that invaded Missouri and nearby slave states in the Trans-Mississippi West. They terrified planters, disrupted the plantation system, and brought hope and liberation to thousands.

Fixico's family members later served in the famed Seminole Negro Indian Scouts. Others became Buffalo Soldiers for the U.S. Army.

Fixico described his mixed heritage: one-eighth Seminole Indian, one-quarter Seminole freedman, one-eighth Creek freedman, one-quarter Cherokee freedman, and one-quarter African-American/white. His ancestral tale brought him unplanned personal fulfillment and led to a successful career as a certified surgical first assistant in the Beverly Hills community.

As president of the Semiroon Historical Society of North America, Fixico continues to spread the story of these early American freedom fighters. He has addressed societies of descendants in the Caribbean, South America, and Mexico. In the United States, he has been a guest speaker at the Smithsonian Institute, Fort Negro in Florida, and many schools and libraries.

William Loren Katz

their Indigenous roots years later from distant relatives, including a great-great-grandfather who served as a buffalo soldier.

In the 1950s, George and Ed formed a gospel group that melted into The Velvets, a rhythm and blues group. They performed at Pete Seeger's Clearwater Festival, sang with The Orioles, and today offer musicals on Black West Pioneers and Black Indian Storytelling. In 1989, they won an AUDELCO Award* for their powerful Korean War drama.

Since 1976, the Tooks brothers and I worked both separately and together. I wrote books and they produced songs, plays, and performances that challenged the John-Wayne, lily-white Hollywood West. As I lectured at colleges and museums, George gave performances for public school students and libraries. When *Black Indians* appeared, George and I introduced it to audiences at the American Museum of Natural History.

As *The Black West* moves into its sixth expanded edition, George has been a most helpful collaborator. When Ed died in 1996, George also continued to offer his acting and singing talents throughout the New York/New Jersey area. And he is still at it... as am I.

For our work needs to continue.

William Loren Katz
2019

George and me,
enjoying a
little time away
from our work.

*The AUDELCO Awards were established in 1973 to give recognition to Black productions, composers, and actors

INTRODUCTION

This book grew out of a phone conversation I had with Langston Hughes shortly before he died in 1967. I had written to request permission to quote from his writing in my first book, *Eyewitness*. He called to ask about the book, and when I explained it was designed as a school text, his response was immediate:

"Don't leave out the cowboys!" I think he said it twice.

"No, I didn't," I said. "In fact, I have two chapters on them."

"Good, good," he said. "That's very important."

Don't leave out the cowboys. Why was that his one piece of advice? From the late 1800s to the dawn of the twenty-first century no phase of our national heritage has been portrayed – in fiction, textbooks, and films – as more typically American than the old West, yet this particular slice of Americana has consistently been pictured as lily-white.

Langston Hughes knew better. He could trace his ancestors to two frontiersmen: John Mercer Langston, an early Ohio lawyer who took part in 1858 in his state's most violent, dramatic, and successful effort to free a fugitive slave, and Lewis Sheridan Leary, a harness maker and student at Oberlin College, who was among the first to volunteer for John Brown's raid on Harpers Ferry. An enslaved African led a European expedition that opened Arizona and New Mexico to colonization. Women and men of African descent got to Helena, Montana, when it was still called Last Chance Gulch; Denver when it was Cherry Creek; and Oklahoma when it was the Indian Territory. They founded towns in half a dozen territories and states.

If African American youths were to feel a part of the country, and if whites were to see them as a part, Langston Hughes was saying, the West's real cast of characters had to be revealed. African American men and women had to ride across the pages of textbooks just as they rode across the Western plains. His insight inspired *The Black West*.

America's frontier tale early became an icon of extraordinary potency that leaped beyond U.S. borders. In eighteenth-century France, Voltaire wrote, "If the American frontier did not exist, it would have to have been invented." In nineteenth-century England, Lord Bryce called it "the most American part of America." Early in the twentieth century President Woodrow Wilson proclaimed, "A frontier people is, so far, the central and determining fact of our national history... The West is the great word of our history. The Westerner has been the type and master of our American life." President John F. Kennedy named his administration's program the New Frontier – and critics have derisively labeled Presidents Lyndon Johnson, Ronald Reagan, and George W. Bush as "cowboys."

In 1893 Frederick Jackson Turner delivered a scholarly paper arguing that the frontier experience shaped American democracy. His "Turner thesis" influenced U.S. historiography more than any other theory. Professor Turner strongly believed in democracy and exhibited no racial malice, but he wrote at the high-water mark of white racial violence in the United States, and accepted the traditional denial of his time there had been any meaningful Black participation in history. Turner even defined his most exhilarating word – "frontier" – in racial terms: "the meeting point between savagery and civilization."

The frontier has been embraced for generations as the greatest American story ever told, an epic victory of the human spirit, the starting point, historical proving ground, and finest hour of our cherished values. The media have used frontier heroes and villains to strum vital chords in our national identity. Swashbuckling cowhands on horseback became the country's greatest folk legends. Cast as archetypal outdoor heroes, cowhands enter the popular mind as the way we were, the way we wanted to be, the way we wished to see ourselves, the way to solve problems. Hollywood studios brewed frontier blood, sacrifice, and conquest into dramatic epics designed to bond white citizens. These "horse operas" established exactly who built the country and who didn't.

This traditional version is slanted and woefully incomplete. It is not subject to Indian claims and has no room for African Americans. This fable usually omits the wanton genocide of Native Americans and glorifies such "Indian fighters" as General William T. Sherman, who in 1866 urged General U.S. Grant to proceed "with vindictive earnestness against the Sioux even to their extermination, men, women, and children." This version of history fails to mention how Southern slave-hunting posses crossed into Free States in the Midwest and Kansas, threatened the peace, and violated constitutional rights.

From nineteenth-century dime novels to Hollywood horse operas and the 2005 TV series *Deadwood*, our media have served up a lily-white West that has transfixed those who sit in public schools, in darkened movie theaters, or before their TV sets.

Africans, as we now know thanks to the books and lectures of Dr. Ivan Van Sertima, landed in the Americas before Christopher Columbus. We also know they rode every wilderness trail – as scouts and pathfinders, slave runaways and fur trappers, missionaries and soldiers, schoolmarms and entrepreneurs, lawmen and members of Native American nations. Some men and women fled westward during slavery with only the clothes on their backs. Some families bearing a few belongings and lofty dreams bumped along rugged roads in Conestoga wagons. Thousands walked up the Chisholm Trail from Texas to Kansas, and others strode across the continent to California. Like white pioneers, some families built a homestead and a few struck it rich, but many found hard toil and humble rewards at the end of their rainbow. Like everyone else, men and women of color reached their goals by dint of hard work, tenacity, and luck.

African Americans had more riding on their journey than white pioneers – they possessed a greater need, carried a heavier burden, and paid a higher price. They pined for a home of their own, teachers to educate their children, and laws that would protect their families, opportunities, and elusive dreams. More than others, African American women needed the shielding arm of the judicial system and government officials. Black men sought a place where a man's worth was judged by his skill, not his skin color.

Pioneers of African descent were a hardy breed, and they had to be. They had to master more than the mountains, rivers, and wild animals. They had to manage their emotions as they sought to survive the wrath of white pioneers and laws that hog-tied their pursuit of happiness.

These men and women did not always realize their dreams, even for their children. But, drawing on a dogged courage, a resilient spirit, family strength, and a supportive church, they kept inching ahead. Their search for the American dream left a unique legacy.

More than others, settlers of color knew their lives depended on amicable relations on all sides. They tried to be good neighbors with everyone, and extended a hand of friendship to Native Americans. Most tried to avoid the murderous land hunger and genocidal bigotry that stained so many white trails. But in the sordid racial world Europeans created, some people of African descent were persuaded to fight Indigenous Americans. Frontiersman James Beckwourth served U.S. forces battling the Seminole alliance in Florida, helped bring U.S. rule to California, and in 1864 was forced at gunpoint to participate in Colonel James Chivington's infamous Sand Creek Massacre of a Cheyenne village. The Buffalo Soldiers were not heroes to Native Americans.

Frontier African Americans are mentioned in explorers' diaries, government reports, frontier newspapers, and pioneers' reminiscences and family letters. Their images are captured in the art of Charles Russell and Frederic Remington, and in the work of early civilian and military photographers.

For more than a century African American scholars have tried to unearth this heritage. In 1882, in the first lengthy study of the African American past, scholar George Washington Williams, a former buffalo soldier, described the "Exodus of 1879" that brought thousands to Kansas. In 1902 Professor Richard R. Wright, Jr., sociologist and early civil rights activist with W.E.B. Du Bois, researched "Negro Companions of the Spanish Explorers" for the *American Anthropologist*. In 1916 Dr. Carter G. Woodson began publication of the pathbreaking *The Journal of Negro History*, which included detailed articles on his people's roles in the West and among Indian nations.

In the late 1920s, Kenneth Wiggins Porter, a white Kansas poet and historian, researched vital aspects of this tale in *The Journal of Negro History* and other publications. Dr. Porter devoted his life to the subject, only to have his fellow historians greet his work with stony silence. For decades Dr. Porter and Dr. Sherman Savage, a Black researcher, wrote articles in *The Journal of Negro History* and *Negro History Bulletin*, but publishers ignored them. Finally, when the civil rights movement lifted the veil, such volumes as *The Negro Cowboys* (Durham and Jones, 1965) and *The Buffalo Soldiers* (Leckie, 1967) began to pry open tightly shut eyes. In the next decade Dr. Ivan Van Sertima's *They Came Before Columbus* offered documentary evidence from

Columbus and other explorers to support his claim that Africans had explored the Americas centuries before 1492.

With the Persian Gulf War and through the influence of General Colin Powell, Washington launched a long-overdue celebration of the Buffalo Soldiers. There was little mention of how shabbily the top brass had treated these brave troopers. Was the army, in the name of ex-slaves who battled Apaches, Sioux, and Comanches, seeking to recruit young men from depressed communities to stem liberation movements in the Third World? That would be a tragic misuse of the past.

In a White House ceremony in 1994, President Bill Clinton introduced surviving Buffalo Soldiers to the public, and the Postal Service issued a stamp commemorating their courage. James Beckwourth and Bill Pickett were included in the U.S. Post Office's "Legends of the West." West Pointers James W. Smith, Johnson Whittaker, and Henry Flipper have won posthumous apologies or exonerations. The African American Western legacy also became an advertising hook to sell cow-country boots, hats, and shirts.

Much remains to be done. With all the kicking up of media dust, belated rehabilitations, and laying down of White House carpets, there are still fans of Tom Mix and John Wayne who have never heard of cowboys who were dark, not from the broiling Western sun but from skin pigmentation.

The African American experience raises a different lens to an old tale. Its close-ups add new dimensions to buried truths and its wide angles reveal heroes who still stand in the shadows. This great American story calls on us to scrutinize anew treasured events and sainted figures, and welcome new heroes.

The Black West is not a campfire yarn but a missing piece of a larger truth. Its information will not make everyone happy, certainly not at first, and may stir hornets from their nests. But only the truth can make us free.

Willian Loren Katz
2005

The Black West

1

Indians and Africans in the Age of Exploration

The Africans who sailed with Columbus, Balboa, and the other major European expeditions in the "age of exploration" helped change the Americas and the world. In 1513 thirty Africans with Balboa hacked their way through the lush vegetation of Panama and reached the Pacific. His men paused to build the first large European ships on the Pacific coast. Africans were with Ponce de León when he reached Florida, and when Cortez conquered Mexico, three hundred Africans dragged his huge cannons in battle. One stayed on to plant and harvest the first wheat crop in the New World.

Africans marched into Peru with Pizarro, where they carried his murdered body to the cathedral. They were with Amalgro and Valdivia in Chile, Alvarado in Educador, and Cabrillo when he reached California. The Europeans destroyed a world, but many Africans peeled away from the devastation to seek a new life. Many found it among Native Americans in Mexico, the Southwest, and elsewhere in the Americas.

The first Africans to enter the chronicles of New World, whom historian Ira Berlin has called "Atlantic Creoles," were men possessed of extraordinary language skills and familiar with life in Africa, Europe, and the Americas. "Fluent in [the Americas'] new languages, and intimate with its trade and cultures, they were cosmopolitan in the fullest sense," Berlin wrote of these intercontinental pioneers. Historian Peter Bakker elaborates on their contributions:

> *Especially in the earliest contact period, Africans were highly valued by Europeans as interpreters with the Native Americans. These*

In 1540, when Coronado reached "The Cities of Gold," Africans played a vital role in his expedition. However, artist Harold A. Wolfenlager Jr.'s 1969 painting marginalizes them.

men of African origins were not slaves but free black men in the employ of various European trading and exploratory ventures.

The use of Africans as interpreters in trading and exploratory ventures was initiated by the Portuguese in the fifteenth century. Prince Henry the Navigator ordered in 1435 that interpreters be used on all such voyages. Portuguese ships thereafter systematically brought Africans to Lisbon where they would be taught Portuguese so that they could be used to interpret on subsequent voyages to Africa.

The Portuguese strategy was imitated by other Europeans.

Hired initially as interpreters, negotiators, and ambassadors, many of these Africans settled in the Americas and struck out on their own. In Latin America the Catholic Church celebrated their souls, consecrated their marriages, baptized their children, and buried their remains in hallowed ground. In the seventeeth century, from Angola to Lisbon to Rio de Janeiro, African settlers formed religious brotherhoods and self-help societies, and by 1650 Havana, Mexico City, and San Salvador had "Atlantic Creole" communities.

Cherokee mother and daughter, around 1931

In North America "both whites and Indians relied heavily on Negro interpreters" writes historian J. Leitch Wright, Jr., and they were considered "among the most versatile in the world." Africans proved highly effective in building peaceful relations with Native Americans. In the Carolinas in the 1710s, Timboe, an African, was "a highly valued interpreter" whose role, historian Peter Woods writes, "is emblematic of the intriguing intermediary position occupied by all Negro slaves during these years."

European officials began to call some Africans impudent and arrogant. They were usually referring to those who successfully advanced

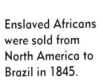

Enslaved Africans were sold from North America to Brazil in 1845.

Brady photograph showing the marriage of two peoples

their own interests, launched merchant businesses, or became independent career diplomats. Matthieu da Costa, an African, may have visited the site of New York as a translator for the French or Dutch before Henry Hudson's *Half Moon* reached it in 1609. Dutch and French officials battled each other in court for the exclusive right to da Costa's services. In New Amsterdam two years before the Dutch built their first fort, Jan Rodriguez, an African, established a trading post among the Algonquins.

Africans and Indians: Slaves and Allies

In their quest for riches, the conquistadores cast the long shadow of slavery on the Americas. On October 12, 1492, Christopher Columbus recorded in his diary: "I took some of the natives by force." Six years later explorer John Cabot seized three Native Americans. The European conquest led to a drive to enslave laborers.

In 1520 Lucas Vásquez de Ayllón dispatched two emissaries to South Carolina's Atlantic coast to build friendship among Native people and locate a site for his colony. Instead, the two seized seventy Native Americans: this made the first European act on what would become U.S. soil the enslavement of free people.

In April 1526, Ayllón sailed to the South Carolina coast to build his dream settlement, San Miguel de Gualdape. He arrived with five hundred Spaniards and one hundred African laborers. But mismanagement, disease, and Indian

This antique print, entitled *America*, used dancing to show peaceful relations between Africans and Native Americans.

hostility dogged his colony for six months and took Ayllón's life. Then Indian resistance and slave defiance tore it apart, and the surviving Europeans retreated to Santo Domingo. The remaining Africans joined with neighboring Native Americans, and together they created the first permanent U.S. settlement to include people from overseas. Their peaceful colony, marked by friendship and cooperation between foreigners and newcomers, introduced an American legacy not born of conquest. The conquistadores soon overran San Miguel de Gualdape, but it came to have many models in the Americas.

Native Americans were the first people enslaved by Europeans in the New World, but they died by the millions of foreign diseases, overwork, and cruelty. European merchants turned next to Africa and seized its strongest men, women, and children to perform the hard work of the new lands.

This meant that Indian and African people first met in the slave huts, mines, and plantations of the Americas. In 1502 Nicolas de Ovando, the new governor of Hispaniola, Spain's headquarters in the Caribbean, arrived in a flotilla that carried the first enslaved Africans. Within a year Ovando reported to King Ferdinand his Africans had escaped, found a new life among the Native Americans, and "never could be captured." He was describing an American tradition earlier than the first Thanksgiving.

In the following decades enslaved Africans and Indians escaped bondage together and began to unite against the common foe. Anthropologist Richard Price studied the sacred legends of the Saramaka people of Dutch Guiana, now Suriname, which date back to 1685. In one, Lanu, an African slave who would become a leader of the Saramakas, escaped, and Wamba, the Indians' forest spirit, entered his mind to lead him to a Native village. "The Indians escaped first and then, since they knew the forest, they came back and liberated the Africans," concluded Price.

Once free of the European conquerors, Africans and Native Americans found they had more in common with each other than with a foe wielding muskets and whips. For both peoples the spiritual and environmental merged. Religion was not confined to a single day of prayer but was a matter of daily reflection and action. Africans and Indians believed that community needs, not private gain, should determine judicial, economic, and life decisions. Both accepted an economy based on cooperation, and were baffled by the conqueror's passion to accumulate wealth.

A successful slave rebellion in Haiti in the 1790s convinced Napoleon that France could not hold its American empire. In 1803 he sold the Louisiana Territory to the United States for four cents an acre.

During the conquest the two peoples brought each other important gifts. The Middle Passage and enslavement gave Africans a multidimensional understanding of European goals, diplomacy, and weaponry. To Native Americans they brought their knowledge of the foe's plans, weaknesses, and often valuable arms and ammunition. Native American societies offered Africans a red hand of friendship, a refuge, a new life – and a base for insurgency.

In the early decades of the sixteenth century, slave revolts in Colombia, Cuba, Panama, and Puerto Rico often found Africans and Native Americans acting in unison. In 1537 Viceroy Antonio de Mendoza of Hispaniola told of a major rebellion that threatened Mexico City, saying the Africans "had chosen a king, and… the Indians were with them." By 1570 Spanish colonial officials admitted that one in ten slaves were living free. Viceroy Martin Enriquez later warned, "the time is coming when these [African] people will have become masters of the Indians, inasmuch as they were born among them and their maidens and are men who dare to die as well as any Spaniard."

In the Southwest, Africans joined the Pueblo Revolt of 1680 as leaders and soldiers, helping to drive out Spain's armies and missionaries and freeing the region for a dozen years. Decades before fifty-five white men met in Philadelphia in 1776 and wrote the Declaration of Independence, people of

A runaway is captured in the French colonies.

color in the continent had revolted against foreign rule, injustice, and slavery. They became the first freedom fighters of the Americas.

"Division of the races is an indispensable element," warned a Spanish official. European governors constantly sought to destroy the alliances in the woods with tactics of divide and rule. In 1523 Hernando Cortez enforced a royal order in Mexico that banned Africans from Indian villages. In 1723 Jean-Baptiste LeMoyne de Bienville, founding governor of Louisiana, urged that putting "these barbarians into play against each other is the sole and only way to establish any security in the colony." In 1776 U.S. Colonel Stephen Bull, saying his policy was to "establish a hatred" between the two races, dispatched Indians to hunt Black runaways in the Carolinas.

Staggering rewards were offered to Africans to fight Indians and Indians to fight Africans. In the Carolinas Native Americans were bribed with three blankets and a musket, and in Virginia it was thirty-five deerskins. Governor Perier of Louisiana offered Indians two muskets, two blankets, twenty pounds of balls, four shirts, mirrors, knives, musket stones, and four lengths of cloth for the recapture of a single runaway. Local warriors often refused to hunt runaways, so Europeans had recruit people from distant regions. "Between the races we cannot dig too deep a gulf," stated a French official.

In 1708 British colonials deployed mounted slave cattle-guards to protect colonial Charleston from Indians. On Virginia's frontier George Washington hired African American "pioneers or hatchet men." In 1747 the South Carolina legislature thanked its militiamen of African descent who "in times of war, behaved themselves with great faithfulness and courage, in repelling the attacks of his Majesty's enemies." But the legislature limited the number of Black men to a third of the total to ensure they would always be outnumbered by armed whites.

Despite divide-and-rule strategies, the lid never closed. In 1721 the governor of Virginia had the Five Nations sign a treaty and promise to return all runaways; in 1726 the governor of New York had the Iroquois Confederacy make a similar promise; in 1746 the Hurons promised and the next year the Delawares promised. None, reports scholar Kenneth W. Porter, returned a single slave.

What for European merchants and planters was a matter of profits had taken on another meaning for Native Americans. They would not sunder the bonds between husband and wife, parent

Slaveholders such as George Washington brought enslaved people to the frontier. Once there, many Africans took the opportunity to learn Indian languages and to escape.

and children, relatives and loved ones. Lacking racial prejudice, Native Americans had welcomed Africans into their villages, then their homes and families. This became clear to careful observers. Thomas Jefferson discovered among Virginia's Mattaponies "more negro than Indian blood." Artist George Catlin found that "Negro and North American Indian, mixed, of equal blood" were "the finest built and most powerful men I have ever yet seen."

To the sputtering fury of European planters, two dark peoples were not only standing as families but uniting as allies. During Pontiac's War in 1763, a white settler in Detroit complained, "The Indians are saving and caressing all the Negroes they take" and warned that this could "produce an insurrection." Af-

African Choctaw in Mississippi photographed in 1908

ricans and Indians faced regimes more mercilessly cruel than the one denounced in the Declaration of Independence. The two peoples of color had to fight off slave-hunting posses dispatched by the men who wrote the great charter of liberty.

Carter G. Woodson, father of modern African American history, would call this genetic mixture of people of color "one of the longest unwritten chapters in the history of the United States." It also pro-

Mohawk Chief Joseph Brant

Interview with a Young Sculptress

One of the most interesting individuals I met at the reception was Edmonia Lewis, a colored girl about twenty years of age, who is devoting herself to sculpture. ... I told her I judged by her complexion that there might be some of what was called white blood in her veins. She replied, "No; I have not a single drop of what is called white blood in my veins. My father was a full-blooded Negro, and my mother was a full-blooded Chippewa..."

"And have you lived with the Chippewas?"

"Yes. When my mother was dying, she wanted me to promise that I would live three years with her people, and I did."

"And what did you do while you were there?"

Wildfire, or Edmonia Lewis, became the first important sculptor of African and American Indian descent.

"I did as my mother's people did. I made baskets and embroidered moccasons and I went into the cities with my mother's people, to sell them..."

"But, surely," said I, "you have had some other education than that you received among your mother's people, for your language indicates it."

"I have a brother," she replied, "who went to California, and dug gold. When I had been three years with my mother's people, he came to me and said, 'Edmonia, I don't want you to stay here always. I want you to have some education.' He placed me at a school in Oberlin. I staid there two years, and then he brought me to Boston, as the best place for me to learn to be a sculptor. I went to Mr. Brackett for advice; for I thought the man who made a brist of John Brown must be a friend to my people. Mr. Brackett has been very kind to me."

She wanted me to go to her room to see... a head of Voltaire. "I don't want you to go to praise me," she said, "for I know praise is not good for me. Some praise me because I am a colored girl, and I don't want that kind of praise. I had rather you would point out my defects, for that will teach me something."

L. Maria Child, letter, *The Liberator,* February 19, 1864

From the Atlantic to California – where these two men lived – Africans and Indians united against the European conquest.

duced a number of talented persons. One gifted individual to emerge from this relationship was Wildfire, born in 1846 in upstate New York to a Chippewa mother and African American father. Until her teenage years she lived with her mother's people; later she attended Oberlin College and began, as Edmonia Lewis, to pursue a career in art and sculpture.

After the Civil War Lewis had a studio in Rome where she produced works based on African and Native American themes. In the next decade her art was sold all over Europe and the United States, and in 1876 her twelve-foot-tall, two-ton *Death of Cleopatra*, exhibited at the Philadelphia Centennial Exposition, was called "the grandest statue in the Exposition."

The Great Dismal Swamp was home to many runaways.

Pioneer Maroon Settlements

From the misty dawn of America's earliest foreign landings, Africans who fled to backwoods regions created their "maroon" (after a Spanish word for runaway) settlements. Europeans saw "maroons" as a knife poised at the heart of their slave system, even pressed against their thin line of military rule. They had a point.

For the daring men and women who built these outlaw communities, however, they were a pioneer's promise. During his first two weeks in the New World, Columbus's diary included the word "gold" seventy-five times. Africans sought something more valuable. From the Great Dismal Swamp to the Florida Everglades, African and Native American maroon enclaves posed a fortified alternative to foreign domination. They served as beacons to discontented plantation slaves and drove slaveholders to fuming anger. They were agricultural and trading centers with armies, and bore names such as "Disturb Me If You Dare" and "Try Me If You Be Men." Maroon songs resonated with pride and defiance: "Black man rejoice/White man won't come here/And if he does/The Devil will take him off."

Guerrilla fighters, such as this Jamaican, fled slavery and picked up European muskets.

In 1719 a Brazilian colonist wrote to King Joao V of Portugal: "Their self-respect grows because of the fear whites have of them." Some maroon settlements, too well hidden and ably defended to be conquered, became trade partners rather than enemies. Many opened commercial relations with slaveholders or other foes, and had slave intermediaries sell their products in local markets.

The Republic of Palmares in northeastern Brazil, founded in the early 1600s by Africans and Indians, became the strongest maroon enclave in the Americas. Courts of justice reigned, children were educated, the elderly were cared for, and a common defense was created under an African form of government. Palmares's monarch, Ganga-Zumba, derived his name from an Angolan word for "great" and a Tupi Indian word for "ruler." By the 1650s the people of Palmares huddled behind their three large wooden walls, fending off Dutch and Portuguese military assaults about every fifteen months.

Two generations later Palmares had ten thousand men, women, and children and constituted one of the largest cities in the Americas, its population twice the size of New York City. Finally, on February 5, 1694, after a forty-two day siege, the walled city was overrun by the Portuguese. White officers not only leveled Palmares as an enemy base but tried to destroy it as a legendary flame of liberty.

The defeat of Palmares coincided with the birth of a new kind of maroon community. Before 1700 maroon settlements were generally ruled by Africans, but after that they were more likely to be governed by children born of African-Native American marriages.

Women played a vital role in maroon settlements. Often in short supply, they were sought as revered wives and mothers who would provide the stability of family life and children, the community's future. Two African women ruled maroon settlements in colonial Brazil. Fillipa Maria Aranha governed a colony in Amazonia, where her uncommon military prowess convinced Portuguese officials it was wiser to negotiate than try to defeat her armies. Aranha was able to win independence, liberty, and sovereignty for her people. In Passanha, an African woman of unknown name successfully hurled her Malali Indian and African guerrilla troops against European soldiers.

The Delawares Respond to Missionaries

They rejoiced exceedingly at our happiness in thus being favored by the Great Spirit, and felt very grateful that we had condescended to remember our red brethren in the wilderness. But they could not help recollecting that we had a people among us, whom, because they differed from us in color, we had made slaves of, and made them suffer great hardships, and lead miserable lives. Now they could not see any reason, if a people being black entitled us thus to deal with them, why a red color should not equally justify the same treatment. They therefore had determined to wait, to see whether all the black people amongst us were made thus happy and joyful before they would put confidence in our promises; for they thought a people who had suffered so much and so long by our means, should be entitled to our first attention; and therefore they had sent back the two missionaries, with many thanks, promising that when they saw the black people among us restored to freedom and happiness they would gladly receive our missionaries.

Dr. Elias Boudinot, cited in Adam Hodgson, *Remarks During a Journey Through North America in the Years 1819, 1820, and 1821* (New York, 1823), pp. 218–220.

British merchants, as part of the plan to seal off Native villages from escaping slaves in North America, introduced African slavery to the Five Civilized Nations: the Cherokees, Chickasaws, Choctaws, Creeks, and Seminoles. Their divide-and-rule tactic worked less than perfectly. In 1765, John Bartram, a famous botanist, found that Native American bondage permitted slaves to marry masters and find "freedom… and an equality." But European intrusions had begun to infect Native American societies, undermining their values, creating racial conflict and class divisions, and producing leaders interested in private gain.

Between the American Revolution and the Civil War, however, in Massachusetts, Rhode Island, New Jersey, New York, Connecticut, Tennessee, Maryland, Virginia, Delaware, and the Carolinas, African Americans, slave and free, often found friendship and a ready adoption among Native Americans. In 1843 whites in Virginia complained to their legislature about the Pamunkeys: "Not one individual can be found among them whose grandfathers or grandmothers one or more is not of Negro blood." The New York legislature announced its Montauk and Southampton Indians "are only Indian in name." Along the Atlantic coast Native Americans were transformed into a biracial people.

Africans and Seminoles

On the Florida peninsula Africans and Native Americans developed a unique and dramatic relationship unmatched in the rest of the country. It began with the last decades of the seventeenth century, when enslaved Africans held on British colonial plantations in the Carolinas fled south. Spanish Florida, often at war with England, granted runaways "complete liberty," and in 1693 the Spanish government issued an edict of liberation designed to draw off enslaved workers from the British. When white masters arrived in St. Augustine to reclaim slaves, they were confronted by Black men and women who taunted them.

By 1739 Florida officials placed Francisco Menendez, an African Mandingo, in command of the key garrison of Fort Mose, his assignment to protect St. Augustine from attack. Fort Mose became the first town governed by people of African descent in North America. In 1740 Menendez's forces helped repulse an invasion led by Georgia governor James Oglethorpe.

When the Seminoles, fleeing persecution as a part of the Creek Nation, fled to Florida at the time of the American Revolution, Africans did more than welcome them. Scholar Joseph Opala claims they taught the newcomers methods of rice cultivation they had learned in Sierra Leone and Senegambia. Then, on this basis, the two peoples formed an agricultural and military alliance that reconstructed the Seminoles as a multicultural nation.

This German print from the 1590s shows people of Florida with an African leader.

Red and Black Seminoles built homes, tended land and flocks, raised families, and provided for the common defense. Though some Africans chose to live in separate villages, intermarriage also marked the Seminole nation. In 1816, U.S. Colonel Clinch reported on the extent of Seminole settlements along the Appalachicola River: "Their corn fields extended nearly fifty miles up the river and their numbers were daily increasing." By this time Colonel Clinch was leading a combined force of Creek mercenaries, regular U.S. Army troops, and U.S. Navy vessels against this alliance.

Since Seminole encampments in Florida appeared to threaten Southern plantations, the U.S. government and planters launched slave-hunting incursions. Finally, in 1819, the United States purchased Florida from Spain to end what General Andrew Jackson called "this perpetual harbor for our slaves."

Washington quickly found itself embroiled in tropical war against a seasoned foe defending its homeland. The "Second Seminole War" of the

In the Florida Everglades, African Americans defended their new, free communities.

1830s cost $40 million, 1,500 American lives, and at times tied up half of the U.S. Army. "The two races, the negro and the Indian, are rapidly approximating; they are identical in interests and feelings…" was commander Major General Thomas Sidney Jesup's perceptive evaluation of the Seminoles.

In 1837 Jesup concluded: "This, you may be assured, is a negro, not an Indian war; and if it be not speedily put down, the south will feel the effects of it on their slave population before the end of the next season." Jesup found the source of Seminole strength

Creek mercenaries captured Black Seminoles from Florida around 1816.

Massacre of the Whites by the Indians and Blacks in Florida.

e above is intended to represent the horrid Massacre of the Whites in Florida, in December 1835, and January, February, March and April 1836, whe near Four Hundred (including women and children) fell victims to the barbarity of the Negroes and Indians.

This is a U.S. version of the warfare in Florida in the 1830s.

easy to identify: "The warriors have fought as long as they had life, and such seems to be the determination of those who influence their councils – I mean the leading negroes."

John T. Sprague, a U.S. soldier who fought in the war, confirmed Jesup's judgment: "The negroes exercised a wonderful control. They openly refused to follow their masters, if they removed to Arkansas. … In preparing for hostilities they were active, and in the prosecution blood-thirsty and cruel. It was not until the negroes capitulated, that the Seminoles ever thought of emigrating."

"The negroes rule the Indians, and it is important that they should feel themselves secure; if they should become alarmed and hold out, the war will be renewed," Jesup warned his superiors in Washington. However, U.S. burn-and-destroy operations, the seizure of hostages, and bribery eventually persuaded a war-weary Seminole Nation to accept removal to the Indian Territory (present-day Oklahoma).

In the Indian Territory the Seminole Nation faced slave-hunting raids by whites and their old Creek enemies. Finally, in 1849 Wild Cat and African Seminole chief John Horse led hundreds of Seminoles across Texas to Mexico. There General Santa Anna welcomed them and hired their young men as "military colonists" to protect the Rio Grande border.

"Negro Abraham" was a leading Seminole interpreter and diplomat when this delegation visited Washington, D.C., in 1824.

The African Seminoles, Kenneth W. Porter notes, had mounted "the most serious Indian war in the history of the United States"; he adds that it "should rather be described as a Negro insurrection with Indian support." In Florida cooperation between Africans and Indians reached its flowering. The Seminole alliance mounted the stongest maroon insurgency, and the most resolute armed resistance to human bondage, in the United States.

The multicultural Seminole Nation had announced that people of color in the Americas would fight until they were free.

Estevan, Explorer and Slave

The first African whose name appears in the historical chronicles of the New World, an explorer of many skills, was Estevan, born

John Horse, chief of the Black Seminole Nation, shown in 1835. He lived until 1882.

in Azamore, Morocco, at the beginning of the sixteenth century. He was the servant of Andres Dorantes and has variously been called Estevanico, Stephen Dorantes, and Esteban. Little is known about his life until June 17, 1527, when Estevan, then about thirty, and his owner boarded a ship in San Lucas de Barrameda, Spain, bound for the Americas. Both men joined a five-hundred-man expedition to explore the northern shore of the Gulf of Mexico, an assignment authorized by King Charles I and under the command of Florida governor Pánfilo de Narváez.

Wild Cat, staunch friend of the Black Seminoles

On April 14, 1528, the Narváez expedition probably landed at Sarasota Bay and immediately floundered on a combination of inept management and natural calamities. Starving members resorted to cannibalism, followed by mass desertions. In one Native American village, which they would rename "Misfortune Island," disease reduced the party to fifteen. Finally only four were left: Estevan, his master, and two other Spaniards.

The four were enslaved by Indian tribes, but this may have saved their lives. During a semiannual Indian gathering the men met and, like slaves anywhere, began to plot their escape. At the next gathering the foreigners escaped together, plunging westward along the Gulf Coast.

The record of their eight years of wandering was recorded by Cabeza de Vaca, their leader. He told how Estevan posed as a medicine man, conducted minor surgery, and learned local languages quickly, and how his skills and diplomacy helped the four gain food and water and find their way. Estevan, Cabeza de Vaca wrote, "was our go-between; he informed himself about the ways we wished to take, what towns there were, and the matters we desired to know." In 1536, eight years after the Narváez party landed in Florida, Estevan led the four to Spain's headquarters in Mexico City.

The three white men had had enough of the Americas and left for Spain. Before he departed, Andres Dorantes sold Estevan to Viceroy Antonio de

Mendoza of New Spain. Estevan's stories, embellished from Indian tales about Cibola, or the Seven Cities of Gold, enthralled the governor, particularly when he produced metal objects to demonstrate that smelting was an art known in Cibola.

In 1539 Governor Mendoza selected Father Marcos de Niza, an Italian priest, to lead his expedition to Cibola, and Estevan was chosen as guide. The African was sent ahead with Indian scouts and two huge greyhounds, and instructed to send back wooden crosses whose size would indicate progress toward Cibola. Estevan, this time bearing a large gourd decorated with strings of bells and a red-and-white feather as a sign of peace, again posed as a medicine man. Some three hundred Native American men and women joined the mysterious and confident African.

One by one, huge white crosses began to arrive in Father Marcos's camp carried by Estevan's guides, who reported that his party, growing in size, was being showered with jewelry and gifts. There was also the evidence of the crosses: each was larger than the last, and every few days another arrived. Father Marcos quickened his march to Cibola. But suddenly there was no further word from Estevan. Then two wounded Indian scouts arrived to tell of Estevan's cap-

In this Jay Datus mural, Estevan is shown with his Native American companions in 1539.

ture and the massacre of his force as they were about to enter an Indian village. They concluded, "We could not see Stephen any more, and we think they have shot him to death, as they have done all the rest which went with him, so that none are escaped but we only." Perhaps he was dead or perhaps Estevan had concocted a clever story, and like many an enslaved African, made his escape.

Estevan's story does not end there. He became the first foreigner to explore Arizona and New Mexico, and legends of his journey led to the explorations of Coronado and de Soto. He brought three races together in the Americas and paved the way for the European settlement of the Southwest.

Estevan Penetrates the Southwest

So the sayde Stephan departed from mee on Passion-sunday after dinner: and within foure dayes after the messengers of Stephan returned unto me with a great Crosse as high as a man, and they brought me word from Stephan, that I should forthwith come away after him, for hee had found people which gave him information of a very mighty Province, and that he had sent me one of the said Indians. This Indian told me, that it was thirtie dayes journey from the Towne where Stephan was, unto the first Citie of the sayde Province, which is called Ceuola. Hee affirmed also that there are seven great Cities in this Province, all under one Lord, the houses whereof are made of Lyme and Stone, and are very great...

Father Marcos de Niza in Richard Hakluyt,
*Hakluyt's Collection of the Early Voyages, Travels,
and Discoveries of the English Nation* (London, 1810)

Lucy and Abijah Prince

America's earliest Atlantic coast frontiers were to the north and south, in Florida and northern New England. In 1735, when five-year-old Lucy Terry was seized in Africa and sold in Deerfield, Massachusetts, the little town stood on the edge of land that stretched from the British colonies to French Canada and was still controlled by Native Americans.

A Rhode Island school for Native Americans and African Americans, around 1860

Of Lucy and the man she would marry, historian George Sheldon has written, "In the checkered lives of Abijah Prince and Lucy Terry is found a realistic romance going beyond the wildest flights of fiction." At the time of their marriage in 1756, he was forty-six. She was twenty-one and had won local acclaim for a ballad she had written when she was sixteen, about a battle with Indians near Deerfield, at a place called The Bars. Her rhymed description of "The Bar's Fight" is the first published poem by an African American, and still is considered the most accurate version of the event.

Abijah Prince had distinctions of his own: For four years he served in the militia during the clash of colonial empires known as King George's War. He later gained his liberty either by this military service or through a grant of his master, and he also obtained his wife's freedom. His original master gave him three valuable parcels of land in Northfield, Massachusetts, and another employer gave him a hundred-acre farm in Guilford, Vermont. By his own application to George III and the governor of New Hampshire, Prince became one of the fifty-five original grantees and founders of the town of Sunderland, Vermont, where he owned another hundred-acre farm.

Two of the Princes' sons saw service in the American Revolution. Caesar, the eldest, served in the militia, and Festus, a fifteen-year-old, falsified his age and served for three years as an artilleryman and a horse-guardsman.

But wartime patriotism did not exempt Abijah and Lucy from peacetime bigotry. In 1785 their farm at Guilford became the target of a wealthy white neighbor, who tore down fences and set haystacks afire. Abijah, close to eighty, stayed at home while Lucy crossed the state on horseback to carry their protest to the governor's council. Though they were aware of the political influence of her wealthy antagonists, the council listened to her plea and on June 7, 1785, found in her favor. Never before had an African American woman challenged the power structure with such success.

However, Lucy Prince tasted defeat when she tried to enroll her youngest son, Abijah, Jr., in the new Williams College. For three hours she addressed the trustees, citing her family's contributions to the Revolution, and her friendship with Colonel Elijah Williams, who had officiated at her own wedding and whose will had established the college. "Quoting an abundance of law and Gospel, chapter and verse," she supported her plea, reported a historian of the time, "but all in vain." The trustees informed her that they had no intention of altering their prohibition against admission of students of color.

Lucy rose again to plead for her right to equal justice before white men. This time she argued a boundary-line dispute with a neighbor who sought to claim part of the Sunderland property Abijah had been granted by George III. Lucy entered Vermont's supreme court advised by Isaac Ticknor, U.S. senator, jurist, and for many years Vermont's governor. Opposing counsel was Royall Tyler, the country's first playwright-novelist, and later chief justice of Vermont's high court, assisted by a legal giant of the Vermont bar, Stephen Row Bradley.

The boundary contest was probably heard by Dudley Chase of Vermont's highest court, though there is uncertainty about the identity of the presiding judge. There is no uncertainty about what the jurist said to the woman in whose favor he ruled: "Lucy made a better argument than he had heard from any lawyer at the Vermont bar." Again she had confronted the powerful, and again she had won.

Abijah died in 1794, and Lucy in 1821 at ninety-one. They had six children. In each of her last eighteen years she rode horseback over the mountains from Sunderland to visit her old friends and her husband's grave on their old Guilford farm.

By 1803 Lucy Prince had lost the farm to the same fence-destroying, haystack-burning neighbors whom she had defeated at the governor's council. The year Lucy died the Massachusetts legislature established a committee to determine whether to pass a law expelling Black emigrants. Cotton had become king and, in strengthening the bonds of slavery, it had weakened claims of free African Americans to equal justice.

Perhaps the frontier experiences of Lucy and Abijah Prince proved that African Americans has less to fear from armed Native Americans than white barn-burning neighbors, college trustees, and state legislators.

The Bar's Fight
By Lucy Terry

August 'twas the twenty-fifth
Seventeen hundred forty-six
The Indians did in ambush lay
Some very valient men to slay
Twas nigh unto Sam Dickinson's mill,
The Indians there five men did kill
The names of whom I'll not leave out
Samuel Allen like a hero fout
And though he was so brave and bold
His face no more shall we behold
Eleazer Hawks was killed outright
Before he had time to fight
Before he did the Indians see
Was shot and killed immediately
Oliver Amsden he was slain
Which caused his friends much grief and pain
Simeon Amsden they found dead
Not many rods off from his head.

Adonijah Gillet, we do hear
Did lose his life which was so dear
John Saddler fled across the water
And so escaped the dreadful slaughter
Eunice Allen see the Indians comeing
And hoped to save herself by running
And had not her petticoats stopt her
The awful creatures had not cotched her,
And tommyhawked her on the head
And left her on the ground for dead.
Young Samuel Allen, Oh! lack-a-day
Was taken and carried to Canada

2

Trappers, Guides, and Mountain Men

In North America the fur trade became a major source of conflict between France and England and the most important reason for Europeans to expand into Western Indian lands. Trappers made a singular if accidental contribution – the discovery of more rivers and mountain passes than all the government expeditions sent into West for that purpose.

A rough, uncouth, and unsung army of trappers entered the wilderness to bargain cheap trinkets for the valuable furs of the beaver, otter, mink, and fox, or the coarse skins of the buffalo, bear, and deer. The trade rested on Native Americans familiar with hunting. The Europeans' appetite for profit and the capacity for dishonesty it spawned would astound these ancient practitioners.

Although aid from the original fur trappers assured the newcomers staggering profits, the arrival of the Europeans meant the end of the American paradise. Foreign trappers were followed by caravans of Conestoga wagons, the crack of axes, the bark of musket fire, and the expulsion of the original inhabitants from the land of their ancestors.

Traditionally, U.S. scholars have described the fur trade as dominated by French and Highland Scots. However, since 1673, when French fur trader Louis Joliet, Father Jacques Marquette, and five men of African descent paddled canoes down the Mississippi to the mouth of the Arkansas River, men of color have played a long, significant, and unheralded role. In 1888 Colonel James Stevenson of the Bureau of American Ethnology, who had spent thirty years living among Native Americans, wrote, "the old fur traders always got a Negro if possible to negotiate for them with the Indians, because of their 'pacifying effect.' They could manage them better than the white men, with less friction." Kenneth W. Porter's research affirms that "Stevenson's opinion… is upheld by… independent and well-qualified observers."

Porter found that people of African descent were represented among the trade's entrepreneurs, voyageurs, and hunters. He concludes, "Any picture of the racial aspects of the fur trade of that period which omits the Negro is so incomplete as to give a false impression, for representatives of that race were to be found in all three groups connected with the trade."

Controversy and false charges unfortunately have cast doubts on the role of African American trappers. For centuries the "tall tale" has been a traditional part of Western lore, but Black frontiersmen have been accused of so distorting personal stories as to blot out the truth. In 1848 General William Tecumseh Sherman met Black trapper James P. Beckwourth and offered this contradictory judgment: "Jim Beckwourth…

Black trapper Jim Pierce, sketched in the 1850s

was, in my estimate, one of the best chroniclers of events on the plains that I have encountered, though his reputation for veracity was not good." Sherman then spent two pages describing how a Beckwourth story, though doubted, led to the capture of four murderers sought by the U.S. Army.

Some scholars assumed the worst about frontiersmen of color. Francis Parkman, the most famous early Western historian, in a scribbled note in his copy of *The Life and Adventures of James P. Beckwourth*, wrote: "Much of this narrative is probably false." Parkman adds: "Beckwith is a fellow of bad character – a compound of white and black blood."

John Brazo, described as a "full-blooded Aethopian" who spoke French, English, and a host of Indian languages and worked for John Jacob Astor's American Fur Company, escaped this negative labeling. During years in the woods of Minnesota he gained a reputation for being efficient, "hardy and courageous."

Edward Rose, on the other hand, has entered the Western chronicles bearing a reputation concocted by his critics. In 1823 one of his contemporaries, Joshua Pilcher, called him "a celebrated outlaw who left this country in chains some ten years before" – reviving an unproved charge Rose had been a Mississippi River pirate. A government report sent on September 20, 1823, by Colonel Henry Leavenworth to Colonel Henry Atkinson contained these contradictory charges about Rose: "I have since heard that he was not of good character. Everything he told us, however, was fully corroborated."

In his novel *Astoria*, Washington Irving cast aspersions on Rose's character, but authority Edgeley W. Todd found, "The bad light in which he appears in *Astoria* may not be justified." Scholar Bernard De Voto has added that Rose "had a reputation for treachery that appears not to have been deserved." H. M. Chittenden, the leading U.S. authority on the fur trade, evaluated Rose's life in these words: "It is apparent, therefore, that Rose bore a bad reputation, but the singular thing is that everything definite that is known of him is entirely to his credit. If judgment were to be passed only on the record as it has come down to us, he would stand as high as any character in the history of the fur trade."

In 1925 Charles L. Camp, editor of the *California Historical Society Quarterly*, wrote of Rose: "Yet even his worst enemies found his services invaluable during Indian troubles, and his bravery then as at other times often rose to the pitch of reckless foolhardiness." Camp concluded that "most accounts of Rose are unsatisfactory."

Rose's experiences indicate that he was much in demand and highly trusted. He served as a guide, hunter, and interpreter for the leading fur trading companies – the Missouri Fur Company of Manuel Lisa, the Rocky Mountain Fur Company of William Ashley, and the American Fur Company of John Jacob Astor. Describing Rose's effort to protect the Henry Atkinson expedition of 1825, fellow trapper Beckwourth wrote: "General Atkinson pacified them through Rose, who was one of the best interpreters ever known in the whole Indian country."

In the *Dictionary of American Biography* (volume 16, p. 158), Kenneth W. Porter's article points to a unique contribution by Rose: "he established [among local Native Americans] a tradition of friendship for the whites." In the 1830s Rose died in the Native American village where he lived.

Edward Rose, Frontiersman

Rose possessed qualities, physical and mental, that soon gained him the respect of the Indians. He loved fighting for its own sake. He seemed in strife almost recklessly and desperately to seek death where it was most likely to be found. No Indian ever preceded him in the attack or pursuit of an enemy...

He was as cunning as the prairie wolf. He was a perfect woodsman. He could endure any kind of fatigue and privation as well as the best trained Indians. He studied men. There was nothing that an Indian could do, that Rose did not make himself master of. He knew all that Indians knew. He was a great man in his situation.

U.S. Army Captain Reuben Holmes, *The Five Scalps* (1848)

What is clear is that Beckwourth and Rose demonstrated both consummate wilderness skills and an ability to cement relations with the Native Americans. In the tradition of Davy Crockett and Daniel Boone – who boasted about the grizzly bears they grinned out of trees and the wildcats they wrestled – many outdoorsmen embellished the truth when it touched on their own powers. To brag about the big one that got away or exaggerate one's strength remains a hunter's cherished tradition.

One African American mountain man who emerged from the wilderness with his reputation intact was Moses Harris. In the 1820s Harris had carved a unique place among many pioneers. Called the "Black Squire," he was described by a white friend as having a "blue-black tint, as if gunpowder had been burnt into his face." Admired for his reflective understanding of Indian life and as one the most reliable Western guides, Harris was highly sought after. Because he was capable and willing to "endure extreme privation and fatigue," he had gained a reputation for his ability to rescue families stranded without food and water in remote areas.

Harris was also an early promoter of settlement in Oregon. In 1841 he offered his services of "twenty years in the mountains" to Eastern migrants. Those who took him up found his thrilling wilderness tales eased travel monotony.

Some African Americans found a new sense of freedom in the wilderness. In 1821 U.S. Major Jacob Fowler's expedition exploring Arkansas and Oklahoma included Paul, an African American. Paul exhibited remarkable independence, riding a horse, carrying a gun, joining hunting and scouting parties, spending his money as he wished, and addressing the party on key issues. In Taos, New Mexico, Paul was pursued by a woman; still cherishing his prized independence, he managed to evade her.

The original site of Chicago in the late eighteenth century

Jean Baptiste Point du Sable

In the world of Daniel Boone and Chief Pontiac, their friend Jean Baptiste Point du Sable was an anomaly. A tall, handsome man, he was both a Paris-educated foreigner and an admirer of European art, and he was known for his skills as a fur trapper and his ease in getting along with Native Americans. However, his particular place in history is based on the trading post he established in 1779 at the mouth of the Chicago River. As the first permanent settlement at the site, his new home made du Sable the founder of today's brash, noisy metropolis. Indians used to laugh and tell visitors the first white man to reach Chicago was their Black friend.

Du Sable was born in Haiti in 1745 to a French seafaring father and an African slave woman. After his mother's death, his father sent the boy to Paris for an education. Later he worked as a seaman on his father's ships, and at twenty he was shipwrecked near New Orleans. Fearful he might be enslaved, he persuaded Jesuits to hide him until he was strong enough to leave the South.

The founder of the city of Chicago

A British report of July 4, 1779, pinpointed both the man's geographical and political position: "Baptiste Pointe Du Sable, a handsome Negro, well educated and settled at Eschikagou, but was much in the interest of the French." Since the British and French were at war, this suspicion led to du Sable's arrest for "treasonable intercourse with the enemy." But an official report admitted Du that the prisoner "has in every way behaved in a manner becoming to a man of his station, and has many friends who give him a good character." Charges were dropped.

Du Sable's sixteen years at the mouth of the Chicago River were busy ones. He expanded his trading business and married Catherine, a Potawatomi Indian woman; the couple had a daughter and a son. The du Sable post grew to include a 40-by-22-foot log house, a bakehouse, a dairy, a smokehouse, a poultry house, a workshop, a stable, a barn, and a mill. Inside he decorated his crude log cabin with twenty-three European works of art. Besides dealing in furs, du Sable was a miller, a cooper, and a husbandman. Though he acquired eight hundred acres of land in Peoria, he considered Chicago his home.

In 1788 Du Sable and Catherine fulfilled an old promise when they were married before a Catholic priest at Cahokia. Two years later their daughter was married and in 1796 they became grandparents. That same year du Sable decided to run for chief of a neighboring Indian village, but he lost. In 1800 he sold his Chicago property for $1,200 and left. He lived on, fearing only two things – that he would become a public charge and that he would not be buried in a Catholic cemetery. As old age overtook him he did have to ask for public relief. But when he died in 1818, he was buried in the St. Charles Borromeo Cemetery in Missouri.

A Charles M. Russell painting of the Lewis and Clark expedition on the lower Columbia in 1805. York is in the front canoe, fifth person from the left.

York

The Lewis and Clark expedition, which spent two and a half years charting the Louisiana Territory, opened this vast new land to fur trapping and eventually to pioneer settlements. Books and TV documentaries have celebrated Sacajawea, the Shoshone woman whose diplomatic skills were invaluable to the forty-four men in Lewis and Clark's mission. More statues celebrate Sacajawea than any other woman in the country.

On the other hand, York, Clark's companion since childhood, and his slave, has largely been unnoticed. Yet York was a hard man to ignore. He was over six feet tall and weighed over two hundred pounds, and for Native Americans he became the expedition's main attraction. Some came from miles around to see York's startling leaps and bounds, and Clark's diary reveals how he utilized his talents: "I ordered my black Servant to Dance which amused the crowd very much, and Somewhat astonished them, that So large a man should be active &c, &c."

On August 16, 1805, when the expedition reached the Lolo Pass through the Rockies, Lewis noted that York, "who was black and had short curling hair… had excited their [the Indians'] curiosity very much. And they seemed quite as anxious to see this monster as they were the merchandise which we had to barter for their horses." While traveling along the Upper Missouri, York allowed a Mandan to wet a finger and try to rub off his color, and artist Charles Russell captured this historic moment in dramatic painting.

York appeared to enjoy his role as an exotic. Wrote Clark: "By way of amusement he told them that he had once been a wild animal, and caught, and tamed by his master; and to convince them showed them feats of strength which, added to his looks, made him more terrible than we wished him to be." Among the Gros Ventres, York was regarded as powerful medicine, his wild leaps and bounds a delight to all who witnessed them. He also worked his athletic magic with the Nez Percé, and along with the other explorers took to an "Indian wife" during their two-week stay in Idaho.

Assisting Sacajawea as the expedition's interpreter, York also proved highly useful in winning the friendship of Native Americans. Lewis and

Clark carried out the most important early U.S. expedition in history, and York was the new nation's first ambassador of good will. A member

When York met the Mandan nation in 1805, some members wanted to see if his color would rub off. (Painting by Charles Russell)

of the Flatheads left this impression of him: "One of the strange men was black. He had painted himself in charcoal, my people thought. In those days it was the custom for warriors, when returning home from battle, to prepare themselves before reaching camp. Those who had been brave and fearless, the victorious ones in battle, painted themselves in charcoal. So the black man, they thought, had been the bravest of his party."

By 1805 Sacajawea and York, having earned an equal voice among the explorers, voted with other members to select the location of a winter camp. The long journey took Lewis and Clark's forty-four men and one woman from St. Louis to the mouth of the Columbia River and back. They gathered a storehouse of information about this vast, challenging wilderness and its people, plants, resources, and rivers.

York returned home to hire out his labor near Louisville so he could be near his wife. Clark eventually freed York and gave him a wagon and six horses so he could start his own business.

James P. Beckwourth

In 1798, the year Daniel Boone left his beloved Kentucky for a home in the Missouri wilderness, James P. Beckwourth was born to a white father and an enslaved mother. Three years before Boone died in 1820, Beckwourth crossed the Mississippi at St. Louis and began a pilgrimage to the Pacific across lands Boone never saw. When legendary pathfinder Davy Crockett abandoned the frontier for a job as a U.S. congressman and stint as full-time humorist, Beckwourth's wilderness reputation was rising.

Beckwourth early demonstrated an ability to turn peril into opportunity. In 1817, when he was a nineteen-year-old apprentice to a St. Louis blacksmith, his boss tried to limit his right to come and go as he chose. Beckwourth slugged him and fled. Then he began five decades of exploration that few would match in dangers faced. Beckwourth was adopted by the Crow Indian nation after an elderly Crow woman insisted he was her long lost son. Named "Morning Star," he married the chief's daughter, and soon became a leader against the Crows' Blackfoot foes. "My faithful battle-axe was red with the blood of the enemy," he boasted. The Crows renamed him "Bloody Arm."

Paul Dorian, Dakota Indian: James Beckwourth

"You are all fools and old women," he said to the Crows; "come with me, if any of you are brave enough, and I will show you how to fight."

He threw off his trapper's frock of buckskin and stripped himself naked, like the Indians themselves. He left his rifle on the ground, took in his hand a small light hatchet, and ran over the prairie to the right, concealed by a hollow from the eyes of the Blackfeet. Then climbing up the rocks, he gained the top of the precipice behind him. Forty or fifty young Crow warriors followed him... The convulsive struggle within the breastwork was frightful; for an instant the Blackfeet fought and yelled like pentup tigers; but the butchery was soon complete, and the mangled bodies lay piled together under the precipice. Not a Blackfoot made his escape.

Cited in Francis Parkman, *The Oregon Trail* (Boston, 1872)

Beckwourth repeatedly crossed the Southwest and the Mississippi and scaled the Rockies. He pushed westward to the Pacific, north to Canada, and south to Florida, where he served as an Army scout. In 1843, traveling sixty miles east of the Rockies with a Spanish wife, he met Pathfinder John C. Frémont. During California's Bear Flag Rebellion, General Kearney sought Beckwourth's aid, saying "You like war, and I have good use for you now." In 1848 Lieutenant William T. Sherman was impressed with Beckwourth when he came upon him as the mail rider from Monterey to San Francisco.

In 1851 a traveling, searching Beckwourth reached the Sierra Nevada northwest of Reno, Nevada, and discovered a pass that secured him an honored place in the history of the West. Beckwourth Pass became a gateway for Eastern gold seekers heading to California, and he personally led the first wagon train of families through. His life continued to be filled with adventure. Five years later his biographer claimed of him, "probably no man ever lived who has met more personal adventure involving danger to life."

In 1859, three years after his biography earned him a reputation as a swashbuckling celebrity, Beckwourth, in his sixties and still vigorous, settled in Denver, Colorado. A journalist who interviewed him the next year

James P. Beckwourth

called him "the most famous Indian fighter of his generation." But the new Beckwourth sought a wife, a home, a family, peace, and a business. He accomplished these goals, but his restless, impulsive nature and demands for his frontier skills repeatedly interrupted his quiet.

In November1864 Beckwourth was forced at gunpoint to accompany Colonel James Chivington's Colorado Volunteers to a sleeping Cheyenne camp at Sand Creek. In an infamous massacre, the colonel ordered his troops to open fire as Cheyenne men, women, and children begged for mercy. People were shot and hacked to death, and prisoners executed. Chivington proclaimed a military victory and recommended his men receive Medals of Honor.

When the U.S. Congress investigated the massacre, Beckwourth, summoned as a witness, described the horror and tragedy, and told how he had retraced his steps to meet with surviving Cheyenne leaders and plead for peace.

In 1866 Beckwourth's own peace was not far off. According to one legend, the Crows, seeking to persuade him to again serve as their leader, invited Beckwourth to a feast. When he turned them down, they poisoned him – reasoning that if they could not have him as their chief, they would keep him in their burial ground.

Accompanied by an army officer, Beckwourth had journeyed to the Crows that year. The officer offers a different story: the old trapper died of natural causes and in Crow tradition was buried on a treetop platform. James P. Beckwourth died as he had lived, among his Crow friends, his trees, and his mountains.

Unlike the popular tales of Boone and Crockett, Jim Beckwourth's saga has been lost. In 1951 Universal International produced its technicolor classic western, Tomahawk, featuring the character Jim Beckwourth. However, the

In 1951, Universal Pictures produced *Tomahawk*. It cast Van Heflin (right) as Jim Bridger and Jack Oakie as Jim Beckwourth. Viewers did not learn that Beckwourth was African American.

pathfinder's role was played by Jack Oakie, a white actor. Everyone learned that Beckwourth was an important figure, but no one learned that he was an African American. The U.S. Postal Service's stamp series "Heroes of the West" finally honored Jim Beckwourth at the end of the twentieth century.

The Bonga (Bonza) Family

At the end of the eighteenth century a British officer brought an enslaved couple, Jean Bonga and his wife, to Leech Lake, Minnesota. Their son Pierre became the servant of Alexander Henry, a Canadian trapper for the Northwest Company in the Red River region. Henry often left Pierre Bonga, together with a white man, in charge of the company fort when he left on business.

When Pierre Bonga married a Chippewa woman, he began a dynasty of African American Chippewas who would place their stamp on northern Minnesota for more than a century. In 1802 near Duluth, the Bongas had a son, George, whom they sent to school in Montreal. He returned, became fluent in English, French, and various Indian languages, married a Chippewa woman, and began to work for the Hudson's Bay Company, which had absorbed the Northwest Company.

George Bonga, trapper and frontier negotiator

George Bonga, a powerful six-foot, two-hundred-pound figure of legendary strength, once carried seven hundred pounds of furs over the portage trails of The Dalles of the St. Louis River in northeastern Minnesota. He also risked his life to track, arrest, and bring an accused murderer to Fort Snelling for trial. He supported his family as a voyageur for the American Fur Company and maintained homes at Lac Platte, Otter Tail Lake, and Leech Lake. Eventually he became an independent entrepreneur.

Bonga also served as an interpreter for Lewis Cass, territorial governor and later a U.S. presidential candidate, and in 1837 at Fort Snelling he negotiated an important treaty for Cass with the Chippewas.

In 1856 a young white adventurer, Charles E. Flandreau, arrived at the Bonga home in Leech Lake after an exhausting canoe trip to the source of the Mississippi. He later wrote of his two exciting weeks as a houseguest of "the blackest man I ever saw."

Not only did Bonga regale him with stories of his early days in the fur trade, but he offered Flandreau a demonstration of "how royally they traveled." Bonga produced "a splendid birch bark canoe" manned by twelve hearty men who paddled "to the music of a French Canadian." After the trip

Bonga continued to amuse his guest with the exciting tales that had made him a local legend. Bonga, the judge reported, "would frequently paralyze his hearers when reminiscing by saying, 'Gentlemen, I assure you that John Banfil and myself were the first two white men that ever came into this country.'"

By this time George Bonga had become "a prominent trader and a man of wealth and consequence." Forty-two years later, Minnesota Supreme Court Judge Charles E. Flandreau wrote in detail about the wit and generosity of "this thorough gentleman" for the Minnesota State Historical Society.

More than a hundred descendants of the Bonga family lived in the Leech Lake region, and some continued to work with Native American fur

Stephen Bonga, of the noted fur-trapping family, photographed in Superior City, Wisconsin, by W. D. Baldwin

trappers into the early twentieth century. The Bongas have lent their name, with its altered spelling, to Bungo Township, Bungo Brook in Cass County, and Lake Bonga on the White Earth Reservation.

3
GOING WEST

Long before the Northwest Ordinance of 1787 opened the Ohio valley to U.S. settlement, pioneers of African descent had made it their home. In 1669 French explorer René-Robert Cavelier de La Salle found Africans in Shawnee villages. Others from the Eastern Seaboard had joined the Delawares, and still others who fled British and French fur traders and slave owners found a sanctuary in other Indian encampments. By 1703 seventy settlers of African descent lived in the Jesuit outpost at Kaskaskia, Illinois.

Early Ohio Valley Settlements

The first large migration to the Ohio Valley, one of the most fertile farm regions in the world, began after Congress awarded land bonuses to Revolutionary veterans. In 1788 Marietta became the territory's first permanent white settlement, and African Americans, such as former private Basil Norman and his wife Fortune, were among its original colonists.

In 1787 James Davis became the first African American child born in the new Northwest Territory (Ohio became a separate territory in 1798). In Dayton, where he became a successful barber and popular violist, he also helped fugitives from bondage find freedom. In 1849 Davis began the American Sons of Protection, the oldest African American self-help society in Ohio.

After the Revolution, hundreds of African Americans traveled to the territory, and many were former slaves liberated by conscience-stricken planters from Virginia, Kentucky, and North Carolina. In some instances emancipation was accompanied by land grants in the valley, and some masters generously provided tools, feed, and livestock for farms. Some owners brought enslaved families across the Appalachians, who then had to work as servants until they earned the money to purchase their freedom and land. Still others made the pilgrimage from Virginia as members of the Shawnee Nation.

Quakers, who were among the first whites to liberate their slaves, also welcomed runaways and helped African Americans build communities and learn skills on the frontier. By 1816 a Quakers' Union Humane Society in Ohio announced it would defend African Americans from injustice and promote their education. Before the Civil War, Ohio boasted thirty Black communities, many located near Quaker colonies.

In 1796 Reverend James Finley of Paris, Kentucky, convinced the Gospel did not justify a minister "living upon the sweat, and blood, and tears of his fellow-beings," freed his slaves. They gathered up their clothes, bedding, cooking utensils, and provisions for the first year. Finley's son James, sixteen, led them on the difficult two-week trip to the Ohio Territory. There they found rich soil and an abundance of turkey, wild ducks, and other game. They immediately went to work planting corn.

In 1818 Samuel Gist of Virginia purchased twelve hundred acres in Brown County, Ohio, so that nine hundred of his former slaves could start a free settlement. In 1832 African Americans and Cherokees forced to leave Northampton County, North Carolina, during the Trail of Tears formed the Roberts Settlement in Hamilton County, Indiana. They built log houses, a church, and a school, and by the Civil War their community produced its share of doctors, teachers, and soldiers.

August Wattles, a white educator, founded a Cincinnati school where he taught two hundred Black children. He spent his own fortune to build schools in Ohio and Indiana, often teaching in them himself, and tried to help his graduates find jobs as mechanics or farmers. In 1838 he initiated a 30,000-acre colony in rural Ohio owned and run by African Americans and noted for its cooperative harvesting, husking bees, and house-raisings.

When African American families found their children barred from public schools, they created their own. One village in Mercer County, Ohio, had "very few farms less than twenty acres and many twice this amount" and boasted "the best library of books in northwestern Ohio." A visiting journalist also found "the panting fugitive is always a welcome visitor here."

Population According to the Bureau of the Census (DC, G.P.O. 1918)

STATE	1810	1820	1830	1840	1850	1860
OHIO						
Black	1899	4273	9574	17345	25279	36673
White	228861	576711	928329	1502122	1955050	2302808
INDIANA						
Black	630	1420	3632	7168	11262	11428
White	23890	145758	339399	678698	977154	1338710
ILLINOIS						
Black	781	1374	2384	3929	5436	7628
White	11501	58837	155061	472254	816034	1704291
MICHIGAN						
Black	144	174	293	707	2583	6799
White	4618	8722	31346	21500	395071	736142
MISSOURI						
Black	3618	10569	25660	59814	90040	118503
White	17227	56017	114795	323888	592004	1063589
WISCONSIN						
Black				196	635	1171
White				30749	304756	773693
IOWA						
Black					188	1069
White					42924	191881
OREGON						
Black					207	128
White					13087	52160
KANSAS						
Black						627
White						106390
WASHINGTON						
Black						30
White						11138
MINNESOTA						
Black						259
White						6038

Eula R. Grey helped publish Black pioneer Emily Grey's diary of her life in early Minnesota.

Black pioneers considered themselves a proud, determined, and educated elite. In 1849 Minnesota's first territorial census takers found that of forty residents of African descent, thirty-eight could read and write. The 1860 U.S. Census for Western territories disclosed that 74 percent of Black women could read and write, and half of Black teenage girls attended high schools.

Race and Justice
On the Frontier

It has been one of our enduring myths that the West offered people – all people – an escape from the inhibiting social customs, mores, and restrictive laws of the East, that the frontier was a fresh stage where individuals would be judged by performance, not ancestry, color, or wealth. Social and geographical mobility, we have been taught, was the frontier's hallmark.

African Americans who ventured west, whether slave, slave runaway, or free woman or man, however, rarely found social or geographical mobility, social acceptance, liberation from inhibiting customs, or a fair legal system. From the Ohio Territory to the Oregon Territory, pioneers of color arrived to find laws that denied them citizenship and equality before the law. In some instances legislators tried to prevent them from even entering. Some white migrants clung with the tenacity of a slaveholder to the folkways, mores, and laws of Southern states. The white Westerners' vaunted antislavery

Advice from a Black Indiana Settler

After leaving you on the 15th day of February, 1830, I feel it a duty for me to write a few lines to inform you of my mind on what you are going to do...

It seems very plain to me that you are now going to make one of the worst mistakes that you ever made, in many ways. The first is that you are taking your children to an old country [North Carolina] that is worn out and to slave on...

...To think that you are going to take your small children to that place and can't tell how soon you may be taken away from them and they may come under the hands of some cruel slave holder, and you know that if they can get a colored child they will use them as bad again as they will one of their own slaves; it is right that parents should think of this, most especially if they are going to the very place and know it at the same time.

I would not this night, if I had children, take them to such a place and there to stay for the best five farms in three miles around where we came from, for I think I should be going to do something to bring them to see trouble and not enjoy themselves as free men but be in a place where they are not able to speak for their rights...

I cannot do myself justice to think of living in such a country. When I think of it I can't tell how any man of color can think of going there with small children. It has been my intention ever since I had notice of such if I lived to be a man and God was willing I would leave such a place.

I wish you well and all your family and I hope that you all may do well, as much so as any people I ever saw or ever shall see, and I hope that you may see what you are going to do before it is too late. This is from the heart of one who wishes you well...

Letter from "Long" James Roberts to Willis Roberts
(Roberts Settlement Collection, Library of Congress)

views often stemmed not from idealism but from racial hatred of Black people, free and slave. "The western settlers did not talk about the sinfulness of slavery," a Kansas historian wrote, "they despised the Negro."

The most pressing question to arise at conventions that met to write state constitutions was not governmental division of power, taxes, spending, or elections, but the legal status to be accorded people of color. In the words of Senator James Harlan of Iowa, "Shall the territories be Africanized?" Pro-slavery and antislavery delegates competed in their resolve to limit the rights and opportunities of people of color. Some delegates proposed laws so total-ly opposed to the wishes of Congress that their passage would have jeopar-dized a state's admission to the Union.

Democracy in America

...the prejudice of race appears to be stronger in the states which have abolished slavery than in those where it still exists; and nowhere is it so important as in those states where servitude never has been known.

Alexis de Tocqueville, *Democracy in America* (1835)

Black Laws

Each Western state enacted a set of harsh Black Laws. First sired in the East-ern states, they denied people of color the right to vote, hold office, serve on a jury, sue in court, testify against a white person, take an oath, or serve in

In the West and the East, Black children were often denied admission to white schools.

the militia. They created a climate that also denied the children of African American taxpayers any right to sit in a public school classroom. Part of an Eastern baggage that bumped along westward trails with the pioneers' pots, pans, and blankets, Black Laws were planted anew from the Ohio Valley to the Pacific coast.

In 1802 the thirty-six white men who assembled at Chillicothe, Ohio, to write a state constitution denied Ohio's four thousand free Black residents the right to vote. The next year the Indiana Territory wrote the West's first Black Law, one that denied people of color the right to testify in court against whites.

When Congress failed to object to Indiana's enactment, in 1804 Ohio legislators passed a law that required any Black person who entered the state to "furnish a certificate from some court in the United States of his actual freedom." The act imposed fines on anyone who hired a person who did not show a certificate, and on anyone who harbored or hindered "the capture of a fugitive slave." The law further required African American residents to register their names and those of their children with a county clerk and pay a fee of twelve and a half cents for each.

A conductor ejects a Black passenger from a train car.

Since Congress said nothing, politicians were emboldened to impose harsher racial laws. In 1807 Ohio prohibited African Americans from entering the state without posting a bond of $500 signed by two white men who would guarantee their good behavior. Few Americans had $500 to leave on deposit, and few people of color could find two whites willing to promise their good behavior.

After Indiana three times failed to enact a Black exclusion bill, legislators passed one that imposed a $3 poll tax on Black adult males. In 1813 Illinois's territorial legislature passed a law that ordered all free African American mi-

"Open the Door of Freedom"

I am a free man of colour, have a family and a large connection of free people of colour residing on the Wabash, who are all willing to leave America whenever the way shall be opened. We love this country and its liberties, if we could share an equal right in them; but our freedom is partial, and we have no hope that it ever will be otherwise here; therefore we had rather be gone, though we should suffer hunger and nakedness for years. Your honour may be assured that nothing shall be lacking on our part in complying with whatever provision shall be made by the United States, whether it be to go to Africa or some other place; we shall hold ourselves in readiness, praying that God (who made man free in the beginning, and who by his kind providence has broken the yoke from every white American) would inspire the heart of every true son of liberty with zeal and pity, to open the door of freedom for us also. I am, &c.

Abraham Camp, 1818, *African Repository*, vol. 1

grants to leave in fifteen days or suffer thirty-nine lashes, to be repeated every fifteen days a person remained. Such officially sanctioned state violence set a dangerous tone throughout the territories.

Illinois, Indiana, Michigan, and Iowa not only forbade interracial marriages but, in violation of the ex post facto provision of the Constitution, nullified those already existing. A Black migrant who remained in Illinois for ten days could be fined $50 or face the public auction of his labor.

In 1854 Arthur Barkshire, an African American from Rising Sun, Indiana, traveled to Ohio and brought back his fiancée, Elizabeth Keith. After the couple was married, Barkshire was charged with bringing a Black person into the state and "harboring" her. His marriage was nullified and he was fined $10. When Barkshire appealed to the Indiana Supreme Court, it ruled against him and stated he must be regarded "only as any other person who had encouraged the negro woman Elizabeth to remain in the state." The Indiana court also warned Mrs. Barkshire she was liable to prosecution in Indiana. "The policy of the state is clearly involved," ruled the jurists. "It is to exclude any further ingress of negroes, and to remove those among us as speedily as possible." The high court concluded, "A Constitutional policy… so clearly conductive to the separation and ultimate good of both races should be rigidly enforced." Any examination of Western democratic institutions has to consider the Barkshire experience.

Throughout the territories, enforcement of Black Laws was haphazard. The Ohio law that required families to post a $500 bond, though rarely enforced, produced mischief. In 1820 Cincinnati had 2,258 Black citizens, mainly congregated in two neighborhoods called "Little Africa." But they were not safe, since Kentucky slaveholders controlled the Ohio River's trade and heavily influenced Cincinnati's white businessmen. When labor competition rose in Cincinnati in 1829, city officials ordered African Americans to leave in six months. Three months later hundreds of impatient whites surged through Little Africa looting and burning. The rioters overcame armed Black resistance and drove away hundreds of residents, especially property owners.

Wisconsin's African American families faced an uphill battle. Whites narrowly approved a Black suffrage referendum in 1849, and eight years later defeated it 60 percent to 40 percent. A Black community of fewer than a thousand repeatedly initiated petition campaigns to remind whites about "taxation without representation" and to denounce "the heel of oppression." In 1865 one hundred Black men petitioned the legislature for "justice," and the next year – after slavery had ended – the Wisconsin Supreme Court ruled that African Americans had had the suffrage since 1849.

Settlers in Pacific Northwest territories with only a few dozen African Americans also enacted Black Laws. In 1853 the territory of Washington limited voting rights to whites. By 1860 legislatures in Nebraska, New Mexico, and Utah, with only two dozen residents of color in each, passed laws that restricted voting or militia service to white men.

In 1857 an editorial in the *Oregon Weekly Times* stated, "Oregon is a land for the white man, refusing the toleration of negroes in our midst as slaves, we rightly and for yet stronger reasons, prohibit them from coming among us as free negro vagabonds." Together with constitutional sanctions prohibiting Black voting and militia service, an Oregon exclusion provision was passed in 1857, and was not officially repealed until 1927.

"Oppression Tracks Our Steps"

From this terrible injustice we appeal to the moral sentiment of the world. We turn to the free North; but even here oppression tracks our steps. Indiana shuts her doors upon us. Illinois denies us admission to her prairie homes. Oregon refuses us an abiding place for the soles of our weary feet. And even Minnesota has our exclusion under consideration…

Black settlers driven from Kansas,
cited in *The Principia*, February 11, 1860

The Struggle for Equal Justice and Education

Without the suffrage, African Americans lacked a political base from which to address politicians. Officeholders had no reason to listen to their protests and most chose to court votes with quiet or noisy appeals to white supremacy. Quakers, abolitionists, and handful of other people of conscience were the strongest allies of Black communities. But they were few in number, difficult to mobilize, and had reason to fear social and economic ostracism and sometimes violent retaliation.

The forces of bigotry could be overwhelming. In 1845 when Tom McGregor, a white man, and Rose Anne, his spirited African American wife, moved from Illinois to Marion County, Iowa, the couple was indicted for violating the ban on interracial marriages. The McGregors managed to have the court venue changed to a Quaker district where a grand jury dismissed the charge.

When Marion County officials then ordered Mrs. McGregor to produce free papers and post a $500 bond "or be sold to the highest bidder," the McGregors defied the order. The sheriff and his deputy waited until Tom was away, then rode out to arrest Rose Anne. She barred the door and warned the men she was armed and a crack shot. At night the lawmen broke open the door and seized her muzzle-loader before she could fire.

The lawmen bound Mrs. McGregor to the deputy's horse, but a mile from her home she dug in her heels and rode into the night. The next day the Tom and Rose Anne posted a bond, but soon they left for a more peaceful home.

Harriet Dorsey and her husband, John Malvin, left Kentucky ready to defy custom and authority. After they reached Ohio, she decided to return for her enslaved father. It was a time when women did not travel alone, transact business, or contradict their husbands, and when African American woman risked seizure by slave hunters. But, Malvin reported, Harriet's father's liberty "lay so heavily upon her that she gave me no rest." With $100 in cash and promissory notes, and over Malvin's objections, Harriet Malvin traveled to Kentucky, where she negotiated and returned with her father.

In Cleveland, Harriet and John Malvin devoted their lives to the fight against injustice. They helped organize the city's First Baptist Church, Malvin preached occasionally to the white congregation, and in 1835 their contributions helped erect its first building on Seneca and Champlain streets. When the church elders voted to establish a segregated balcony, the couple vigorously protested. "If I had to be colonized," John said, "I preferred to be colonized in Liberia, rather than in a House of God." Offered a return of their seats, the Malvins rejected any compromises, and after a year and a half won full desegregation. In church or out, this was a rare victory for open seating.

Sunday morning had become the most segregated time in the United States. East or West, African American worshippers faced what was commonly called the "African corner," with seats marked "B.M." and "B.F." (for Black male or female), or space in the gallery.

As their numbers grew, African Americans in the Midwest mounted organized protests. They sent representatives to annual nationwide Black conventions to protest the Black Laws and slavery. Then, beginning in 1839 with Ohio, African Americans in the West initiated their own statewide conventions to demonstrate their resolve to gain citizenship rights. When Ohio's first convention launched a petition campaign for repeal of the Black Laws, state legislators denied that African Americans had a right to petition "for any purpose whatsoever." Over the next two decades Black Ohioans, stronger in numbers and bolder in approach, convened seven statewide conventions, six in Columbus and one in Cincinnati.

Western conventions focused on state Black Laws, particularly the denial of court testimony, and the denial of education to children of color. Delegates denounced prohibitions against jury service, suffrage, and militia service, and called poll taxes "taxation without representation." Conventions repeatedly advocated the education of Black children. In 1843 an African American convention in Michigan spoke as an "oppressed people wishing to be free… and by our correct, upright and manly stand in the defence of our liberties, prove to our oppressors, and the world, that we are determined to be free." Two Illinois conventions in 1853 and 1856 sought to raise public awareness of how the Black Laws affected white citizens who could not call Black witnesses during criminal trials.

In 1857 in Muscatine, Alexander Clark and thirty-two other men launched Iowa's first statewide convention to demand equal rights and affirm that education led to "the moral and political elevation of the colored race." They gathered 122 Black and white signatures on their petition to repeal Iowa's Black Laws.

The African American church, as it had in the East, became a source of spiritual solace and a port in many storms. Ministers helped parishioners learn to read and write from the Bible, gain job skills, and advance their interests. In church basements and attics runaways were fed, nurtured, and hurried along their way. Strategies and demands for civil rights first echoed in church buildings.

A Call to Michigan's First Black Convention

As we are an oppressed people wishing to be free, we must evidently follow the examples of the oppressed nations that have preceded us: for history informs us that the liberties of an oppressed people are obtained only in proportion to their own exertions in their own cause… Shall we not meet together and endeavor to promote the cause of Education, Temperance, Industry, and Morality among our people; and by our correct, upright and manly stand in the defence of our liberties, prove to our oppressors, and the world, that we are determined to be free?

Yes! yes! let us assemble – let us come together, and pledge ourselves in the name of God and bleeding humanity and posterity, to organize, organize and organize, until the green-eyed monster Tyranny, shall be trampled under the feet of the oppressed…

William Lambert, Minutes of the State Convention
of the Colored Citizens of the State of Michigan, 1843

Black pioneers often focused on the education of their children as much as owning land and financial success. Since African Americans paid school taxes, they first tried to enroll their children in public schools. When most administrators barred their children, communities took command of Black education. For a few months a year, teachers, sometimes in homes or church rooms, followed a curriculum of reading, writing, arithmetic, grammar, and geography.

In 1829 the Woodson family and others launched the community of Berlin Crossroads, Ohio. It soon boasted a church, day school, and Sunday school. In 1832 John and Harriet Malvin joined other Cleveland residents to organize a school for African American children with men and women instructors. In 1835 Black families in Ohio formed a School Fund Society that built educational facilities in Columbus, Springfield, Cincinnati, and Cleveland.

Sarah Jane Woodson was the first Black education graduate of Oberlin College.

That same year, another early Ohio farming settlement that began on swampy, unproductive land surrounded by hostile white neighbors was able to support a school.

In Cincinnati, Peter H. Clark, a short wiry, intense nineteen-year-old graduate of Gilmore High School, the Ohio Valley's first secondary school, became a teacher there. In 1857, Clark was appointed principal of Cincinnati's Western District Colored School. He continued to advocate more schools. By the Civil War, Cincinnati's African American community, with women in the lead, had founded five churches, five schools, eleven self-help societies, and an orphanage.

Peter H. Clark, Ohio educator

In 1831, Indiana's Mount Pleasant Church opened a school and one of the first circulating libraries in the state; after 1842 it served citizens of both races. Samuel Smothers, Indiana's leading Black educator, championed his people's "rapidly rising talents and aspirations," but the state ignored his efforts. It spoke of its duty "to elevate" African American children and claimed integrated schools would "degrade our own race." Not until 1852 did Indiana open its public schools to children of color. By 1860 a fourth of the state's African American children attended school, most run and funded by Quakers or their own communities.

In Detroit in 1846, George DeBaptiste, a successful barber, opened a school for children in his large home. In Illinois in the 1840s, when they found their children were denied admission to public schools, the Bass family built a church and school in their community. In 1858, Minnesota had fewer than three dozen African American residents when Black parents in St. Paul pressured the Board of Education to pay for a three-month segregated school.

The slave state of Missouri outlawed the education of slaves, but the law was often violated. Nuns at the St. Louis Catholic Cathedral in 1847 conducted a secret school; one graduate, James M. Turner, entered Oberlin College. Turner later taught in Missouri's first tax-supported school for African Americans, founded Lincoln University, and after the Civil War was appointed state superintendent of Missouri schools for children of color.

Reverend John Berry Meachum, a former slave, built a steamboat with a library anchored in the Mississippi River at St. Louis. His floating school illegally taught pupils to read and write. In 1856 Hiram Revels opened a school in St. Louis to 150 people who paid a dollar a month for their education.

Black men, women, and children faced greater opposition than their white counterparts as they headed into the wilderness. Their will to survive also had to defeat an opposing white will armed with the force of law.

Greenbury Logan

Long before Moses and Stephen Austin arrived in Texas, African Americans lived and worked on its broad plains. In 1792 a Spanish census found 263 men and 186 women of African descent among the province's 1,600 residents, people with Spanish names who spoke the language and fully exercised their rights. This would change with the birth of the Lone Star Republic.

In 1835, when white Americans in Texas demanded independence from Mexico, Greenbury Logan was among the Black Texans who agreed to shoulder arms for the Americans. His heroic and tragic story had begun in 1831, when he answered Stephen Austin's call for U.S. settlers. After a meeting with Austin, Logan was granted a quarter-acre plot and Texas citizenship. He came to love the country where he felt himself more "a freeman than in the states."

Logan and others then found that Texas's successful struggle for independence strengthened the hand of its leading slaveholders and reduced rights for free people of color. And his military service for Texas left him

Greenbury Logan: "In Behalf of Texas"

I hope you will excuse me for taking the liberty of riting to you. I knew not of you being in the county until the night before you left for Austin. It was my wish to see you from the time you was elected but in consiquence of your absence I co[u]ld not. I presume it is unecessary to give you eny information abought my coming to Texas. I cam[e] here in 1831 invited by Col. Austin. it was not my intention to stay until I had saw Col. Austin who was then in Mexico. after se[e]ing him on his return and conversing with him relitive to my situation I got letters of sittizen ship. having no famoly with me I got one quarter League of land insted of a third. but I love the country and did stay because I felt myself mower a freeman then in the states. It is well known that Logan was the man that lifted his rifle in behalf of Texas as of fremans righted. it is also known that Logan was in everry fite with the Maxacans during the camppain of 35 until Bexhar was taken in which event I was the 3rd man that fell. my discharge will show the mar[n]er in which I discharged my duty as a free man and a sol[d]ier but now look at my situation. every previleg dear to a freman is taken a way and logan liable to be imposed upon by eny that chose to doo it. no chance to collect a debt with out witness, no vote or say in eny way, yet liable for Taxes [as] eny other [person]. the government

permanently disabled. In a letter Logan bitterly told a Texas congressman that "every thing that is deare to a freman is taken from me," that he could not even collect a debt without aid from a white person, and that he had "no vote or say in eny way, yet liable for Taxes…." Since he could no longer work on his land, he appealed for tax exemption.

Logan also asked for restoration of "what has been taken from me in the constitution," and said he "would be willing to leave the land though my blood has nearly all been shed for its rights" if his debts were erased and taxes paid. But those who ruled the new Texas no longer showed any appreciation for the sacrifices made by Logan and other patriots of color. There is no record of what happened to this Texas pioneer, but the slide of Texas toward slavery and discrimination is documented.

has giv[e] me a Donation and Premium [land] and now in short I must loose it for its taxes is well known. it is out of my pour to either settle on my land or to sell them or to labour for money to pay expenses on them. I am on examination found perment injurd and can nom[o]re than support by myself now as everry think that is deare to a freman is taken from me. the congress will not refuse to exempt my lands from tax or otherwise restoure what it has taken from me in the constitution. to leave I am two poor and imbarrased and cannot leav honerable as I came. I am too old and cr[i]ppled to go on the world with my famaly recked. if my debts was payd I wo[u]ld be willing to leav the land though my blood has nearly all been shed for its rights – now my dear friend you are the first man I hav ever spoken to for eny assistance. I hombely hope you as a gentleman whose eze is single towards individuel is well noted al good will look into this errur and try if you cannot effect – something for my relief. I know I have friends in the house if a thing of the kind was brought u wo[u]ld be willing to git me sum relief. as to my caracter it is well known and if enything is wanted of that kind I am prepared – please use your best exertions and what ever obligations it may leave me unde[r], I am yours to acer the same. yours with respe[c]t, G. Logan.

Greenbury Logan letter, November 22, 1841, in Document No. 2582, File 28, Sixth Congress, Republic of Texas

John Jones (1817–1879), painted after the Civil War by Aaron E. Darling

Mary Richardson Jones (1819–1910), painted after the Civil War by Aaron E. Darling

John and Mary Jones

In 1845, John and Mary Richardson Jones, after four years of marriage, arrived in Chicago from North Carolina with $3.50. They set up a home and a tailoring establishment, and Jones taught himself to read and write.

Fellow residents admired their prosperity and accepted their forthright stand against bigotry, but few knew the Jones couple was involved in the dangerous work of the Underground Railroad and John Brown's revolutionary conspiracies. John Jones's aristocratic manner and business acumen cloaked a fine hand for intrigue, and the couple was discreet.

Although the Joneses devoted time to business and amassed a fortune of $100,000, their hearts were devoted to aiding their fellow citizens of color. They became active in the Underground Railroad, and their home became one of its many "stations." As people who had much to lose, they were able to persuade less fortunate people of color to assist the cause.

In 1853 the state of Illinois passed a law halting Black migration to the state. Jones lectured, donated money, and campaigned against the law. In

1864 he published a pamphlet, *The Black Laws of Illinois and a Few Reasons Why They Should Be Repealed*. He pointed out that since whites employed African American wagon drivers, they stood to suffer significant losses if their wagons were robbed because the law prohibited Black testimony. He also pointed out his family personally paid taxes on $30,000 in assets and yet he was denied the ballot.

During the Civil War the Jones family escalated their civil rights campaign, speaking to people in every part of the state and lobbying in the state capitol for repeal of the Black Laws. In January 1865, Illinois revoked the odious laws and, a few months later, became the first state to adopt the Thirteenth Amendment abolishing slavery.

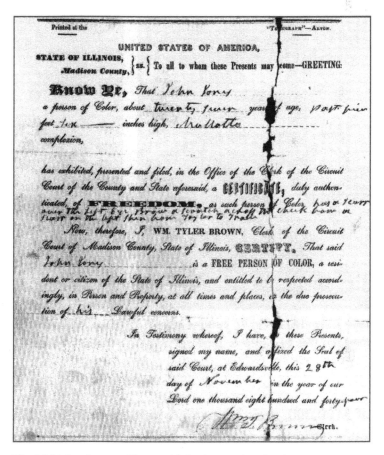

The 1844 freedom certificate of John Jones when he was twenty-seven

John Jones stepped forward to run for a seat on the Cook County Board of Commissioners; he was elected and reelected. From his public rostrum he fought to integrate Chicago's public schools. In 1874, his last year in office, he achieved his goal.

In 1875 the Jones family celebrated thirty years of labor for liberty and justice. John Jones died in 1879 a man of wealth and prominence, mourned alike by Black and white citizens. He was buried at the Graceland Cemetery near the grave of his friend Allan Pinkerton, head of the Union Army's secret service, with whom he had worked in the Underground Railroad.

George Washington of Centralia, Washington

In 1817 George Washington was born in Virginia to a slave father and white mother. After his mother agreed to let a white family adopt him, his new family headed westward. By the time he was a teenager, he was six feet tall, weighed almost two hundred pounds, was known for his strength, and had become an expert shot with rifle and revolver. He had learned to read and write and was skilled as a miller, distiller, tanner, cook, weaver, and spinner. In Missouri the legislature granted him most of the rights of a citizen.

In 1850 Washington and his adoptive parents joined a train of fifteen wagons for a four-month journey to the Oregon Territory. The next year, as an independent homesteader on a 640-acre plot twenty miles south of Bush Prairie purchased for him by his parents, he grew cereal and vegetable crops. Washington held off marriage until

George Washington, founder of Centralia, Washington

A fiddler plays for an Oregon pioneer dance in the 1850s.

after he had repaid his adoptive parents and after they had died, and was fifty when he wedded an attractive African American widow, Mary Jane Cooness.

In 1872, when the Northern Pacific Railroad decided to build across his land, he founded Centerville (later Centralia), a town halfway between the Columbia River and Puget Sound. To ensure its growth, he sold lots at only $5 to buyers who would agree to build a house worth at least a hundred dollars. He donated his profits to build churches and a cemetery and to aid less fortunate citizens. In 1890, two years after his wife May Jane died, he remarried, and the new couple, when Washington was in his mid-seventies, had a son.

In the Panic of 1893 Washington became a one-man relief agency. His wagons brought rice, flour, sugar, meat, and lard from as far away as Portland to his starving town. He provided jobs and, stated one authority, "he saved the town."

In 1905 and still in good health, Washington was thrown from his horse and buggy, and died. Centralia's mayor proclaimed a day of mourning and the city's biggest funeral was held in a church and on ground Washington had donated. He was laid to rest in a cemetery that was his gift to the town. A city park bears the name of this compassionate man whose skilled hands and resourceful mind had done much to build the West.

George Washington Bush

In 1844 a wagon train pushed across the plains toward the Columbia River valley. Officials of this British area tried to keep the region safe for the Crown and the fur-trading Hudson's Bay Company and free of American settlers. But this wagon train ignored the British protests and pushed northward to Puget Sound.

A combination of personality and political factors powered the defiance. One of the expedition's leaders was Michael T. Simmons, an Irish immigrant who resented both the British and being told where to settle. Another was George Washington Bush, an African American whose independent spirit might have begun in 1815 when he served at New Orleans under Andrew Jackson. Bush had become wealthy trading cattle in Missouri by the time he, his white wife, and five children joined the Oregon train. From the expedition's first day Bush had contributed to the welfare and happiness of his fellow voyagers. One of the party, John Minton, reported that "Bush was assisting at least two" other families to make the trip. This also may account for the group's united opposition to any mistreatment of the Bush family.

Bush's advice, recalled by another traveler, was short, sound, and long remembered: "Boys, you are going through a hard country. You have guns and ammunition. Take my advice: anything you see as big as a blackbird, kill and eat it."

Pioneer Sarah Grose (left) arrived in Seattle in 1860.

As the Bush-Simmons party neared Oregon they learned that a new law denied admission to settlers of color. But since Simmons was determined that the Bush family enter Oregon with him, long before the caravan reached the border, he and others decided they would not settle anywhere without Bush.

To avoid the Oregon exclusion law, the Simmons-Bush party pushed northward beyond the Columbia River. The U.S. Congress had passed a homestead law granting 320 acres to each "white settler," and this invalidated any claim Bush would stake. Ezra Meeker, a white pioneer, spoke with him: "George Bush doubtless left Missouri because of its virulent prejudice against his race in the community where he lived. He knew well that the English and French Canadians treated him different. We may readily believe that Bush would prefer the English rule rather than the Americans."

In 1898 Mrs. Mary B. Mason joined the Yukon gold rush and returned with a claim and $5,000 in gold dust.

Two years after the Bush-Simmons party settled on Puget Sound, a U.S.-British compromise was reached over the disputed Oregon boundary. The successful American claim to the Puget Sound Territory was based on the Bush-Simmons settlement, but it brought Bush under Oregon law. In 1853 twenty-five Oregon white citizens petitioned the Territorial Legislature to ask Congress to validate Bush's land claims. In 1854 Simmons, as an elected member of the legislature, sponsored a bill to exempt the Bush family from the laws and asked Congress to grant him a homestead. Both bills were passed, and in 1855 Congress granted Bush a 640-acre homestead. The Bush family, living on what is today called Bush Prairie, breathed easier.

Once the Bush family settled down, they became renowned for their skills and their generosity to neighbors. He is credited with introducing the region's first sawmill, gristmill, mower, and reaper. An amiable man, he di-

"On Account of His Color"

I struck the road again in advance of my friends near Soda Springs. There was in sight, however, G. W. Bush, at whose camp table Rees and I had received the hospitalities of the Missouri rendezvous. Joining him, we went on to the Springs. Bush was a mulatto, but had means, and also a white woman for a wife, and a family of five children. Not many men of color left a slave state so well to do, and so generally respected; but it was not in the nature of things that he should be permitted to forget his color. As we went along together, he riding a mule and I on foot, he led the conversation to this subject. He told me he should watch, when we got to Oregon, what usage was awarded to people of color, and if he could not have a free man's rights he would seek the protection of the Mexican Government in California or New Mexico. He said there were few in that train he would say as much to as he had just said to me. I told him I understood. This conversation enabled me afterwards to understand the chief reason for Col. M. T. Simmons and his kindred, and Bush and Jones determining to settle north of the Columbia [River]. It was understood that Bush was assisting at least two of these to get to Oregon, and while they were all Americans, they would take no part in ill treating G. W. Bush on account of his color.

John Minton, "Reminiscences of Experiences on the Oregon Trail in 1844," *Quarterly of the Oregon Historical Society*, vol. 2 (September 1901)

vided his crops with needy friends, saying, "Return it when you can," and maintained good relations with neighboring Indians. During the winter of 1852, when the grain supply was low on Puget Sound, speculators had accumulated much of the wheat crop, and prices were soaring, Bush was put to a test. Speculators rode out to Bush Prairie and offered him a high price for his crop. "I'll keep my grain," he told them, "so that my neighbors will have enough to live on and for seeding their fields in the spring. They have no money to pay your fancy prices, and I don't intend to see them want for anything I can provide them with."

Bush died in 1863, the year of Emancipation, but his sons carried on his tradition of farming and public service. One of his sons raised a prize wheat

William Owen Bush in his store

crop that was exhibited at the Smithsonian Institution. He was also twice elected to the Washington legislature (1891–1895).

Aunt Clara Brown

Aunt Clara Brown, who saw her husband, son, and four daughters sold to different owners, was deeply religious and not easily discouraged. Born in Virginia in 1803, three years later she and her mother were sold to an owner who headed west. In 1856 she was freed in another owner's will, made her way to Kansas, and in 1859 persuaded prospectors heading to Pike's Peak to hire her as a cook.

At fifty-nine Clara Brown found herself with her pots and pans in the back of a covered wagon, part of a thirty-wagon caravan winding its way for eight weeks across the plains to Cherry Creek, today known as Denver. In June, and before Colorado had a territorial government, the party reached their destination.

"I go always where Jesus calls me," said Clara Brown, and she helped two Methodist ministers found the Union Sunday School. In 1861 she moved to

Washington state pioneers Sally and George Davis, with their Bibles

Central City, opened a laundry that catered to miners, served as a nurse, and organized the first Methodist Church in her home. She donated money for a Catholic church and opened her home as a hospital and a refuge for the poor, including hungry Native Americans.

Brown soon owned sixteen Denver lots and seven houses in Central City, and by 1865 – and despite the fact that she had never turned down anyone in need – she had saved $10,000. That October she began to search for her family in Kentucky. Though she failed to locate relatives, she brought back twenty-six formerly en-slaved men, women, and children, paying for their travel to Leavenworth by steamboat and by wagon to Denver. She helped each to settle down, find work, and secure an education.

In 1882, as her money began to run out, Brown was able to locate one daughter, Eliza Jane, living in Iowa. The two returned to Denver and together continued to help others.

In 1885 when Clara Brown died, the Colorado Pioneers Association conducted her funeral, which was attended by the mayor of Denver and the governor of Colorado. A bronze plaque in the St. James Methodist Church told of how her home was the first church.

Colorado pioneer Clara Brown

A chair at the Opera House is named in her memory. Clara Brown was respectfully remembered in Colorado in the hearts of the many families she helped.

Clara Brown: "Loved by All"

"She came to Colorado in 1859 and accumulated quite a large fortune, but has spent most of it for the relief of her own race. She is one of the best old souls that ever lived and is respected and loved by all who know her."

Letter from Colorado Governor Frederick Pitkin
to Kansas Governor John St. John, August 8, 1879

4

SLAVERY ON
THE FRONTIER

The Constitution

Slavery marched into the West as a result of repeated compromises with slaveholders. These began in the summer of 1787, when representatives of the new United States met, some in New York City and others in Philadelphia, and "settled" the slavery issue. In New York the Continental Congress passed the Northwest Ordinance, which included an article that forbid human bondage in states to be carved out of the Ohio Valley. And in Philadelphia fifty-five men wrote the U.S. Constitution, which protected slave property and granted exceptional powers to slaveholders.

Northern states had begun the process of emancipation during the Revolution. But in 1792 the invention of the cotton gin revitalized the South's "peculiar institution." Slaves soon constituted the country's largest financial asset, and a slaveholding elite wielded a political whip over eleven Southern states and all three branches of the new government.

At the Constitutional Convention men talked eloquently of liberty and justice, but many delegates were either slaveholders or represented Northern businesses dependent on profits from the slave trade and the plantation economy.

Until the election of Abraham Lincoln, slaveholders dominated the federal government. Two-thirds of the time they controlled the White House, the Speaker of the House, and the president of the Senate. Twenty of thirty-five Supreme Court Justices were proslavery Southerners.

Embarrassed that every fifth American was enslaved, the Founding Fathers, at James Madison's request, wrote a document that did not use the word "slave" and instead used such euphemisms as "other persons" or "persons held to labor." The Constitution failed to stem the slaveocracy. It also highlighted the gulf between promise and democratic performance in America, forever tarnished the claims of its creators, and ensured, as Lincoln said in 1864, that "with every drop of blood drawn the lash shall be paid by another drawn with the sword."

Slavery in the Ohio Valley

The shadow of slavery lengthened across the land with the first treaty signed under the new Constitution. In Section III of the Creek Nation Treaty of August 1, 1790, the U.S. government required the return of slave runaways among the Creeks.

The Northwest Ordinance ban on slavery had its first test when a Black couple owned by Judge Henry Vandenburgh in the Ohio Territory sued in court for "illegal enslavement." Judge George Turner ordered their immediate release, but Vandenburgh seized them. Turner then appealed to Arthur St. Clair, the newly arrived territorial governor, who had played a leading role in passage of the Northwest Ordinance. St. Clair used his high office to wave aside the Ordinance's clear antislavery meaning. He stated it did not apply to people enslaved before 1787. This left the couple in bondage and it allowed masters to bring thousands of people to the Ohio Valley as slaves, and opened a western path to the Civil War.

Slaveholders in the Ohio Territory began to clamor for a legal return of bondage, and between 1803 and 1807 the Indiana territorial legislature three times passed laws permitting retention of slaves as "indentured servants." By 1810 the Indiana and Illinois territories listed 405 indentured men and women, and by 1820 Illinois alone had 917 – individuals who had been forced to sign thirty- to ninety-nine-year contracts of indenture. Kentuckian William Henry Harrison, Indiana's first territorial governor and later a president of the United States, was among the first to import "indentured servants."

The slavery issue brought Illinois to the verge of armed conflict. Violent disputes, reported Judge Gillespie, an eyewitness, "for fierceness and ran-

THE FREEMAN'S DEFENCE.   Page 284.

An abolitionist sketch shows armed resistance by fugitives and their white allies. The illustration is from the novel *Uncle Tom's Cabin*.

cor excelled anything ever before witnessed. The people were at the point of going to war with each other." Another Illinois citizen reported: "Old friendships were sundered, families divided and neighborhoods arrayed in opposition to each other. Threats of personal violence were frequent, and personal collisions a frequent occurrence. As in times of warfare, every man expected an attack, and was prepared to meet it."

By 1822 proslavery forces had elected a lieutenant governor, controlled both houses of the legislature, and demanded a constitutional convention to legalize slavery. Governor Reynolds wrote: "The convention question gave rise to two years of the most furious and boisterous excitement and contest that ever was visited on Illinois. Men, women and children entered the arena of party warfare and strife, and the families and neighborhoods were so divided and furious in bitter argument against one another, that it seemed a regular civil war might be the result."

Enslaved men and women in the territories waged their own battle for freedom. In 1807 in frontier Detroit, Peter and Hannah Denison, learning that their master's will freed them, sued for the liberty of their eight children.

When a court rejected their plea, friends helped two of their children, Elizabeth and Scipio, escape to Canada.

Women Against Slavery

African American women struggled to be free in Western territories and states. Some escaped, others worked at extra jobs to pay for their liberty, and still others hired attorneys and sued for freedom in the judicial system.

When Indiana entered the Union in 18116 as a state, fifteen "indentured" African Americans sued for their liberty, but only one was successful. When Mary Clark brought her case to trial a document was produced showing that in 1821 she had signed an indenture. The Ohio Supreme Court ruled that since her suit "declared her will," this proved she was held against her will, and she became a free woman.

Over a forty-year period that began in 1820, the federal Circuit Court in St. Louis, Missouri, heard 200 cases in which enslaved people sued for freedom, and 120 of the cases were brought by women. Some women in St. Louis took illegal action. In 1824, Caroline Quarelles, sixteen,

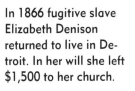

In 1866 fugitive slave Elizabeth Denison returned to live in Detroit. In her will she left $1,500 to her church.

decided to flee the city after her owner cut off her long black hair. As she fled to Wisconsin, a $300 reward notice was posted for her capture and a posse rode in pursuit. Ever resourceful, Quarelles took a steamboat to Alton, Illinois, a stagecoach to Milwaukee, and from there was guided by Underground Railroad agents to Detroit and then Canada.

In Indiana, women repeatedly appealed to the courts to nullify their indentures. In Harrison County a Kentucky slave sued her master for assault and false imprisonment and a jury awarded her liberty and $14. In 1816, Lydia, born in Indiana and sold three times, brought suit and finally was freed by the Indiana Supreme Court. In 1820 a slave named Polly hired an attorney and sued her master; acting on her appeal, the Indiana Supreme Court freed Polly and ended slavery in the state.

Some battles ended in bloodshed. In 1856 Margaret Garner and her children crossed the Ohio river from Kentucky with seventeen other fugitives. Surrounded by a posse, Garner killed one of her children rather than see her return to slavery. When she was shipped back to Kentucky, Garner drowned another child. Later, after she ended her own life, her husband reported, "and is free."

Slavery in Texas

The first Texans of African descent were not enslaved but free, and some were ranchers in the sprawling Mexican province. In 1810 Narciso la Baume had a ranch near Nacogdoches, and Pedro Ramirez herded cattle along the San Antonio River.

Mexico began to move toward emancipation soon after it freed itself of Spanish control, in 1811. But matters changed in the early 1820s, when Mexico invited U.S. citizens to settle in Texas if they agreed to become Catholics and accept its ban on slavery. Defiant Southern slaveholders brought along thousands of slaves, some insisting they were "indentured servants." By 1836, when settlers declared Texas free, enslaved African Americans were a fourth of the population, and fourteen East Texas counties had an enslaved population of 50 percent or more.

The Lone Star Republic was annexed by the United States in 1845. The new state's economy was based on slave labor, and the Texas House of Repre-

Rhoda Beaty, enslaved in Jasper County, was a free person when she moved to Travis County, Texas.

sentatives called its 5,000 slaves "the happiest... human beings on whom the sun shines." Those in chains spoke differently: "Slavery time was hell!" said Mary Gaffney. At thirteen Jeff Hamilton was sold in an auction: "I stood on the slaveblock in the blazing sun for at least two hours... my legs ached. My hunger had become almost unbearable... I was filled with terror, and did not know what was to become of me. I had been crying for a long time." Cotton labor in East Texas began at sunup and did not end until sundown. "You went out to the field almost as soon as you could walk," recalled Adeline Marshall.

Some enslaved people were house servants, midwives, skilled artisans, and others helped to run ranches and plantations. Some were cowhands. "I doubt if Texas has ever seen finer cowboys than those black men," recalled Nan Alverson of her father's ranch near Fort Worth. Near Hondo in the 1850s, Moses Brackens was proud of his cowhand talents: "Bout the only way I'd get throwed was to get careless."

Enslaved men and women tried to resist harsh conditions, preserve families, and improve their lives. In 1846 nineteen slave and free men and women inaugurated Galveston's First Colored Baptist Church. In 1858 Mrs. M. L. Capshaw, a white woman, taught reading and writing classes in the African Methodist Church, and by 1860 an estimated 5 percent of Texas's 186,000 slaves could read.

Masters such as Mary Maverick claimed to be kind and fair, but found people just wanted to be free: "I have owned many slaves, yet I can't see that one loves me or cares consistently to please me."

Some enslaved people sued to gain liberty. In 1838 in Harris County, Sally Vince brought Allen Vince to court for holding her in bondage after her owner's will had bestowed liberty. A county judge freed her and ordered Allen to pay court costs. In 1847, also in Harris County, when Emeline and her two children sued for liberty, a white jury ruled in their favor, and awarded Emeline liberty and $1 in damages.

Resistance often turned violent. "Aunt Angeline," a relative recalled, battled "anybody that tried to whip her." Reward notices for runaways reveal tales of pain and defiance: "Bill [twenty-eight]… a bright mulatto knocked down the overseer" and "ran off with a double-barrell shotgun." Martin, a forty-eight-year-old blacksmith, fled with whip marks on his back, neck, and both temples. When Tempie Cummings and

Victoria C. Lofton was born into slavery in Kaufman County, Texas.

her mother ran away, their owner fired at them. With bullets whizzing over their heads, they slid down a ravine and escaped.

In 1850, though Rachel was pregnant, she and two other armed slaves fled to Mexico. By the Civil War Mexico's Black Texan population had risen to four thousand, and a white U.S. visitor described them as among the healthiest and most intelligent people he had ever seen. But planters, such as John "Rip" Ford, were furious: "Slaves are treated with respect and with more consideration than either [white] Americans or Europeans."

Ford and others led raids across the border to seize fugitives. U.S. presidents James Polk and Zachary Taylor pressured Mexico to extradite runaways, but Mexican officials replied: "No foreign government would be allowed to touch a slave who had sought refuge in Mexico." Pitched battles and heated diplomatic exchanges kept the Rio Grande border in turmoil.

An African American woman is among those waiting outside a post office in the Texas panhandle. (Date unknown)

Slavery in Utah

Slavery was both legal and important to the economy of Utah. In 1847 Reverend Brigham Young led members of the Church of Jesus Christ of Latter-Day Saints, known as the Mormons, from Eastern states to sanctuary in Salt Lake City. Since its founding in 1830, African Americans, slave and free, had been recruited by the church.

Among the pioneer Mormon settlers of Utah were African Americans Green Flake, Hark Lay, and Oscar Crosby. Two weeks after Mormon wagons rolled into the territory, Crosby was baptized in the church. When Flake returned to the East with Young, the other African Americans helped build the colony's homes, prepared soil for planting, and constructed irrigation dams.

In early Salt Lake City, Black Mormons pitched in as farm laborers, house servants, carpenters, store clerks, midwives, and teamsters. Frontier hardships found people of both races sharing food and the small, crude, dirt homes they had dug into hills.

By 1850, twenty-six enslaved and twenty-four free African American Mormon men, women, and children lived in the Utah Territory. The church fathers agreed to set aside a building so they could develop their own activi-

The Mormon migration to Utah included African Americans.

ties and societies. Some formed an "African Band" to provide music and entertainment that would help ease the boredom and tediousness of desert life.

Despite the African American contributions to Mormon migrations and settlements, Young cited the Bible as a justification for slavery and said African people were condemned to be "servants of servants." Though he personally was not an owner, Young said his colony could not prosper without enslaved workers and he welcomed slaveholders.

Slavery among the Mormons, however, granted many rights to the enslaved. African Americans lived in Young's home, and others could take complaints directly to church elders. In 1851 the Mormon paper, the *Millennial Star*, reported that since no laws existed for or against slavery, anyone could leave. Its white editors also claimed that "All the slaves… appear to be perfectly contented and satisfied."

Oklahoma

The slavery that flourished in Oklahoma among the Cherokees, Choctaws, Chickasaws, Creeks, and Seminoles began in the Southern colonies, their ancestral home. By the time the U.S. government drove these Five Nations to the Indian Territory during the Trail of Tears, slavery dominated their once-peaceful economic, political, and social life.

Although most Native American masters were not motivated by the profit-driven, mean-spirited bondage that marked Southern planters, issues of race bitterly divided the Five Nations and sparked class divisions and notions of superiority based on blood. And in 1842 dozens of enslaved Cherokees launched a rebellion that also gained support among Black Creeks and Choctaws. It took a hundred Cherokee militiamen to crush their drive for liberty.

In the 1850s the Oklahoma Indian Territory was ruled by proslavery federal Indian Agents and surrounded by Southern states. However, in interviews conducted during the 1930s, African Americans held by Native Americans testified they fared far better than their sisters and brothers in the South. They shared their owners' resources, problems, and good times, they said, and were, in the words of one, "eating out of the same pot."

Slaves of Oklahoma Indians, 1853

These new disciples of civilization have learned from the whites to keep Negro slaves for house and field labour; but these slaves receive from the Indian masters more Christian treatment than among the Christian whites. The traveller may seek in vain for any other difference between master and servant than such as Nature has made in the physical characteristics of the races; and the Negro is regarded as a companion and helper, to whom thanks and kindness are due when he exerts himself for the welfare of the household.

M. H. Wright and G. H. Shirk, "Artist [Heinrich B.] Mullhausen in Oklahoma," *Journal of Negro History* (1953)

To the Pacific Shores

In 1846 slavery was outlawed in Oregon, but banning it was one matter, stopping slaveholders was another. Masters, overseers, and slaves operated in plain sight, no one was arrested, and officials refused to act. Citizens, deeply divided over this issue, joined private militias that ominously marched, shouted, and drilled, but in Oregon no one seemed ready to fire a weapon or start a battle.

During Oregon's first legislative session delegates introduced three bills to safeguard slave property. Masters needed legal protection, insisted legislator William Allen. "There are slaves here, but no laws to regulate or protect this kind of property."

While masters defied the law, enslaved people mounted a resistance. In 1846 Robin and Polly Holmes began a long struggle to free their growing family from the grip of Nathaniel Ford, a Missouri sheriff who had promised to liberate them in Oregon. Each time they raised his promise, Ford threatened to drag them back to Missouri. In 1850 Ford finally agreed to liberate Robin, Polly,

A slave couple prepares to fight bloodhounds and posses. (From an 1853 British publication)

and their infant son, but still claimed ownership of their two other daughters and a son.

When the anguished parents went to court for their children, Ford filed to keep the entire family, claiming Robin and Polly were too poor and ignorant to care for their children. An Oregon judge permitted Ford long delays and asked each side for a bond of $1,000, which the Holmeses did not have. Finally the Holmes family brought their plea before George H. Williams, the state's new Supreme Court chief justice. He not only returned the children to their parents, but ruled slavery in Oregon was illegal "without some positive legislation establishing slavery here."

Western Abolitionism

The West was destined to become the first battleground of the Civil War. A host of abolitionists, such as John Brown, who first rose in the East, became antislavery leaders in Western territories. Agitators in New England could be ignored, but frontier citizens unwilling to cooperate with slaveholders spelled doom for the expansion of their system. Western men and women who aided escapees, confronted slave-hunting posses, and demanded local governments cease any surrender to Southern interests, made Western bondage costly and precarious.

Some frontier legislators boasted of their militant antislavery views and actions. Ohio representative Joshua Giddings told Congress how he defied the Fugitive Slave Law of 1850 by aiding runaway slaves: "as many as nine fugitives din[ed] at one time in my house. I fed them, I clothed them, gave them money for their journey and sent them on their way rejoicing." His two sons, he proudly noted, served as their guides. Giddings's Senate colleague, Salmon P. Chase, provided aid to so many escapees that in Ohio courts he was known as "the attorney general of the fugitive slaves." As punishment for their activities, Congress denied both Giddings and Chase appointments to key committees. When John Brown traveled east to raise funds among New England abolitionists, he carried a note of recommendation from the new Ohio governor, Salmon P. Chase.

President Buchanan faced a determined man in Chase. When a Mechanicsburg, Ohio, white man hid a slave in his home and fired on a slave-hunting posse, the federal government issued a warrant for his arrest. Governor Chase countered by securing a warrant for the arrest of the posse members. President Buchanan agreed Chase had checkmated him, and canceled the warrant.

The Western antislavery movement produced its share of antislavery societies. By 1837, Ohio's 213 antislavery groups placed it second only to New York's 274 and ahead of the 145 in Massachusetts.

Reverend Elijah Lovejoy, who had been driven out of St. Louis for publishing denunciations of bondage, brought his printing press to Alton, Illinois, and continued to issue fierce antislavery editorials. Twice at Alton, mobs attacked Lovejoy's office and threw his press into the river. The third

Frederick Douglass in Indiana, 1843

At our first meeting we were mobbed, and some of us had our good clothes spoiled by evil-smelling eggs. This was at Richmond… At Pendleton this mobocratic spirit was even more pronounced. It was found impossible to obtain a building in which to hold our convention, and our friends, Dr. Fussell and others, erected a platform in the woods, where quite a large audience attended. As soon as we began to speak a mob of about sixty of the roughest characters I ever looked upon ordered us, through its leaders, to be silent, threatening us, if we were not, with violence. We attempted to dissuade them, but they had not come to parley but to fight, and were well armed. They tore down the platform on which we stood, assaulted Mr. White and knocked out several of his teeth, dealt a heavy blow on William A. White, striking him on the back part of the head, badly cutting his scalp and felling him to the ground. Undertaking to fight my way through the crowd with a stick which I caught up in the melee, I attracted the fury of the mob, which laid me prostrate on the ground under a torrent of blows. Leaving me thus, with my right hand broken, and in a state of unconsciousness, the mobocrats hastily mounted their horses and rode to Andersonville, where most of them resided.

Frederick Douglass, *The Life and Times of Frederick Douglass* (1892)

In 1837 a white mob in Alton, Illinois, attacked and killed Elijah Lovejoy for publishing an antislavery newspaper.

time in 1837, Lovejoy and his brother Owen waited with guns; but the mob killed Elijah and destroyed his press. Owen Lovejoy was later elected to Congress. During a meeting to commemorate Elijah Lovejoy's martyrdom a young John Brown raised his hand and pledged to fight slavery to the death.

In Ohio, housewife Harriet Beecher Stowe interviewed escapees who crossed the river from Kentucky, and used this material to write her worldwide best seller, *Uncle Tom's Cabin*. And a tall, gaunt former slave, Sojourner Truth, spent two years driving her horse-drawn buggy along the Ohio riverfront speaking to whoever would listen about their duty to help runaways who crossed the river. She supported herself by selling six hundred copies of her slave narrative.

Frederick Douglass tries to fight off an Indiana mob.

The Underground Railroad

Men and women who successfully escaped from bondage usually found they had to rely on themselves and free people of color. Most did not find the famous Underground Railroad but simply followed the North Star from their plantations and towns. Others took different paths. Some fled southward from Georgia and the Carolinas to Florida, from Texas to Mexico, from Virginia and North Carolina to the Great Dismal Swamp. Many found a refuge in Native American villages, or in Quaker or African American frontier communities, or in Texas, Arizona, and New Mexico.

In the Midwest an Underground Railroad began after the War of 1812 and moved passengers northeast from Ohio and Indiana to the shores of Lake Erie, and from Illinois and Iowa to the southern shore of Lake Michigan. Conductors found riverboat pilots who were willing to bring escapees to Canada. William Wells Brown, a runaway himself, piloted a boat that moved people from Detroit and Buffalo to Canada. "In the year 1842," he wrote, "I conveyed from the first of May to the first of December, 69 fugitives over Lake Erie to Canada."

Indiana stations were kept busy and on the defensive. From 1839 Reverend Chapman Harris, his wife, and their four sons, African Americans from Virginia, directed their rescue mission work from a cabin in Madison. Indiana and Kentucky residents across from each other on the Ohio river used bonfires to communicate. For refusing to reveal where he had hidden slaves in Indiana, African American Griffith Booth was beaten by a Madison mob, and on another occasion, thrown into the Ohio River. For aiding fugitives in Indiana, three African Americans were sentenced to the Kentucky state prison at Frankfort and one died there.

By the 1840s African Americans in Indiana had formed military units. In 1849 a Black militia and armed whites confronted a

William Wells Brown

Kentucky slave-hunting posse, ordered it to leave, and watched the men gallop off.

In frontier Detroit, community resistance started early. In 1833 Thornton Blackburn and his wife, who had fled Kentucky to settle in Detroit, were jailed as runaways after a Kentucky posse complained to a judge. Black men packed the courtroom and others deployed near the jail armed with clubs and guns. Black women devised their own strategy. On Sunday a women's delegation visited Mrs. Blackburn in her cell. After Mrs. George French secretly changed clothes with her, Mrs. Blackburn left with the delegation. On Monday Black men attacked the sheriff, fractured his skull, and freed Thornton Blackburn. By evening the Blackburns had been reunited in Canada.

Detroit's mayor Marshall Chapin summoned a company of the U.S. Fourth Artillery Regiment to restore order. Thirty people were arrested for aiding the fugitives, but none was convicted.

By 1846 William Lambert and George DeBaptiste, both born free, successful businessmen and community leaders in Detroit, recruited and trained an "African-American Mysteries: the Order of the Men of Oppression." Their first military operation was a daring daylight raid on a courtroom that seized fugitive Robert Cromwell and spirited him to Canada. "Our law point was bad," Lambert conceded, "but we were many in numbers and resolute."

To protect their society Lambert and DeBaptiste swore recruits to secrecy and devised tests for membership. "The general plan was freedom," Lambert explained, and this included "arranged passwords and grips, and a ritual, but we were always suspicious of the white man, and so those we admitted we put to severe tests…" The African American society did admit two whites, a trustworthy local friend and abolitionist John Brown.

Fugitives were hidden near Lake Huron, Lambert recalled. "There they found food and warmth, and when, as frequently happened they were ragged and thinly clad, we gave them clothing. Our boats were concealed under the docks, and before daylight we would have everyone over [to Canada]. We never lost a man by capture at this point, so careful were we…" Slave catchers often were hot on their trail. "It was fight and run – danger at every turn," Lambert remembered, "but that we calculated upon, and were prepared for."

The Ohio branch of the Underground Railroad may have been the most active in the nation. Rutherford B. Hayes, who had served as an attorney for runaways, believed that during the months the Ohio River was frozen, so many people crossed the ice from Kentucky that stations suffered serious congestion.

Underground Railroad hero William Lambert

Reverend William Mitchell escaped to Ohio, where he and his wife devoted their lives to liberation. They would send posses who appeared at their door back for search warrants, and then whisk fugitives to safety before they returned. One Saturday Mitchell mobilized his friends among both races to help rescue a runaway. During a heated trial argument the courtroom became unruly and Mitchell's allies whisked the man to safety. On Sunday, Mitchell brought the prisoner to church and collected enough money for him to reach Canada.

From 1843 to 1855 Mitchell's life was dedicated to liberty: "Many are the times I have suffered in the cold, in beating rains pouring in torrents from the watery clouds, in the midst of the impetuosity of the whirlwinds and wild tornadoes, leading on my company, not to the field of sanguinary war and carnage, but to the glorious land of impartial freedom, where the bloody lash is not buried in the quivering flesh of the slaves."

In 1860 in *The Underground Railroad from Slavery to Freedom*, pubished in England, Mitchell told his story. It was the first book to appear at a time when the Fugitive Slave Law required the arrest of all participants. His book celebrated his secret conductors as "patriotic men, white and colored, voluntarily going into the Slave States and bringing away their fellow men." He told of John Mason, a fugitive himself, who "brought to my house, in 19 months, 265 human beings" whom "I had the privilege of forwarding to Canada."

Ripley, Ohio, a mecca for former slaves and whites opposed to bondage, boasted at least one church "for repentant slaveholders" and became a leading station. In 1849 former slave John Parker, an iron worker, turned his house into a refuge for escapees and reported for the next dozen years he and his guests saw "adventurous nights together." When Southern posses rode in, Ripley became a disputed territory. Parker recalled violent street brawls, shootouts, and times when "I never thought of going uptown without a pistol in my pocket, a knife in my belt, and a blackjack handy."

Oberlin College and its town in northern Ohio acted as a junction of five different routes for the underground railroad. Founded in 1833, the

A woman and her child are seized by slave catchers.

college was the first to admit African Americans and women as students. One posseman called Oberlin an "old buzzard's nest where the negroes who arrive over the underground railroad are regarded as dear children." Students proved so successful in moving fugitives through town that four times the Ohio legislature tried to repeal the college's charter. During a trial, a Southerner compared Painesville, Ohio, to Oberlin: "Went there and found a worse place than Oberlin. Never see so many niggers and abolitionists in any one place in my life! Dayton was with me. They give us 20 minutes to leave then wouldn't allow us that! Might as well try to hunt the devil there as to hunt a nigger. Was glad to get away as fast as I could."

Wilbur Siebert's famous 1898 study, *The Underground Railroad*, confirmed the daring record of Ohio's Underground Railroad stations. It established that Ohio's 1,540 runaway-aiding agents almost matched the total number, 1,670, active in the rest of the country. Siebert estimated that the total number of fugitives who entered Ohio from 1830 to 1860 was "not less than 40,000."

Dred, Harriet, Lizzie, and Eliza Scott

For more than a century after his death in 1858, Dred Scott was the only person of color mentioned in school history books and social studies classes.

Dred Scott and Harriet Robinson met and were married at Fort Snelling. For eleven years they fought the U.S. legal system to win freedom for their two daughters and themselves.

He was pictured as an unlikely candidate for immortality – a confused man without normal roots or feelings, lazy, and stupid enough to become a pawn for white fanatics bent on disrupting the Union.

Scott did not fit this image, and little mention was made of his devoted family. In 1836 he was taken by his owner to Minnesota, where the Northwest Ordinance, the Missouri Compromise, and the territorial laws barred bondage. At Fort Snelling he met Harriet Robinson, the slave of an Indian agent, and the couple were married in a civil ceremony.

Dred and Harriet Scott became members of the Second Baptist Church in St. Louis. They proved courageous and persistent in their quest for freedom. Once Dred Scott fled to the Lucas swamps near St. Louis, a haven for runaways, and was recaptured. Working at extra jobs, he saved $300, which in 1846 he offered his new owner as a down payment on his family's freedom. It was rejected. Then Harriet and Dred Scott sued in court for their liberty and that of their two daughters, Eliza and Lizzie, and for $10 in damages for false imprisonment. In 1850 they won their case. Two years later the Missouri Supreme Court reversed the ruling, and they appealed. Abolitionists then assisted with legal and financial aid.

The Scotts were simply another family who wanted to be free. They had no idea their case would stoke the fires of the new Republican Party, advance the career of Abraham Lincoln, and help precipitate the country's bloodiest war.

After a legal battle of ten years and ten months, a seven-to-two Supreme Court majority denied their plea in 1857. In a stunning ruling, Chief Justice Roger B. Taney declared the Missouri Compromise – and all congressional regulation of slavery in the territories – unconstitutional. He also stated that Black people even if free "had no rights which the white man was bound to respect." President-elect James Buchanan, in secret violation of the Constitution's separation of powers, secretly communicated to Justices Taney, Catron, Grier, and Wayne his desire for a proslavery ruling. His wish was granted, but the national reaction was so strong it eventually led to the Fourteenth Amendment.

After Taney had spoken, the Scotts were purchased and freed by white friends. They continued to live in St. Louis, Dred as a hotel porter who also assisted Harriet with her laundry business. Years of bondage, old age, and deteriorating health had taken their toll. Dred died the year of his liberation, Harriet, a year later.

In *The Dictionary of American Biography*, scholars Ray Allen Billington and Richard Bardolph have dismissed Dred Scott with the redundancy "shiftless" and "lazy." Pulitzer Prize–winning historian Bruce Catton called Scott "a liability rather than an asset" to his owner. None mention a life of hard labor and dedication to family, church, and liberty. Dred Scott was hardly a stupid, lazy dupe.

Despite repeated failures, endless delays, and the collusion between a president and his Supreme Court, Dred Scott was able to gain his family's freedom. School texts have labeled "heroic" those who have done far less. The Scott family never had their day in court. Scholars have tried to strip Dred Scott of his manhood and resistant spirit. This is a tragic comment on the way our American story has been distorted and whitewashed.

5
THE CRISIS YEARS

The Compromise of 1850 admitted California as a Free State but it also set the stage for a decade of civil strife. A resounding victory for proslavery forces, the law welcomed slavery into the huge land area taken from Mexico by war. It also provided a stringent new Fugitive Slave Law and sent posses led by U.S. marshals into Free States and mandated fines and prison for citizens who aided runaways or refused to assist in their capture.

After escaping, a hundred former slaves wrote or dictated their life stories as their part in the battle against human bondage.

In this picture from *Uncle Tom's Cabin*, Eliza reveals she is going to flee in order to save her child from slavery.

The response was not what the white South had expected. Ohio's Green Plain Quaker yearly meeting declared that its members would aid fugitives "in defiance of all the enactments of all the governments on earth... If it

is really a constitutional obligation that all who live under the government shall be kidnappers and slave catchers for Southern tyrants, we go for revolution." Eight states, including Michigan, Wisconsin, and Kansas, passed "Personal Liberty Laws" that allowed citizens to defy the law. Near Oberlin, Ohio, Lewis and Milton Clarke, themselves escapees, trained a Black militia to challenge "kidnapping" posses. Abolitionists in the North and West prepared for combat.

In Cincinnati, young Harriet Beecher Stowe learned about slavery as she helped fugitives escape across the Ohio River.

September 13, 1858, was "at once the darkest and the brightest day in the Calendar of Oberlin," wrote Black Ohio attorney John Mercer Langston. Two dozen Black and white citizens of Oberlin and Wellington rescued fugitive John Price from three U.S. marshals. Langston, whose brother Charles was one of the two tried and convicted for the crime, wrote: "Names must not be mentioned. The conduct of particular individuals must not be described. It is enough for us to know, just now, that the brave men and women who came together in hot haste, but with well-defined intention, returned as the shades of night came on bringing silence and rest to the world, bearing in triumph to freedom the man who, but an hour before, was on the road to the fearful doom of slavery."

Charles Langston: "A Court That Was Prejudiced"

"I was tried by a jury who were prejudiced; before a Court that was prejudiced; prosecuted by an officer who was prejudiced...

"One more word, sir, and I have done. I went to Wellington, knowing that colored men have no rights in the United States, which white men are bound to respect; that the Courts had so decided; that Congress has so enacted; that the people had so decreed."

John M. Langston,
Anglo-African Magazine,
Vol. I (July 1859)

Attorney and later congressman, John Mercer Langston

Crisis Years: Free People of Color

The Compromise of 1850 ushered in a fearful time for free African Americans that undermined their efforts for equality. In 1853, the Washington Territory, with little more than a dozen African American families, limited voting rights to white men. California passed its own harsh Fugitive Slave Law. In 1860 Nebraska, New Mexico, and Utah, with only a dozen or so African American families in each territory, voted to deny Black pioneers any right to vote, hold office, or serve in the militia.

In 1848 Wisconsin joined the Union with several hundred African American families, and as the only state to enter without passing Black Laws. But in 1857, when Wisconsin's 770,000 white residents elected a Republican governor, they turned down equal suffrage by 40,106 to 27,550.

At the 1850 Indiana Constitutional Convention, feverish outbursts marked debates about race. One delegate suggested that "it would be better to kill them [Black residents] off at once, if there is no other way to get rid of them…" He pointed to a precedent: "We know how the Puritans did with the Indians who were infinitely more magnanimous and less impudent than the colored race." A proposed equal suffrage was voted down 122 to 1. Instead,

An abolitionist depiction of the Fugitive Slave Law of 1850

the convention passed a provision denying entrance to emigrants of color; the Indiana electorate approved it by a vote of 113,628 to 21,873, or five to one.

In 1855, as war raged over slavery in Kansas, antislavery delegates heard their Topeka convention president, James H. Lane, triumphantly predict "a decided majority" of voters "will favor" exclusion of African Americans. The African, Lane added, was a connecting link between man and the orangutan. In an election boycotted by proslavery forces, an exclusion provision passed three to one. A Free State man explained to a *New York Tribune* reporter: "First, then be not deceived in the character of the anti-Slavery feeling. Many who are known as Free-State men are not anti-Slavery in our Northern acceptation of the word. They are more properly negro haters, who vote Free-State to keep negroes out, free or slave; one half of them would go for Slavery if negroes were to be allowed here at all. The inherent sinfulness of slavery is not once thought of by them."

On Admitting Free People of Color to Oregon, 1850

This is a question of life and death to us in Oregon, and of money to this Government. The Negroes associate with the Indians and intermarry, and, if their free ingress is encouraged or allowed, there would a relationship spring up between them and the different tribes, and a mixed race would ensue inimical to the whites; and the Indians being led on by the Negro who is better acquainted with the customs, language, and manners of the whites, than the Indian, these savages would become much more formidible than they otherwise would, and long and bloody wars would be the fruits of the comingling of the races.

Congressman Samuel Thurston, Letter of the Delegate from Oregon to the Members of the House of Representatives, First Session, 31st Congress, in Oregon Historical Society Manuscript Collection

In Oregon, the idea of "popular sovereignty" prompted legislators to introduce three bills to safeguard slave property. "There are slaves here, but no laws to regulate or protect this kind of property," lamented legislator William Allen. In 1857, Oregon's constitutional convention voted to restrict people of color from the militia and the suffrage. Voters sanctioned the constitution by 4,000 votes, rejected slavery by 5,082 votes, and approved exclusion of African American migrants by an eight-to-one majority – in a land with only few dozen Black families. Oregon became the only state to enter the Union with a constitutional provision that denied admission to African American emigrants. The shadow of slavery had lengthened to the Pacific.

Free people of color in Texas had faced mounting hostility since the early days of the Lone Star Republic, when the Ashworth family of Jefferson County ran a successful ranch. Aaron Ashworth owned 2,570 cattle and Mrs. Ashworth owned land valued at $11,000. The family's wealth and friendship with influential whites enabled them to defy certain racial laws. Then, in the 1850s, a Texas Vigilance Committee tried to drive the Ashworths away. *New York Times* reporter Frederick Law Olmsted told how the family armed 150 men, including whites and Spaniards, and prepared for a war. For weeks homes were burned, men assassinated, and anarchy and violence reigned. Men fired away in broad daylight and a sheriff and a deputy were among the slain. State militia units finally had to quell the disorder.

Slave discontent, another barometer of the rising tension in the 1850s, led to more patrols and stronger Slave Codes and Black Laws. But white Texans still spent many sleepless nights.

The arguments over Kansas, "popular sovereignty," and the Supreme Court's Dred Scott decision intensified sectional strife. In 1860, Sylvester Gray, who had homesteaded a 160-acre farm in Wisconsin since 1856, was informed by a U.S. land commissioner that his homestead was revoked because he was "a man of color."

The next year, when Mrs. Mary Randolph was put off a Colorado-bound stagecoach because of her color, it was hard to determine whether it was a result of the Dred Scott decision or narrow-minded attitudes. All Mrs. Randolph knew was that she was left behind as the stagecoach rolled on to Denver, and had to spend a lonely night on the Kansas plains snapping her umbrella open and shut to frighten away coyotes.

Though the Republican Party was pledged to halting slavery in the West, it loudly committed itself to a white country. Senator Lyman Trumbull of Illinois said: "We, the Republican Party, are the white man's party. We are for the free white man, and for making white labor acceptable and honorable, which it can never be when negro slave labor is brought into competition with it." Abraham Lincoln emphasized that Republicans want the territories "for homes of free white people."

During the 1850s Black emigrationist sentiment soared in the East and West, and thousands of free people of color sought refuge in Canada, some in Mexico. In August 1954 a Black emigration convention drew 102 enthusiastic delegates, including 29 women, to Cleveland, Ohio, with a president from Michigan, the first vice president from Indiana, and the second vice president, Mrs. Mary E. Bibb, from the Midwest. Mrs. Bibb had moved to Canada with her husband, Henry Bibb, where they had started *Voice of the Fugitive*, a paper advocating a Black exodus from the United States. Delegates denounced "our white American oppressors," "refused submission" to the Fugitive Slave Law, and scorned attempts to open new land to slavery as "contemptible."

Fugitive Henry Bibb edited a Canadian paper, *Voice of the Fugitive*, that called on his people to flee to Canada.

An "Alien" in Illinois

I can hate this Government without being disloyal because it has stricken down my manhood, and treated me as a saleable commodity. I can join a foreign enemy and fight against it, without being a traitor, because it treats me as an ALIEN and a STRANGER, and I am free to avow that should such a contingency arise I should not hesitate to take any advantage in order to procure such indemnity for the future.

H. Ford Douglass, *Proceedings of the National Emigration Convention of Colored People* (1854)

Still other African Americans responded to the turmoil of the 1850s by heading westward. The number of free people of color in the West had increased sharply, according to the 1860 U.S. Census: 36,673 in Ohio, 11,428 in Indiana, 7,628 in Illinois, 6,799 in Michigan, 1,171 in Wisconsin, 1,069 in Iowa, 259 in Minnesota, 128 in Oregon, 82 in Nebraska, 46 in Colorado, 59 in Utah, 45 in Nevada, 30 in Washington, 85 in New Mexico, and unrecorded but smaller numbers in Arizona, Idaho, Wyoming, Montana, and the Dakotas. The Census also found increased numbers of free people of color in Western slave states: 355 in Texas, 3,572 in Missouri, 7,300 in Tennessee, and 10,684 in Kentucky (Bureau of the Census, Negro Population 1790–1915. [Washington, D.C.: Government Printing Office, 1918], p. 44).

In 1863 Rev. Robert Hickman organized a massive slave flight from Missouri to St. Paul.

Proslavery Missouri raiders cross into Kansas in 1856.

"Bleeding Kansas"

For those who hoped sectional differences could be resolved through further compromises, the 1850s had a terrifying answer. Senator Stephen A. Douglas's Kansas-Nebraska Act offered his "popular sovereignty" solution to the issue of slavery in the West. Popular sovereignty, he believed, would turn an inflammatory national issue into a peaceful local vote. He also hoped that his device of letting residents of a territory decide the issue would land him in the White House.

The new law, however, nullified the Missouri Compromise, opened all of the West to slavery, and created new conflicts. In Kansas popular sovereignty ignited a miniature civil war. Grumbling farmers along the up-

A Slave Auction at Iowa Point, Kansas

I was required to mount a box in front of the store, and, then the auction began. "How much am I offered for this black boy," the auctioneer cried. "See, he is a fine boy, he is about twenty years old, we guarantee his health, he is strong, and he will give you years of service. Step right up and feel his muscles and look at his teeth. You will see that he is a fine specimen of young manhood."

The first bid was $100 and the auctioneer kept asking for other bids, first 25, then 10 and even $5 until they ran the bids up to $200. Then, as he could get no other bids, he sold me for $200. While the auction was going on I noticed a group of twenty-five or thirty men armed with clubs and riding horses hurrying down the ravine. I noticed one of the men was leading a saddled horse without a rider; the two crowds came together with a clash and there was much brawling and cursing. There were many bloody noses, and some heads cracked by the clubs. It was a bunch of "free soilers" who were determined to break up the auction. The man leading the riderless horse rushed up to me and shouted, "The moment your feet touched Kansas soil, you were a free man," and, then, he ordered me to mount the horse and we rode at a fast gallop, leaving the two groups of men to fight it out.

Uncle Mose, quoted in *Negro History Bulletin* (March 1955)

per Mississippi Valley, determined to close Western lands to slaveholders, formed the Republican Party to oppose any extension of slavery to the West.

In Kansas both sides prepared for war. A New England Emigrant Aid Society began to ship rifles to Kansas Free-Staters and pledged to send twenty thousand settlers before the year was out. On election day of 1855, five thousand heavily armed Missouri "Border Ruffians" rode in, seized voting booths and cast four times as many ballots as there were legal voters. Missouri posses killed six Free-Staters and no one was arrested. The next year eight hundred "deputized" Missourians attacked and burned the Free State capitol at Lawrence, and destroyed two newspapers.

John Brown and his raiders arrived too late to save the city, but three days later they calmly executed five proslavery men by sword. Scholars have recoiled in horror at this cold-blooded act, but Free-Staters welcomed the retaliation, and Brown's name became a rallying cry. When 150 Missourians attacked and burned Brown's camp at Osawatomie, Brown told his son Jason

what he saw in the flames: "God sees it. I have only a short time to live – only one death to die, and I will die fighting for this cause. There will be no more peace in this land until slavery is done for. I will give them something else to do than to extend slave territory. I will carry the war into Africa." This pledge would lead Brown to Harpers Ferry and martyrdom.

As guerilla warfare raged in Kansas, President Franklin Pierce and his secretary of war, Jefferson Davis, declared the Free State movement a rebellion. When Governor Andrew H. Reeder protested the Missourians' wanton disregard for elections, he had to flee Kansas disguised as a peddler. A newly elected proslavery Kansas government rammed through laws that limited free speech, press, and officeholding to men who favored slavery. At one point two governors ruled Kansas.

Kansas governor Andrew Reeder dressed as a peddler to escape capture by proslavery militia.

On Christmas night, 1858, John Brown's Kansas band freed eleven Missouri men and women, concealed the women on a frontier farm and the men in shacks used for corn, and then guided the party to Canada.

John Brown in Kansas

On Sunday, December 19 [1858], a negro man called Jim came over the river to Osage settlement, from Missouri, and stated that he, together with his wife, two children, and another negro man, was to be sold within a day or two, and begged for help to get away. On Monday (the following) night, two small companies were made up to go to Missouri, and forcibly liberate the five slaves, together with other slaves. One of these companies I assumed to direct. We proceeded to the place, surrounded the building, liberated the slaves, and also took certain property supposed to belong to the estate. We, however, learned before leaving that a portion of the articles we had taken belonged to a man living on the plantation as a tenant, and who was supposed to have no interest in the estate. We promptly returned to him all we had taken. We then went to another plantation, where we found five more slaves, took some property and two white men. We moved all slowly away into the Territory for some distance, and then sent the white men back, telling them to follow us as soon as they chose to do so. The other company freed one female slave, took some property, and as I am informed, killed one white man (the master), who fought against the liberation.

John Brown, letter from Trading Post, Kansas, January 1859

In 1859, six months before Brown's raid on Harpers Ferry, underground agents in Lawrence, Kansas, were in dire need of help. So many fugitives had crowded its stations, wrote Colonel J. Bowles to Franklin B. Sanborn that April, that only massive financial aid could end congestion. In the last four years, Colonel Bowles wrote, "nearly three hundred fugitives" passed through Lawrence. In 1860 the number of African Americans in Kansas rose to sixty-two, and during the Civil War it swelled to more than twelve thousand, almost a tenth of the total population.

For his raid on Harpers Ferry, John Brown had raised money and recruits in the East and West. His band of seventeen whites and five Blacks included John Copeland and Lewis Sheridan Leary, an ancestor of Langston Hughes, both from Oberlin, and five of his own sons. Brown's plan failed. He was convicted of treason and hanged as John Wilkes Booth, Robert E. Lee, and Stonewall Jackson looked on. In eighteen months these witnesses

Lewis Sheridan Leary
fought and died during
John Brown's raid on
Harpers Ferry.

and others helped form the Confederacy and initiate the Civil War. Not long after that, Union soliders marched into battle singing the "Battle Hymn of the Republic" with new lyrics about John Brown – "His truth goes marching on." By the war's end U.S. soldiers would complete the bloody work begun at Harpers Ferry.

The murder and turmoil in Kansas swelled the ranks of the Republican Party and dashed the hopes of Senator Douglas. In 1856 John C. Frémont, the Republican Party's first presidential candidate, carried all states but five north of the Mason and Dixon line, unifying Northerners and Westerners as never before. In 1858 a political unknown, Abraham Lincoln, almost toppled Douglas from his Illinois Senate seat. Only an antiquated electoral system saved Douglas from defeat. When Douglas became the Democratic Party's presidential candidate in 1860, his party's Southern wing split off to back another candidate, ensuring the election of Lincoln.

Slaveholder Expansion

Planters knew they faced a choice between growth and death, since their plantation system had ruined the South's soil. Less than two generations after Mississippi entered the Union, a soil expert reported that "a large part of the state is already exhausted; the state is full of deserted fields." Judge Warner of Georgia told the U.S. Congress, "There is not a slaveholder in this House or out of it, but who knows perfectly well that whenever slavery is confined within certain specified limits, its future existence is doomed."

The Southern plantation system handed the reins of state power to a slaveholding elite. It also undermined the chances of hard-working and skilled whites. "Slavery drives free laborers – farmers, mechanics, and all, and some of the best of them too, – out of the country and fills their places with Negroes," said the president of Virginia College. Southern roads were clogged with unemployed farmers and skilled mechanics, driven into exile, heading to the frontier. Wrote an Alabama politician: "Our small planters, after taking the cream off their lands, unable to restore them with rest, manures or otherwise, are going further west and south, in search of other virgin lands, which they may and will despoil and impoverish in like manner."

By the 1840s leading planters advocated foreign expansion as the answer for the slave system. In April 1844, Secretary of State John C. Calhoun told a British diplomat he believed the annexation of Texas was necessary to protect slavery. As U.S. officials conspired to seize Texas, Texas's president, Anson James, charged the U.S. with "unholy" attempts at "manufacturing a war with Mexico." Mexican officials repeatedly warned that admitting Texas to the Union would be an act of war. But planters deemed Texas crucial to their economic and political power. In 1845 the United States admitted Texas and war broke out with Mexico. A young officer in the war, Ulysses S. Grant, later wrote: "I do not think there was ever a more wicked war than that waged by the United States on Mexico. I thought so at the time, when I was a youngster, only I had not moral courage enough to resign… Texas had no claim beyond the Nueces River, and yet we pushed on to the Rio Grande and crossed it."

SOUTHERN CHIVALRY _ ARGUMENT versus CLUB'S.

After Senator Charles Sumner of Massachusetts denounced Southern raids on Kansas, Congressman Preston Brooks of South Carolina beat him to the Senate floor.

Frederick Douglass's Solution For Kansas

Let it be known, throughout the country, that one thousand Colored families, provided with all the needful implements of pioneers, and backed up by the moral influence of the Northern people, have taken up their abode in Kansas, and slaveholders, who are now bent upon blasting that fair land with Slavery, would shunt it, as if it were infested with famine, pestilence, and earthquakes. They would stand as a wall of living fire to guard it. The true antidote, in that Territory, for black slaves, is an enlightened body of black freemen – and to that Territory should such freemen go.

Frederick Douglass opposed any U.S. invasion or expansion that would bring slavery to other lands.

To the question, Can this thing be accomplished? we answer – Yes! Three cities can, at once, be named, in which, if proper means be adopted, nine hundred of the one thousand families can be obtained in three months, who would take up their abode as permanent settlers in Kansas the coming spring. New York City and its vicinity could send three hundred families. Philadelphia and its vicinity would gladly spare three hundred families more. Cincinnati and vicinity could afford three hundred families for such a purpose; and Boston, with the aid of New England, could easily send the additional one hundred – making an army of One Thousand families... The line of argument which establishes the right of the South to settle their black slaves in Kansas, is equally good for the North in establishing the right to settle black freemen in Kansas.

Frederick Douglass's Paper, September 15, 1854

The invasion of Mexico stirred the conscience of freshman Congressman Abraham Lincoln; he challenged President Polk to justify his war by showing where American blood was shed on American soil. Philosopher Henry David Thoreau chose prison rather than pay taxes to support the war. "Abandon [your] murderous plans, and forsake the way of blood," Frederick

Douglass told U.S. officials, and called for "the recall of our forces." Congressman Horace Mann said the war had a "twofold purpose of robbing that republic of its territory, and then robbing that territory of its freedom."

In the Treaty of Guadalupe Hidalgo, Mexico surrendered half of its national domain and opened an area from Texas to California for slaveholder expansion. Congress repeatedly defeated a Wilmot Proviso that sought to prohibit slavery in the new lands. Planters enjoyed support in the North. Secretary of State James Buchanan of Pennsylvania and Northern Democrats wanted to annex all Mexico for slavery.

Slaveholders adopted the jingoist cry "Manifest Destiny" and announced that their goal was "to overspread the continent allotted by Providence." In 1842 Virginia Congressman Henry A. Wise, an administration spokesman in the House, declared, "slavery should pour itself abroad without restraint, and find no limit but the Southern ocean." In 1854 the U.S. ambassadors to Britain, France, and Spain met in Ostend, Belgium, and issued a declaration that if Spain did not sell Cuba to America "by every law human and divine, we shall be justified in wresting it from Spain if we possess the power."

Voices of Southern imperialism became more unrestrained. Mississippi Governor John Quitman, under indictment for aiding an 1850 invasion of Cuba, resigned his post to visit Baltimore, New York, and Philadelphia to drum up support for another foreign adventure. Senator Sam Houston of Texas urged the United States to seize Mexico and use it as a base to impose slavery and domination on South America.

Words soon led to action for William Walker, a Tennessee doctor and career militarist who planned "filibustering" expeditions to extend the slaveholders' empire. He tried to seize Lower California and Sonoma from Mexico to launch incursions into Central America. In 1855 Walker captured Nicaragua, declared himself dictator, restored slavery, and had his diplomats received by President Pierce. Walker also proclaimed "a formal alliance with the seceding states." But Central American forces united against Walker, and by 1857 his invasion had collapsed.

In 1860 Walker invaded Central America, but the British Navy intercepted him and turned him over to Honduran officials. Three months before eleven Southern states seceded from the Union, a firing squad representing the three races of the Americas ended Walker's violent life.

6

THE CIVIL WAR
IN THE WEST

The Civil War has been called the Second American Revolution. It emancipated four million slaves. It enacted three constitutional amendments granting Black people citizenship and Black men the right to vote. But these lofty goals were policy changes forced on President Abraham Lincoln. For two years he fought to defeat the Confederacy, restore seceded states to the Union, and not "free a single slave." It was a stalemate. When Congress passed the Corwin Amendment to extend slavery into the future, the president promised his support.

Both the Union and Confederate governments were as fiercely committed to white supremacy as any slaveholder. Like the earlier battles in "Bloody Kansas," this war was about the new Western territories: Would they enter the union as free or slave states? Lincoln and the Republican Party pledged to save Western lands for white pioneer families.

By early 1861 betrayal was in the air, as thirteen slave states formed a confederacy, wrote a constitution, and chose a congress and president. Seceded states seized federal forts and property as they left. Treason even reached New York City,

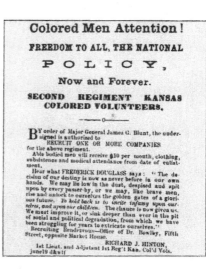

Colored Men Attention!

FREEDOM TO ALL, THE NATIONAL

P O L I C Y,

Now and Forever.

SECOND REGIMENT KANSAS
COLORED VOLUNTEERS.

BY order of Major General James G. Blunt, the undersigned is authorized to RECRUIT ONE OR MORE COMPANIES for the above regiment.
Able bodied men will receive $10 per month, clothing, subsistence and medical attendance from date of enlistment.
Hear what FREDERICK DOUGLASS says: "The decision of our destiny is now as never before in our own hands. We may lie low in the dust, despised and spit upon by every passer-by, or we may, like brave men, rise and unlock to ourselves the golden gates of a glorious future. To hold back is to write infamy upon ourselves, and upon our children. The chance is now given us. We must improve it, or sink deeper than ever in the pit of social and political degradation, from which we have been struggling for years to extricate ourselves."
Recruiting Rendezvous—Office of Dr. Bowlby, Fifth Street, opposite Market House.
RICHARD J. HINTON,
1st Lieut. and Adjutant 1st Reg't Kan. Col'd Vols.
june19 d&wtf

Abolitionist Richard J. Hinton, commander of the First Black Kansas regiment, used this poster to recruit a Second Regiment of Black Kansas Volunteers.

where Mayor Fernando Wood urged his city council to unite Manhattan, Long Island, and Staten Island as the Free State of "Tri-Insula" and join the Confederacy.

White supremacy guided Union war policies. When free Black men in the North and West rushed to enlist in the Union army, recruiters told them, "This is a white man's war!" When enslaved families fled to Union lines seeking freedom (and offering to help), they were handed back to their Confederate owners. Union generals Butler and McClellan promised to crush slave revolts in their sectors, and Washington nodded in approval.

The Oklahoma Peace March

Commanding an army of 13,000 men and officers, and anticipating a brief conflict, President Lincoln called for 75,000 volunteers to serve for three

"Our Strong Black Arms Would Be Needed"

I was a student at Wilberforce University, in Ohio, when the tocsin of war was sounded, when Fort Sumter was fired upon, and I never shall forget the thrill that ran through my soul when I thought of the coming consequences of that shot. There were one hundred and fifteen of us, students at that university, who, anxious to vindicate the stars and stripes, made up a company, and offered our services to the governor of Ohio; and, sir, we were told that this was a white man's war and that the negro had nothing to do with it. Sir, we returned -- docile, patient, waiting, casting our eyes to the heavens whence help always comes. We knew that there would come a period in the history of this nation when our strong black arms would be needed.

Congressman Richard H. Cain,
Congressional Record, 43rd Congress, First Session

months, the time he thought it would take to crush the rebellion. He was among 31 million other Americans who never expected a four-year carnage that would take 750,000 lives and leave no family untouched.

Frederick Douglass and his fellow abolitionists denounced Union policy for inviting defeat and encouraging treachery. He called for a "people's revolution" – arm the enslaved and overthrow the slaveholder system. Lincoln and the vast majority of Americans considered abolitionists unrealistic fanatics.

But during the fateful spring and summer of 1861, a people's revolution began to explode in Oklahoma that shook the Trans-Mississippi West. It first stirred when U.S. troops were recalled from the Indian Territory to fight back East. Oklahoma's Native American Nations, surrounded on three sides by slaveholding states, were now unprotected by the Union treaties. Confederates sent their diplomat Albert Pike in with troops. He forced Confederate treaties on Native American leaders as his soldiers arrested men for work details or as conscripts for their army. As Native American leaders caved in, they, African Americans, and whites alike tried to flee to safety.

Creek Chief Opothleyahola decided to free his slaves and offer refuge to all neutrals in Oklahoma.

"The Trail of Blood on Ice"

Few Oklahomans, it was soon clear, wanted any part of a war to defend slavery. Leading the resistance were the Keetoowah, or PINS, a secret antislavery network of Indians and African Americans within Native American Nations. Opothleyahola, a wealthy Creek chief, also called "Old Gouge," favored neutrality and opened his 2,000-acre North Fork stock-raising and grain plantation for people fleeing Confederate control.

Opothleyahola had fought U.S. slaveholder armies in two Seminole wars. He became an inspired voice defending his people's traditional values. As ten thousand people of all colors raced to North Fork, he freed his slaves. With one in seven residents of Oklahoma in his plantation, it looked a refugee camp and sounded like a community meeting.

When Confederate colonel Douglas Cooper marched on North Fork with fourteen hundred troops, Opothleyahola's neutrals began an exodus. Their plan was to circle northern Oklahoma recruiting more neutrals. Their enemies had other plans.

Cooper's army dogged their trail. At Round Mountain on November 19, 1861, neutrals used bows and arrows and their few rifles to drive the enemy back to Fort Gibson. On December 7, while their officers were away, a large force of conscripted Indian Confederates visited Opothleyahola's camp. What began with warm greetings ended the next morning with most Native American conscripts leaving for home and some joining the marchers.

During the Civil War, slaveholders drove their captives into Texas, away from advancing Union armies.

On October 29, 1862, a clash at Island Mound, Missouri, became the first Civil War battle for African Americans.

Then a savage winter of wind and snow, one of the worst in years, swept in. At Chustenahlah on the day after Christmas Confederate troops opened fire on the march. Hundreds were slain. Cattle, ponies, and sheep died and survivors fled, leaving their food, supplies, wounded, and dead in the snow. One Seminole chief recalled: "At that battle we lost everything we possessed: everything to take care of our women and children with, and all that we had."

As the neutrals headed toward Union lines in Kansas, their flight became "The Trail of Blood on Ice." In early 1862 about 7,600 ragged, wounded, and traumatized people straggled into southern Kansas. It had few relief facilities, with only small tents for shelter and the cold, hard ground as a bed.

Devastating losses changed many young survivors who now wanted to fight to liberate slaves. Runaways from Arkansas, Missouri, Kentucky, and Tennessee also began fleeing to freedom in Kansas. By 1865 the state's Black population had swelled to 12,527.

Abolitionist Officers Greet Recruits of Color

This multicultural force found Kansas stocked with abolitionist officers who had arrived in the 1850s with John Brown. The white officers embraced these men of Native American and African ancestry as the freedom fighters that Brown had always wanted to lead against slaveholders.

Jim Lane Meets the President

"...We need the services of such a man out there [in Kansas] at once – that we better appoint him a brigadier-general of volunteers today, and send him off with such authority to raise a force... [and] get him into actual work quickest."

President Abraham Lincoln, June 1861

General James Lane (center) Lincoln's choice for commander of Kansas Recruiting, recruited, trained, and led Black and Indian soldiers on raids into Missouri.

Their commander was General James Lane, the same committed racist who served as Topeka convention president in 1855. He was an Iowa general during the Mexican invasion that claimed a huge portion of Mexico for U.S. slaveholders. By 1856 Lane rode in "Bleeding Kansas" with Brown's antislavery raiders to make Kansas a free state. Lane was later appointed one of its two U.S. senators.

In Washington in 1861, President-elect Lincoln met Lane as he prepared for his inauguration amid rumors of assassination plots. Lane offered to recruit 116 armed Kansans for the White House. For twenty days his men camped in the East Room while Lane slept outside the president's bedroom. Lincoln eventually named him commander of Kansas recruiting.

General James Blunt, a doctor, became John Brown's leading officer in Bleeding, Kansas. During the Civil War, he was an aggressive major general.

Grim-faced, impulsive, a man anchored only by his ambition, Lane followed a ruthless fighting code that his men admired and many others feared. He won the support of his officers and men as he built a freedom-fighting army of many races.

By the summer of 1861 Lane led the First Regiment Kansas Volunteer Cavalry, which included the first ex-slaves to fight in the war, into Missouri. His 30 men defeated 130 mounted Confederate guerrillas. He called his men "the finest specimens of manhood I have ever gazed upon."

Lane authorized General Blunt, a doctor and Brown's highest-ranking officer, to recruit more African Americans. By fall Blunt and other officers were leading troops of color eager to free Missouri slaves. To recruit runaways for his armies, Lane offered certificates of freedom and threatened those reluctant to take up arms.

By July 1862 Lane authorized Blunt to recruit all men in Kansas "willing to fight." He picked two other officers he met in the 1850s: Colonel William Phillips, one of Brown's two brigade commanders, and Captain Richard J. Hinton, Brown's biographer. They trained and led invasions of slave territories. Kansas's officers were now defying policies set by President Lincoln's War Department. As soldiers rolled up victories, the War Department did not appear to notice.

After each invasion Lane guided or pushed some into his Kansas ranks. They were joined by runaways fleeing slave states, free men of color, and Native Americans. The appearance of Black soldiers inspired many escape plots and disrupted plantation life.

Kansas monument to its African American soldiers who fought for freedom

Kansas monument to John Brown

Between 1860 and 1863 Missouri's enslaved population fell from 114,000 to 78,000. Runaways began to find refuge in Iowa, Illinois, and Kansas. To avoid the advancing Black troops, planters force-marched enslaved families as far away as Texas.

In such units as the Indian Home Guards and Indian Brigades, Black Indian members served as interpreters between their Native American brothers and white officers. The new troops continued to defeat or hold their own against seasoned Confederate units.

On July 17, 1863, Blunt's multicultural army of 3,000 faced 6,000 Missouri State Guard, Confederate cavalry, and guerilla units at Honey Springs in the largest battle of the Indian Territory. Confident that the mere appearance of armed Confederates would cause Black soldiers to surrender, some Confederate soldiers arrived with 300–400 pairs of handcuffs. Instead the new Union soldiers routed the enemy in what the *New York Times* headlined their "desperate bravery."

A U.S. officer reported, "They fought like tigers." Six Killer, a Black Cherokee, shot two Confederates, bayoneted another, and clubbed a fourth with his rifle butt. Sergeant Edward Lowry, ordered to surrender by three Confederates, instead knocked all three from their horses.

From other trans-Mississippi battlefields, Union generals and Northern journalists reported the "extraordinary courage under fire" of the new troops of color. Clearly these soldiers were fighting for something more fiercely personal than saving the Union.

So too were Lane and his white officers. They repeatedly petitioned the War Department to pay their men the $13 a month granted to whites, and urged their best soldiers be appointed officers. Colonel James Montgomery's "colored brigade" – Indians, whites and ex-slaves – fought for nine months without any wages to protest unequal pay. But equal pay came only after Emancipation and formal recruitment.

On Emancipation Day, January 1, 1863, Lane's men and officers held their own celebration of the Union's new policy. In a richly symbolic ceremony, Lane's multicultural army honored their victories and saluted their hero, John Brown. Wives and children cheered their courage and the rescue of enslaved families. Blunt's men sang the John Brown song, and added a fi-

The decisive victory of the multicultural Kansas forces at Honey Springs in 1863 secured Union control of the Indian Territory.

John M. Langston of Ohio (center) recruited Blacks as soldiers. In 1863 he presented the regimental colors to the Fifth Infantry Regiment of the United States Colored Troops at Camp Delaware.

nal line – "John Brown sowed, and the harvesters are we." Men and officers, Blunt wrote, then shared a barbecue and "strong drink."

The Impact of Emancipation

Lincoln's mass recruitment of former slaves and free men of color arrived as both sides were running out of reserves. Enslaved families that had provided food for Southern citizens and soldiers, or picked cotton to sell abroad, became runaways. Confederate desertions rose and Southern cities faced food riots.

Emancipation also brought Frederick Douglass and the abolitionists to the fore as Union recruiters. Almost 200,000 Black men served in 150 regiments. With less training and fewer medical officers and facilities, recruits of color suffered 37,000 battlefield deaths. Runaways also served as spies, and others, including women, labored in Union Army camps.

The military success of Kansas soldiers of color "mostly from Missouri," historian James M. McPherson notes in a letter to the author, was one of the "factors in the summer and fall of 1862 that moved Lincoln" toward issuing the Emancipation Proclamation.

These runaways and free men of color, when joined by more than 150,000 others, tipped the war's balance. African American troops liberated Petersburg, Wilmington, Charleston (the heart of the Confederacy), and finally Richmond, its capitol. To cheering crowds of liberated slaves, Black Union cavalrymen escorted President Lincoln through the streets of Richmond.

Without his Black soldiers, the president said, he would have been forced to withdraw from the war in three weeks. In November of 1864, their success in battle helped persuade voters to elect him president for a second term. By then General Howell Cobb, whose Confederacy did not dare arm its slaves, wrote, "If slaves make good soldiers our whole theory of slavery is wrong."

The First Black Officers

In 1862 Lane appointed African American William D. Matthews to artillery officer. Mathews's life of daring had begun in running a Maryland station of the Underground Railroad. In Kansas he rode with John Brown and ran the busy Waverly House station. In January 1863, the Union formally commissioned him as a captain and its first official Black officer. In July 1864 Lane made officers of African Americans Patrick Minor and H. Ford Douglass. In Illinois, July 1862, Douglass became the only Black man to raise and command his own company. Minor had served as a recruiter.

William D. Mathews, born a slave, ran an Underground Railroad station and then recruited and became a lieutenant of the First Kansas Colored Volunteers.

The three Black men began to assert their new authority and investigative powers to probe the treatment of soldiers of color. Commander Lane, they found, often forced enlistments with threats, or ordered former slaves beaten and starved. On August 3, 1862, he publicly threatened a thousand Black men to join the First Kansas Colored Infantry Regiment, saying, "If you won't fight we will make you." They exposed and ended this Lane practice.

Next the three found that their commander jailed Black soldiers too traumatized to fight for "shirking official duty," whereas white soldiers suffering similar mental problems were discharged to their families. Matthews, Minor, and Douglass won Black men the right to return home.

The War Ends

In 1865 peace saw Commander Lane returning to his white supremacist roots. Kansas legislators again chose him as their senator. The next year Lane fired one more shot, taking his own life. Fellow Kansans named Lane University in his honor.

Matthews, Minor, and Douglass settled into Kansas African American society. With Richard Hinton they organized the first Kansas Colored Convention to promote equal education and citizenship. Its delegates announced to white Kansas, "Our misery is not necessary to your happiness." Kansas became the first state to erect monuments to John Brown and soldiers of color.

The Union armies of the Trans-Mississippi West blazed a historic trail. They were the first to enroll men of every race, the first to appoint officers of color, and the first to enter the Civil War as liberators.

Richard J. Hinton fought in Kansas with John Brown and commanded Kansas troops of color during the Civil War.

7
CALIFORNIA

Africans first arrived in California in 1697, traveling from Mexico with Indians and Jesuit missionaries. In 1768 King Charles of Spain, fearing Imperial Russia was about to send troops southward from Alaska, ordered Captain Gaspar de Portola's army to California. The expedition's servants were recruited from Rosario, Bolivia, where two-thirds of the population was of African descent.

In Mexican California, a tolerant Catholic Church sanctified interracial marriages and did not rigidly oppose racial mixing. This became clear on September 4, 1781, when, of forty-four persons who founded Los Angeles, twenty-six were of African ancestry, two were Caucasians, and the others were Indians, some mixed with Caucasians. Maria Rita Valdez, whose African grandparents were among the city's founders, owned Rancho Rodeo de Las Aguas, today known as Beverly Hills. Francisco Reyes, of African descent, owned the San Fernando Valley, and in the 1790s became mayor of Los Angeles.

By 1790 a Spanish census recorded many people of African descent in California: 18 percent of San Francisco, 24 percent of San Jose, 20 percent of Santa Barbara, and 18 percent of Monterey. Color did not prove a bar to wealth or high office. Andreas and Pio Pico were born to an African American landholding family in the Simi Valley. Andreas Pico, a general during the U.S.-Mexican War, inflicted a stunning defeat on U.S. forces at San Pascual. Pio Pico, who twice served as governor of California, owned a large San Diego ranch (which later became the Marine base of Camp Pendleton). In 1846, as California's last Mexican governor, Pio Pico surrendered to the United States.

Governor Pio Pico and his wife. Pico had to surrender California to U.S. forces.

William Leidesdorff

When William Leidesdorff sailed his 106-ton schooner *Julia Ann* into San Francisco harbor in 1841, the town was called Yerba Buena, a sleepy Mexican province of 200 residents with unpaved, dusty streets. Young Leidesdorff would do much to change that.

Born in 1810 in St. Croix, Virgin Islands, to a Danish planter and his enslaved African wife, Leidesdorff arrived as an experienced sailor and merchant. His spent his first four years trading goods between Hawaii and San Francisco, and in 1844 he became a naturalized Mexican citizen.

Leidesdorff purchased land in town, and at thirty-six he owned Rancho Rio de los Americanos, 35,000

California pioneer William Leidesdorff

acres on the banks of the American River just east of John Sutter's sawmill. His landholdings and power brought him in contact with leading Californians, from Governor Pio Pico to explorer John C. Frémont, and he soon owned estates throughout the growing city.

Leidesdorff was drawn to businessmen who wanted to make California part of the United States, and in 1845 U.S. consul Larkin appointed him a vice-consul, making him the first African American in the U.S. diplomatic service. Part of the inner circle of men promoting U.S. intervention, he denounced Americans who opposed a seizure of California as "more Mexican than the Mexicans themselves." That April he provided a boat for U.S. marine lieutenant Archibald Gillespie and told him to bear "Glorious news for [John Charles] Frémont" that war with Mexico was inevitable.

In 1846, when pro-U.S. forces seized power in Sonoma, Leidesdorff's report helped guide U.S. policy toward support. In July, Captain John Montgomery landed in San Francisco with seventy U.S. Marines and spent an evening discussing strategy with Leidesdorff. The next day he raised the American flag in the town plaza and read a proclamation in Spanish that Leidesdorff had translated. By September the new rulers were securely in power, and Leidesdorff hosted a celebration for U.S. officers and "over 100 ladies, Californian and American."

Leidesdorff owned the famous City Hotel in 1847.

In 1849 Leidesdorff established San Francisco's first school in this building.

Leidesdorff prospered under the new administration and increased his role in civic affairs. He was appointed a member of the City Council, and on a prominent city lot he constructed the City Hotel, San Francisco's first hotel. In 1847 he supervised the building of a spacious house at the corner of California and Montgomery streets, where he would live for the rest of his life.

That year Leidesdorff also launched the first steam-powered ship, the thirty-seven-foot *Sitka*, to sail into San Francisco Bay. In 1848 he organized the city's first horse race, and as treasurer of San Francisco's City Council, he helped establish California's first public school.

An 1848 San Francisco street map shows Leidesdorff as owning choice waterfront properties on Yerba Buena Cove, an area since filled in as part

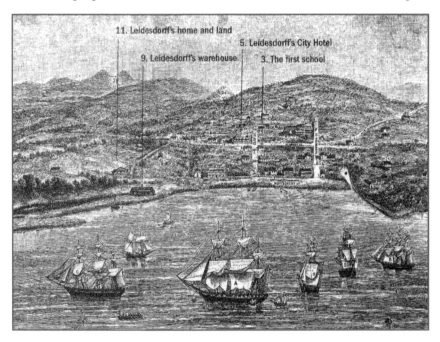

An 1847 map of San Francisco showing Leidesdorff's key properties

of the expanding city. On Block 8 he owned the beach area; on Block 9 he owned building A, an adobe house; on Block 13 he built a warehouse on the beach, on what later would be called Leidesdorff and California streets.

In May 1848, Alexander Leidesdorff was stricken with typhus. He died at thirty-eight at the height of his wealth and influence. Flags flew at half-mast, businesses closed for his funeral, and cannons were fired. He was buried beneath the floor of the city's Mission Dolores, and a memorial plaque was placed to the right of the mission's door. Gold had been discovered five months earlier at Sutter's Mill near Leidesdorff's property. California was about to change forever.

The Gold Rush

The feverish pursuit of gold overwhelmed California in 1848, and opportunity suddenly beckoned to people around the globe. In their eagerness to find wealth, white people who rushed in failed to build the racial walls that marked other states. By 1860 four thousand African Americans lived in California, and two thousand called themselves prospectors.

Eastern emigrants pushed westward across the perilous Death Valley, the Mojave Desert, and the Humboldt Sink. Along parched trails they passed broken wagons, skeletons of cattle and horses, and shallow human graves.

People hurtled excitedly toward the Mother Lode. As their wagon bumped along, two German immigrants and two African Americans "had von good fight," reported one of the Germans. Though the brawl left the four men "bruised, mashed, scratched, gouged, torn and almost literally cut to pieces," they made up and pushed on. At the western end of the Mojave Trail a former African American soldier managed a ranch that welcomed pioneers and sold them beef.

By the end of 1850 California's population had soared to 100,000, and two years later it stood at 225,000, including 100,000 prospectors. That year gold production peaked at $80 million. A passion for it gripped African Americans no less than others. In 1850 a white woman at the Humboldt Sink described "a Negro woman… tramping along through the heat and dust, carrying a cast iron bake stove on her head, with her provisions and a blanket piled on top – all she possessed in the world – bravely pushing on for Cal-

Gold seeker at Auburn Ravine in 1852

ifornia." That year Frederick Douglass's widely read *North Star* paper called California a magnet for the daring and ambitious, and reported that forty Black prospectors had recently set out from New Bedford, Massachusetts.

African Americans were lured by success stories. In April 1849, Reuben Ruby of Portland, Maine, mined $600 in gold, and after four months at the diggings two African American men returned to Philadelphia with $30,000. William H. Hall, who also arrived that year, returned home to New York in a year with enough cash to pay for a wedding a local paper characterized as "perhaps without a parallel in the history of the coloured society in New York." Hall also made a fortune delivering a thrilling lecture, "Hopes and Prospects of Colored People in California."

African American prospectors often labored alongside Native Americans; emigrants from Latin America, China, and Europe; and white Americans. Some negotiated cooperative arrangements with Mexicans, Kanakas Indians, and immigrants from France, Wales, Portugal, and China. One encampment of miners included African Americans and a hundred Chinese immigrants. Near the Yuba River a partnership of two whites and seven Af-

MINES D'OR DE LA CALIFORNIE.

A French paper depicting the multiracial mix at California's Mother Lode

rican Americans, including two runaways, found gold. At a Feather River camp a white man reported working with "two doctors, a lawyer, two negroes, and an Indian."

Few prospectors found instant wealth, and the glamour of the gold fields faded with the arrival of desperate men. Even those who struck it rich feared for their lives and fortunes. Where law reached, it did so with vigilante committees' ropes that separated "guilty" from "innocent" with scant attention to evidence. Wealth in California was not gathered by eager prospectors scratching in hills but by calculating town merchants. Eggs sold for a dollar each, strong shovels cost a fortune, and gambling casinos gathered gold from miners.

Men who clawed at the countryside by day encountered others in town who clawed at their pockets at night. In muddy, shabby, and ungoverned towns, prospectors found that the rainbow trail to California led to unhappiness more often than to a pot of gold. Drawn by the Mother Lode's huge magnet, two thousand African Americans and seventeen thousand Chinese had reached California by 1852.

Spanish Flats miners of two races, 1852

Peter Brown: "The Best Place for Black Folks"

I am now mining about 25 miles from Sacramento City and doing well. I have been working for myself for the past two months... and have cleared three hundred dollars. California is the best country in the world to make money. It is also the best place for black folks on the globe. All a man has to do is work, and he will make money.

Letter from Peter Brown to Alley Brown, December 1851,
Missouri Historical Society, St. Louis

Building a White State

By September 1, 1849, when forty-nine delegates assembled at Monterey to write California's constitution, the most bigoted voices represented mining districts. Would his constituents dig alongside people of color? one delegate asked. "No, sir, they would leave this country first." White prospectors, recalled settler Walter Colton, were not concerned with "slavery in the abstract or as it exists in other communities; they must themselves swing the pick, and they won't swing it by the side of negro slaves." The state's two papers, the *Californian* and the *California Star*, condemned both slavery and free people of color. "We desire only a white population in California," wrote the editor of the *Californian*.

White miners had circulated a rumor that African Americans had an internal antenna that enabled them to detect gold, so they should not be allowed in the gold fields. Black prospectors hoped it was true. In 1850, when Thomas Green and fellow Texas slaveholders arrived with fifteen enslaved people, they ran into trouble. No sooner had they staked out claims at Rose's Bar when white miners met to protest that "no slave or negro should own

California gold seekers, as shown in the *London Illustrated News*, January 1849

claims or even work in the mines." A second meeting warned the Texans that unless they left, they and their slaves would be forcibly removed. They left.

To preserve the gold fields for whites, California's legislature imposed a "Foreign Miners Tax" of $4 a month. The category included Native Americans, African Americans, South Americans, and other people of color. Corrupt collectors demanded extra payments, and occasionally shot those slow to comply. The Foreign Miners Tax paid for the new state's first decade.

The presence of African American miners in California is affirmed in documents and photographs, and in thirty place names such as Negro Hill, Negro Flat, and Arroyo de los Negros. In his "A Miner's Sunday in Caloma," eyewitness Charles Gillespie wrote about "mulattoes from Jamaica" and "Negroes from the Southern States swaggering in the expansive feeling of runaway freedom."

Some enslaved men bargained with their owners for a chance at prospecting. In 1849 Alvin Coffey, twenty-seven, was brought to California by Dr. Bassett, his Missouri master. In two years Coffey panned $5,000 in gold and earned $700 more washing clothes. But when Coffey handed Basset his money for his family's freedom, Bassett kept the cash and sold Coffey in Missouri. His new owner sent Coffey back to the gold fields, where he began all over. This time he earned $1,500 in gold at placer mining, which he used to liberate himself, then produced more to buy his wife and two daughters. Coffey's family resettled in a mining town, and the all-white California Pioneer's Association of Forty-Niners later elected him its first African American member.

Daniel Rogers, like Coffey, first had to survive a double-dealing owner. After he handed the Arkansas man a thousand dollars in gold dust for his liberty, he simply pocketed it. But this so incensed other whites in Arkansas they raised the cash for Rogers's liberty and handed him a certificate testifying to his "honesty, industry and integrity." Rogers then purchased his family's liberty and they settled in California.

In 1849 Emmanuel Quivers bought his freedom and that of wife and their children from his employer, Virginia's Tredegar Iron Works. With little more than his free papers, he left for Stockton, where he ran a successful blacksmith shop. But the Quivers family goal was to have their five children enrolled in a public school. They fought a long battle to end the town's

Diary of a Black Forty-Niner

I started from St. Louis, Missouri, on the 2nd of April in 1849. There was quite a crowd of neighbors who drove through the mud and rain to St. Joe to see us off. About the first of May we organized the train. There were twenty wagons in number and from three to five men to each wagon...

Alvin A. Coffey wrote a memoir of his daring trip to California.

We got across the plains to Fort Larimie, the 16th of June and the ignorant driver broke down a good many oxen on the trains. There were a good many ahead of us, who had doubled up their trains and left tons upon tons of bacon and other provisions...

Starting to cross the desert to Black Rock at 4 o'clock in the evening, we traveled all night. The next day it was hot and sandy...

A great number of cattle perished before we got to Black Rock... I drove our oxen all the time and I knew about how much an ox could stand. Between nine and ten o'clock a breeze came up and the oxen threw up their heads and seemed to have a new life. At noon we drove into Black Rock...

We crossed the South Pass on the Fourth of July. The ice next morning was as thick as a dinner-plate...

On the morning of the 15th [of October] we went to dry-digging mining. We dug and dug to the first of November, at night it commenced raining, and rained and snowed pretty much all the winter. We had a tent but it barely kept us all dry. There were from eight to twelve in one camp. We cut down pine trees for stakes to make a cabin. It was a whole week before we had a cabin to keep us dry.

Reminiscences of Alvin Coffey, **Society of California Pioneers**

segregated educational system, and in 1877 the school board admitted the Quivers children and abolished segregation.

One of the Quivers's daughters married Moses Rodgers, a former slave who, as a mining engineer, made a fortune during the Gold Rush. A respected metallurgist, he served as superintendent of the Mt. Gaines Mine and also purchased mines in Mariposa County. In 1978, the Stockton City Council declared the Rodgers family home, built in 1898 at 921 San Joaquin Avenue, a landmark.

In Southern California an African American named Dick staked off a rich vein, sold off a portion for $100,000, and bought a home in Sacramento. Far less lucky was another Black prospector named Dick, who staked a claim near Tuttlestown. It yielded $1,000 in gold, but he lost it gambling and killed himself.

The Free People of Color

California entered the Union in 1850 with 91,635 whites, largely men without families, and 952 people of color, also largely men. Among African Americans, men from Free States outnumbered those from slave states, and prospectors, adventurers, and wanderers outnumbered farmers.

Some rejected mining for other jobs. Two African Americans carried the mail for the Pony Express. William Robinson rode the mail from Stockton to the Mines. After serving for many years as a Pony Express rider between Merced and Mariposa, George Monroe, son of a prospector, became one of the state's most renowned stage drivers. In 1879 Monroe was chosen to drive President Ulysses S. Grant along the treacherous S curves of the Wanona Trail into Yosemite Valley. Monroe Meadows in Yosemite is named after him.

Pony Express rider
William Robinson

People of color also sought city jobs, since wages were high and the work was more dependable than prospecting. African Americans who enjoyed

Pony Express rider George Monroe

reputations as excellent cooks were able to command exorbitant salaries. Others owned or worked in hotels, restaurants, and stores.

The Gold Rush attracted a highly diverse and worldly Black population. Northerners and Southerners, free and enslaved men and women, intellectuals, cooks, and menials, made the new state their home. They also began to discuss how to advance their goals of equality, justice, and fair treatment. Before the 1850s ended, California had become the country's richest African American community.

Within a year of the Gold Rush, Black self-help and cultural organizations began to sprout. In December 1849, thirty-seven San

A *London Illustrated News* artist captured California's racial mixture during a night at a Sacramento casino.

Francisco men formed a Mutual Benefit and Relief Society, the city's first African American community associa- tion. They wrote a constitution, held meetings, and recruited new arrivals. In an open letter the soci- ety claimed its members were "making from one hundred to three hundred dollars per month."

In 1853 prominent African Americans opened a San Francisco cultural center, the Ath- eneum. With a saloon on the first floor for reve- nue, the community's great pride was a flight above – an 800-book library, a museum, and a lecture hall designed to attract women and men and promote the pursuit of education, progress, and piety. Members were expected to be moral and intelligent and improve them-

Pioneer Biddy Mason

selves through reading. By the following year the city boasted three Black churches, and by the end of the Civil War, Black California had given birth to three newspapers, each well edited and militant on the subject of civil rights.

One of the most prominent Californians of the day, Biddy Mason, thir- ty-two, trudged from Georgia with three daughters to Utah and then Cali-

The Biddy Mason home in Los Angeles

fornia behind the dozens of wagons of Robert Smith, her Mormon owner. During the long journey she served as a midwife and cook, and also was assigned to keep the cattle together.

In 1856, when Smith decided to return to the South, Mrs. Mason and her oldest daughter had other ideas. They persuaded a local sheriff to serve Smith with legal papers. After he failed to appear in court, Biddy Mason gave two days of testimony. She and her three daughters were freed.

Using earnings from her lucrative work as a midwife, Mrs. Mason acquired large parcels of Los Angeles real estate. As her fortune grew, she donated money to schools, churches, and nursing homes; aided flood victims ;and delivered food to prisoners in the dank jails. In 1872 she helped found the First African Methodist Episcopal Church of Los Angeles, then a daycare center and a nursery. By her death in 1891 her investments had made the family one of California's wealthiest. Many knew and few forgot the generosity of Biddy Mason.

Daring Educators

From 1854, when Elizabeth Thorn Scott opened the first African American schools in Sacramento and Oakland, the Black community's struggle for education was part of its fight for justice and economic opportunity. No figure better represented this combination of interests than J. B. Sanderson, a tall, slim, eloquent young man who was born free in Massachusetts, where he became an ordained Methodist minister and worked with Frederick Douglass.

In California, Sanderson quickly rose to leadership. He organized schools in San Francisco, Oakland, Sacramento, and Stockton, and often served as teacher until others could be hired. As a civil rights activist, he was a commanding presence in three Black statewide protest conventions during the 1850s.

Sanderson conducted a two-front war for education. Charging that denial of education to young people of color threatened the state's future, he prodded officials to create or fund schools for children of color. When officials refused, Sanderson and others shouted "taxation without representation." Then he mobilized people to build schools with private funds, a huge burden for poor communities. In April 1855, Sanderson secured enough

"Today I Opened a School"

Today I opened a school for colored children. The necessity for this step is evident. There are 30 or more children in Sacramento of proper age and no school provided for them by the Board of Education. They must no longer be neglected, left to grow up in ignorance, exposed to all manner of evil influences, with the danger of contracting idle and vicious habits. A school they must have. I am induced to undertake this enterprise by the advice of friends and the solicitation of parents. I can do but little, but with God's blessing, I will do what I can.

J. B. Sanderson *Diary*, April 20, 1855

donations to open a school on Fifth and O streets in Sacramento with an enrollment of twenty-eight children and a daily attendance of twenty-two.

In 1859 Sanderson began to teach in St. Cyprian's elementary school in San Francisco. Although two hundred children had enrolled, daily attendance was only about thirty-two, largely because classes were conducted in a dank basement, a loud band practiced music above, street noises interrupted lessons, and the school lacked maps, blackboards, and other instructional tools. In vain Sanderson searched for a suitable building. "Who would sell a lot for a colored school?" he wondered in his diary. "Property holders usually object to a school upon or contiguous to their property or homes. They dislike the crowds and the noise of children. Added to this was the old prejudice against the Negro."

Some young Californians battled for the right to an education. After graduating from the white San Francisco Spring Valley school, Sarah Lester, fifteen, the light-skinned daughter of civil rights activists, enrolled in a white high school in 1858. In her first year she scored second highest in academic achievement and first in art and music.

Then, an anonymous letter to the *San Francisco Herald* demanded her expulsion. For months debate roiled the city. Tempers rose as other families sought admission for light-skinned children, white neighbors petitioned to let Sarah complete her studies, and white students threatened a boycott if their popular classmate was expelled. Each day her activist mother, Nancy Lester, walked Sarah to school.

"A Death Blow to Our System"

Our public school system permits of no mixture of the races. ... Whilst I will foster by all proper means the education of the races, I should deem it a death blow to our system to permit the mixture of the races in the same school.

California state school superintendent Paul K. Hubbs, quoted in the *Sacramento Daily Union*, January 30, 1855

Tensions rose when the school board voted to expel Sarah and the superintendent refused to act. After threats and further turmoil, the Lesters withdrew their daughter from school and left for Victoria, Canada. Sarah Lester wrote a friend, "I can scarcely bear to talk about schools."

In 1859 Sacramento's African American families united to start "Mixed School #2." They hired a white teacher, and enrolled thirty to thirty-five pupils, mostly girls, with an average attendance of twenty-three. Despite a dilapidated building that foul weather often shut down, by 1860 three students,

Educator Jeremiah B. Sanderson

Nancy Lester walked her daughter, Sarah, to school each day.

daughters of a barber, an expressman, and a hotel steward, each won silver achievement medals from the Sacramento Board of Education. In 1863 the school had a new building, but it soon was destroyed by an arsonist and was not rebuilt until 1866.

Battles Over Bondage

Something in the California air fanned the flames of freedom. Enslaved men and women fought for liberty on its streets, in its courts, and aboard the ships in its harbors. The struggle began before the United States took California from Mexico. In 1846 a woman known only as Mary, who may have been the first African American to arrive in California from the East, was brought to San Jose by her Missouri owner. Mary was the first person of African descent to sue in court and win her liberty in the West.

In Sacramento in 1849, a man named Charles twice had to win his freedom. He sued for liberty and a judge invoked Mexican law to free him. But his enraged "owner" tried to beat him into submission on the street. Charles went before another judge, this time represented by two white attorneys, and again won.

The state's free people of color often provided valuable assistance to escapees. Local African Americans, wrote a German visitor, "exhibit a great deal of energy and intelligence in saving their brothers" and were "especially talented" in aiding runaways. Peter Lester, for example, invited enslaved people he met on the street to his home and taught them about their rights, and they left singing antislavery songs.

California enforced its own Fugitive Slave Law.

In February 1850 the first fugitive case to reach public attention came from a brawl on a San Jose street in which a master beat his slave with a club and both men were arrested. Contact with free people of color, the master complained to the judge, had led to the disobedience. The court ruled in the master's favor, and before defense lawyers could arrive with writs, he spirited the man out of town. Another street brawl in Sacramento led to a court hearing in which the slave was represented by two white attorneys, and won his liberty.

Civil rights activist Mary Ellen Pleasant

The earliest case in San Francisco involved Frank, who admitted he was a Missouri slave. White attorneys defended Frank, and Judge Morrison set him free, claiming California laws against slavery outweighed the federal Fugitive Slave Law. The judge ruled, perhaps with an inward twinkle, that Frank's words were inadmissible since state law banned Black testimony.

In April 1852 legislators reacted to the Morrison decision by passing a state Fugitive Slave Act. The next year in Auburn, when Mr. Brown, a Missourian, invoked state law to plead that "Lucy" was his slave, Lucy was prepared. Her white attorney appeared with the freedom papers she left with him – papers signed by Brown's father, her former owner – and her case was dismissed.

The excitement over Frank and Lucy and the new fugitive law also convinced Mary Ellen Pleasant, a wealthy free woman of color and abolitionist from New England, to enter the fray. Year after year she rode her wagon into rural districts to rescue enslaved people.

Though California's Supreme Court upheld its Fugitive Slave Law, in 1855 antislavery agitation mounted and the law lapsed into disuse. Two years later, in the Archey Lee case in San Francisco, the California Supreme

Court ruled Lee deserved his freedom and then returned him to his master anyway. The African American community exploded in anger and the legislature considered registering Black residents and banning further emigration to the state. Neither Lee nor his community nor white abolitionists were ready to give up. Antislavery forces mobilized inside and outside the court, and Lee eventually won his freedom. His jubilant friends carried him off to a victory celebration arranged by Mary Ellen Pleasant.

Civil Rights Campaigns

General William Tecumseh Sherman liked to tell about his friend, General Persifer F. Smith, who would "take off his cap and make a profound bow to every colored man whom he met in San Francisco in 1849, because he said, they were the only gentlemen who kept their promises." General Smith was in a minority. Not many white Californians believed that no matter how honest, reliable, hardworking, or wealthy he or she might be, their neighbors of color deserved the same rights. The blurred racial lines that marked Mexican rule became fixed in stone under the new U.S. government.

Changes began in 1849 at California's constitutional convention. One delegate denounced African Americans as "a brutish and depraved race."

Senator Daniel Broderick, challenged to a duel because he opposed slavery, fired into the air — like a gentleman. Then he was shot by Chief Justice Terry. "They killed me because I was against slavery," he said before he died.

Another warned of "a black tide over the land… greater than the locusts of Egypt." Whites feared they would be unable, as one delegate said, "to compete with the bands of negroes who would be set to work under the direction of capitalists. It would become a monopoly of the worst character. The profit of the mines would go into the pockets of single individuals." Delegates rejected exclusion 33 to 9, but the constitution, by reserving voting rights and militia service for white men, initiated a white supremacy state.

In his first speech as governor, Peter H. Burnett warned against a "heterogeneous mass of human beings," and asked legislators to exclude African Americans. John McDougal, the second governor, refused to pardon Black prison inmates and warned the gold fields "would bring swarms of them to our shore." In 1851 the legislature passed a Homestead Act that barred African Americans from purchasing public land.

The next year legislators denied African Americans the right to testify against whites in court. This made it impossible for a woman or man to appear in court and identify a rapist, thief, murderer, or arsonist. It left the Black business class without legal protection.

In the law's first year wealthy San Francisco entrepreneurs Mifflin Gibbs and Peter Lester were robbed and assaulted and had no recourse. Two white men walked into the Gibbs and Lester imported shoe and boot store. One selected an expensive pair of boots and asked Lester to put them aside. A few hours after they left, the customer's partner returned, tried on the boots, and walked out without paying. Then both men returned with weapons, the customer demanded his boots, and began to beat Lester.

Lester was among those who organized San Francisco's Franchise League and launched its petition campaign asking the legislature to repeal its ban on Black testimony. Despite signatures from many Black and white Californians, only one representative voted to receive what another called "a petition from such a source." A year later more petitions arrived. One legislator suggested they be thrown out the window, others suggested faster ways of disposal.

Then, in 1856, in *People v. Hall*, a state court extended the denial of Black voting rights and testimony to all people of color. Speaking for "the European white man," judges declared the state's obligation to "shield" him from "the corrupting influence of degraded castes." Without these restrictions, the

Grafton Tyler Brown came to San Francisco to paint landscapes of the Pacific Northwest.

court warned, "we might soon see them at the polls, in the jury box, upon the bench, and in our legislative halls." The jurists concluded, "This is not a speculation which exists in the excited and overheated imagination of the patriot and statesman, but it is an actual and present danger."

African Americans began to realize their problems were statewide, and as they had in the East and Midwest, summoned state conventions aimed at repeal of the hated Black Laws. On November 21, 1855, the first convention convened at Sacramento's African American Methodist Episcopal Church with forty-nine delegates – lawyers, businessmen, journalists, ministers, teachers, and community leaders. J. B. Sanderson delivered the keynote speech, a stinging call for action: "the laws scarcely recognize us; public sentiment is prejudiced against us; we are misunderstood, and misrepresented; it is needful that we should meet, communicate, and confer with each other upon some plan of representing our interests before the people."

Delegates were told of African American prospectors who had been driven from their claims and denied help from the legal system. In San Francisco a Black man had been stabbed by a white man in front of twenty Black people, delegates heard, only to be exonerated since there were no white witnesses.

The convention listened to a report that the state's African American population stood at 4,815 people who owned $2,413,000 in real and personal property. "Immense sums," the report noted, had been paid by individuals to purchase the liberty of loved ones. The data, unknown until then, were issued to instill confidence in communities and impress white residents. Delegates also proposed creating a community newspaper and a bank, and urged public demonstrations against discrimination.

In September 1855, California's first Black newspaper, *Mirror of the Times*, appeared and was circulated weekly by agents in thirty counties from the Mexican border to the Oregon line. When legislators ignored petitions signed by three hundred lawyers and others, the paper's editorial called them hypocrites and "liars."

Advice to Black Californians

Let every Colored resident of the State… abandon such positions as boot-black, waiters, servants, and carriers, and other servile employment, and if they cannot engage in trading, mechanical pursuits or farming, let them pitch into mining from which they have not yet been debarred; although it perhaps remains for the notorious Taney to determine how soon that will be done. Money can be made if followed with industry, accompanied with strict economy. And money will purchase stock farms, and certainly our people are as well, if not better qualified for that calling as any on the face of the earth.

Mirror of the Times, San Francisco, December 12, 1857

The next year, sixty-four delegates attended the second statewide convention in Sacramento, which again emphasized the right of testimony. Murderers and arsonists, a delegate explained, "may go unpunished because only a colored man saw the act or heard the plot… When will the people of this state learn that justice to the colored man is justice to themselves?"

Representing Nevada County's mining and farming community, delegate Booth proudly detailed his constituents' ownership of $300,000 in mining claims, their new church, and plans to build a school. "We are showing to our white fellow-citizens that we have some natural abilities," he said.

A heated dispute flared when a delegate offered a resolution to "hail with delight" America's progress. William H. Newby, editor of *Mirror of the Times*, responded, "I would hail the advent of a foreign army upon our

"Only Just and Right"

The necessity of establishing schools for the education of our youth, would seem too evident to need urging. And yet there is scarcely a village or town in California that possesses a common school for the education of Colored children. It is true that we are compelled to pay taxes for the support of those already established, and from which our children are excluded; but that is of course, only just and right. It is also true that we are denied our portion of the public school-fund, but as we are not possessed of any rights which the white man is bound to respect, it is perhaps only right and proper that we should continually give and never receive.

Without schools for the education of those who are to compose the next generation of actors on this great stage, we cannot expect our condition to be permanently improved – for it is upon the present youth of the country that we must make impressions that will perfect what we can only hope to commence.

Thomas Duff, *Mirror of the Times*, December 8, 1857

shores, if that army provided liberty to me and my people in bondage." He concluded, "If we are capable of hailing such a progress, we were fit for nothing else, and ought to be enslaved." Some delegates admonished Newby, but the "hail with delight" resolution was defeated.

Following the convention, another petition campaign brought hundreds of signatures from San Francisco, Sacramento, and five mountain counties to the state legislature. But the ban on testimony from Blacks remained.

In October 1857 a third convention assembled in San Francisco, the largest having seventy delegates from eighteen counties and the longest, lasting five days. But it also met after two defeats: the Dred Scott decision had escalated the sectional crisis, and the United States land office in California had denied African Americans any right to claim unsurveyed land.

Eliminating the testimony ban was still paramount for delegates, and education was second. A petition campaign for the right of testimony collected eighteen hundred signatures in San Francisco, again to no avail. The *Mirror of the Times*, burdened with financial problems, first cut back to four pages and then closed the next year.

In 1858 the state legislature again tried to ban Black emigration. This produced a Black exodus. A gold rush in Fraser Valley, Canada, also beckoned. The next year the San Francisco correspondent for the *Weekly Anglo-African* wrote of people of color needing a territory "by conquest or purchase" so they could send their leaders "to be recognized in our own country as men and women… respectfully asking or demanding an interview with the governments of Mexico or the United States, or any other Government that might have territory to dispose of."

Ten years of aggressive struggle had given people a taste for combat, and before the guns of war were silenced, California's Black Laws were repealed. In 1866, though she usually rode in her carriage, Mary Pleasant sued two San Francisco streetcar companies that denied entrance, and won $500 in damages. Her victory later resulted in a California ruling that ended segregation.

State politics, however, retained its bigoted core. In 1865 the majority Union Party in Yuba County objected to removal of the Black Laws, insisting "we still believe this to be a white man's government and the extension of the natural rights to the negro is degrading, impolitic and unnatural."

A half century later, Mrs. Mary Johnson of Los Angeles felt a chilling hand after she moved into her new home in a white neighborhood. One day, while Mrs. Johnson and her family were away, neighbors invaded her home and heaved her belongings on her front lawn. A hundred African

Gold Rush California became the wealthiest Black community in the United States. Captain William T. Shorey, his wife Julia (right), daughter Zenobia (left), and baby Victoria.

American women then formed a vigilance committee to guard the Johnson home. In Pasadena during the 1920s, Jackie Robinson recalled, "we saw movies from segregated balconies, swam in the municipal pool only on Tuesdays, and were permitted in the YMCA on only one night a week. Restaurant doors were slammed in our faces." California's Golden Gate had a "whites only" welcome sign.

Mifflin W. Gibbs

During the early years of the Gold Rush the men in front of the Union Hotel in San Francisco had their shoes shined by an enterprising young bootblack named Mifflin W. Gibbs. Little did they or he realize that he would establish a fancy imported boot store, help launch California's first Black newspaper, and after the Civil War become the first African American judge in the United States. Mifflin Gibbs's story has a Horatio Alger flavor.

Born in Philadelphia in 1828, the son of a Methodist minister who died when he was eight, Gibbs early took an interest in cultivating his literary talents and aiding his fellow citizens. A member of the Underground Railroad and the Philadelphia antislavery society, at twenty he was persuaded by Frederick Douglass and Charles Lenox Remond to join the lecture circuit. But the Gold Rush caught his imagination and he raced to California in 1850 with ten cents. Gibbs rode with explorer John C. Frémont and shined shoes. Then he and Peter Lester, a Philadelphia friend, opened their Pioneer Boot and Shoe Emporium to sell imports from London and New York. The two also threw themselves into the fight for citizenship rights.

Mifflin W. Gibbs arrived in California at twenty-two to dig for gold. He became a civil rights advocate and a successful businessman.

In 1851 Gibbs, Lester, and others publicly denounced the new Black Laws. In 1855 Gibbs and others began publication of California's *Mirror of the Times*, which lasted for three years. When goods were seized from their Emporium because they refused to pay the poll tax, Gibbs and Lester denounced this "flagrant injustice" against "disfranchised, oath-denied, outlawed colored Americans." The government, they said, compelled them to "pay a special tax for enjoyment of a special privilege and break[s] their heads if they attempt to exercise it."

When their goods were seized and placed on public auction, a white friend, Gibbs revealed, "moved through the crowd, telling them why our goods were there, and advising them" not to bid. There were "no bidders" and "our goods were sent back to our store."

"We Refused to Pay"

Among the occasions continually occurring demanding protests against injustice was the imposition of the "poll tax." It was demanded of our firm, and we refused to pay. A sufficient quantity of our goods to pay the tax and costs were levied upon, and published for sale...

I wrote with a fervor as cool as the circumstances would permit... closing with the avowal that the great State of California might annually confiscate our goods, but we would never pay the voters tax... Our goods were sent back to our store... No further attempts to enforce [the law] upon colored men were made.

Mifflin W. Gibbs, *Shadow and Light*, 1902

By then Gibbs was a crusader for equality, riding to the capital in Sacramento and elsewhere in the state to rouse support for repeal of the Black Laws. He played a prominent role in his people's protest conventions. Of their many petitions to the legislature, Gibbs later wrote, "We had friends to offer them and foes to move they be thrown out the window."

In 1858 Gibbs was again smitten by gold fever, this time in the Fraser River valley in British Columbia. In Canada he opened a store, and by 1866 the white and wealthy James Bay district elected him as its councilman. The next year he was reelected without opposition.

Gibbs began to pursue an interest in law. He first studied in Arkansas and in 1869 graduated from Oberlin College. The next year he was admitted to the Arkansas bar; in 1873 he was elected a city judge in Little Rock. For his service to the Republican Party, Presidents Hayes and Arthur rewarded him with minor diplomatic appointments, and toward the end of his life, he was appointed a U.S. consul to Madagascar.

Mifflin Gibbs died in 1903, the year after the appearance of his autobiographical *Shadow and Light*. From the crouch of a bootblack in vigilante-dominated San Francisco, Mifflin Gibbs had fought for his people and scaled high walls.

8
THE COWHANDS

Africans skilled with horses were among the earliest to ride alongside the New World's cattle herds. In 1598 when Juan de Oñate's expedition imposed Spanish rule on New Mexico, at least five African Americans, two soldiers and three enslaved women, accompanied him. Others, riding in cattle crews from the Mexican highlands, drove the cows and horses of mixed African, European, and American breeds that would ensure that European settlements survived.

Through an outdoor mix of talent, stamina, and sweat, Africans, Europeans, and Native Mexicans created the Southwest's cattle industry. These

Cowhands assemble around 1910 for a Bonham, Texas, fair.

Shoshone Indians
and their friend
One Horse Charley
(second from left) in
Reno, Nevada (1886)

men were first
known by the Span-
ish word *vaqueros,*
then the English
word "drovers,"
and finally as "cow-
hands." Some au-
thorities believe the
word "cowboy" de-
rives from the fact
that so many were African Americans – and whites would not dignify them
with the term "men." Historically the language of trail and ranch was Mexican Spanish, using such terms as *lariat, morral* (feed bag), *bosal* (rope), and
rodeo. The *sombrero galoneado* became the famous "ten-gallon hat."

The great era of the cattle crews began after the Civil War in Texas,
where five million cattle roamed free and ready for coralling. In an expanding country, prices for beef cattle soared to $30 or $40 dollars a head, urban
markets beckoned, and new railroads provided a fast means of transportation. So many cowpuncher jobs opened to so many youths that rarely was
race an issue in hiring. For African Americans the cattle industry offered
one of the few chances for equal, exciting, manly labor in a country that
increasingly closed other doors to people of color.

In 1866 Bose Ikard, born a slave in 1847, rode with Charles Goodnight
and Oliver Loving when they charted the Goodnight-Loving Trail to New
Mexico, Colorado, Wyoming, and Montana. At nineteen Ikard had valuable riding, roping, and shooting skills and Goodnight called him "the most
skilled and trustworthy man I had." He continued: "There was a dignity, a
cleanliness, and a reliability about him that was wonderful. He paid no atten-

Cowhands at
Rio Grande Plain,
early 1900s

tion to women. His behavior was very good in a fight, and he was probably the most devoted man to me that I ever had. I have trusted him farther than any living man. He was my detective, banker, and everything else in Colorado, New Mexico, and the other wild country I was in. The nearest and only bank was at Denver, and when we carried money I gave it to Bose, for a thief would never think of robbing him – never think of looking in a Negro's bed for money."

Bose Ikard was one of thousands of African American cowpunchers who drove cattle up the trails from 1865 until 1890. They whisked Texas beef to urban markets for "thirty dollars a month and grub." A largely unhindered outdoor life, fair treatment, and decent pay attracted thousands of African Americans, Mexicans, Indians, and poor whites.

But these intrepid Westerners often had to ride a largely ungoverned and violent trail. Periodically, as if from sheer exhaustion, the cattle frontier would lapse into peace and tranquility. In Texas, a visitor noted, "men were seldom convicted, and never punished… if you want distinction in this country, kill somebody." By 1877 the Texas "wanted" list numbered five thousand men and every race, religion, and color was included.

The first man shot in Dodge City, Kansas, was a tall cowhand named Tex, and he was African American. Tex was standing on a Dodge street, there was gunplay, and a stray bullet took his life. The first man arrested and jailed in Abilene's new stone jail was Black and he was not innocent. Infuriated by his imprisonment, his white and Black trail crew rode into town,

Texas cowboys
on horseback

pulled the bars out of his cell, rescued their buddy, shot up the place, and rode back to camp.

Estimations of the number of African American cowhands vary, but the most reputable source on the subject has been George W. Saunders, president of the Old Time Drivers Association. He estimated that from 1868 to 1895, "fully 35,000 men went up the trail with herds" and "about one-third were negroes and Mexican." Recent authorities accept Saunders's figures, and have agreed that at

Judge Roy Bean of
Texas tries a horse
thief as four Black
cowhands (left)
look on.

least a fourth of the riders were of African descent. The average trail crew of eleven probably included two or three African Americans, and one or two Mexican Americans or Native Americans. Some African Americans served in all-Black trail crews and others worked alongside whites as drovers, cooks, and scouts.

Some cowhands of African descent had begun as enslaved people and were roping and branding cattle before they became free. Others headed west after Emancipation, seeking a life where skill would count more than skin color. Most came to live by the law, but a few rode in to break it.

Cowhands were ordinary men who possessed outdoor skills and a strong love of horses and cattle. Daily life on the range was more often hard, tedious, and lonely than filled with high adventure. However, danger lurked at any turn in the road or ford of the river, herds became unruly, and nature repeatedly offered the shocking and unforeseen.

Cowhand Arthur L. Walker

A rough outdoor fairness grew out of the work's inherent cooperative nature and interdependence. Cowmen had to help and stand by each other. Sleeping arrangements often found ranch owner, trail boss, drovers, and cooks of every race under the same blanket. Thwarted by lack of capital and racial barriers, only a few men of color were able to rise to foreman, trail boss, or ranch owner.

A Colorado cowpuncher (date unknown)

Saloon Life

A fancy Telluride, Colorado, bar and game room, with a Black man on his knees doing some cleaning

Dodge City's Long Branch saloon had bartenders of both races in the 1800s.

Johnnie Deivers's Place in Breckenridge, Colorado, in 1895. Bob Lott is standing alongside his white friends.

The multicultural patrons of this Klondike, Alaska, saloon pose for the camera in 1901.

Though historian Kenneth W. Porter believes that the Black range riders probably suffered less discrimination than they would have in any other occupation open to them at the time, discrimination did exist on the trail and at the ranch. Many were hired, according to a white cowhand, "to do the hardest work around an outfit" – as broncobusters. In his 1936 "Tribute Paid to Negro Cowmen" in *Cattlemen* magazine, Hendrix wrote, "They did as much as possible to place themselves in the good graces of the [white] hands." He told of cowhands who would take "the first pitch out of the rough horses... in the chill of the morning, while the [white] cowboys ate their breakfast." When subjected to hazing, African American cowmen relied on a tactful restraint rather than retaliatory fists and six-guns.

But not all. John B. Hayes, or "The Texas Kid," born in Waco in 1881, responded to "For Whites Only" signs in saloons by asking for a drink, and when refused, would back his horse through the swinging doors and shoot out the lights. Jess Crumbly of Cheyenne, six foot four and 245 pounds of simmering temper, was nicknamed "Flip," because, recalled a friend, "when he hit you you'd flip." Crumbly could settle disagreements by showing two brawny fists that knew no color line. Henrietta Williams Foster, who also rode as a cowhand, reportedly killed a man who raped her.

Since existence was perilous enough without needless gunplay, cowhands tried to reach peaceful solutions. Despite the presence of former Confederate soldiers among trail crews, clashes between Black and other

Cowhands assemble at a Bonham, Texas, fair.

Jess (right) and his Apache friends

cowboys were few. More white gunfire was directed at Native Americans and Mexican Americans.

Racial discrimination, however, repeatedly appeared, arriving in the wagons that brought large numbers of white wives, daughters, and their families from Eastern states. These newcomers, particularly men, began to demand the East's "protective" barriers. The larger and more stable a Western community became, the more likely it would exude intolerance, practice forms of discrimination, and demand segregation. In newer settlements, particularly those with few white women, cowhands of color were less likely to encounter barriers. Cattle drive towns, even in Texas, enforced only an informal segregation in saloons. They served Blacks at one end and whites at the other, and cowhand camaraderie repeatedly challenged this barrier. This was particularly true in multicultural Oklahoma. However, when it came to houses of prostitution, Black men often faced warnings or entered at their own risk.

Some Black cowpunchers developed extraordinary talents, and a few were cut in the heroic mold. John Slaughter's fearlessness matched his giant frame. When Tombstone, Arizona, murderer Frank Leslie tried to jump his claim, he chased him away. When boxing champion John L. Sullivan came to Tombstone in 1884 and

John Slaughter was a large, strong, and fearless cowhand who lived a long, eventful life.

Jesse Stahl,
rodeo
champion

offered $500 for anyone who would last two rounds with him, Slaughter volunteered. He even landed the first punch. But once the champ got busy, Slaughter was carried out of the ring.

Britton Johnson, described by a friend as "a shining jet black negro of splendid physique," was considered the best shot on the Texas frontier. In October, 1864, Johnson returned home to find Comanches and Kiowas had raided his community, killing his infant son and carrying off his wife, their three other children, and some white settlers, including children. Johnson persuaded the survivors he could rescue their loved ones, and rode off. He was able to enter the Indian village posing as a warrior-recruit or as a man willing to trade horses for prisoners. One tale holds he bartered for their liberty with horses, but another claims he conducted a harrowing night escape that rescued everyone.

In 1874 Willie Kennard, forty-two and a former U.S. cavalryman, rode into Yankee Hill, Colorado, a fearful town in the grip of hardened criminals. When he applied for the marshal's job, the mayor told him that Yankee Hill's white citizens would drive him out before he could confront a gunslinger. When Kennard insisted on a chance, the mayor slyly proposed a test – that he arrest Caswit, a vicious outlaw who had raped a teenager and shot her father. Kennard strode into Gaylord's saloon and confronted Caswit, who drew his two Colt .44s. Kennard blasted them out of his hands and marched him to jail. For three years Marshall Kennard tamed Yankee Hill before he rode into the sunset.

On February 1, 1898, an African American was publicly lynched in Paris, Texas.

It would be a mistake to assume from the tales of Johnson and Kennard that cowhands were particularly good marksmen. Most were poor shots, few were skilled at handling guns, and some were trigger-happy. A cowpuncher named Ben and his white comrades became so furious when an Indian stole Ben's horse, they galloped into the thief's village guns blazing. When the smoke cleared, no one was wounded, but Ben's horse lay dead.

In the early decades of the twentieth century the frontier saga had its reincarnation in Wild West shows and rodeo performances. Crowds thrilled at acts of incredible strength, recklessness, and macho guts, but in a Jim Crow age they rarely saw cowhands of color. Prejudice had kept some from entering, and others lacked the cash or amiable contacts with the white rodeo promoters.

Peerless Jesse Stahl, riding a bronco named Glasseye in California in 1916, was considered one of the best riders of wild horses in the West.

Some, however, burrowed into rodeos. Mose Reeder of Cheyenne became "Gaucho the Coral Dog… because they wouldn't allow colored to ride, and I would pass when I used that name." The two Mosely brothers, though top rodeo artists, adopted Indian names. Robert J. Lindsay of Clarksdale, Texas, found "You could ride all-right, but they would give you the worst horse." Or, as Mose Reeder recalled, "those that didn't buck so no points could be scored." Barriers were more rigidly enforced as the era of segregation moved toward the 1930s. Black towns, such as Boley, Oklahoma, had to stage their own rodeos.

Texas Jack – a rare example of a Black cowhand hero in a nickel-Western novel

The Black Jockeys

Africans carried vital traditions in handling horses and cattle which they then imported to Central and South American ranches and the plantations of the colonial South. These traditions surfaced when enslaved men and boys became horse trainers, stableboys, and jockeys. Therefore there was nothing unusual in 1875 when the winning jockey in the first Kentucky Derby at Churchill Downs was African American. Hardly anyone would have bet the winner would be white, and the reason was simple arithmetic. Of the fourteen horses that lined up at the starting gate, thirteen carried Black jockeys.

The greatest jockey of the nineteenth century was Kentucky-born "Ike" Murphy, who began racing horses when he was fourteen. In 1882 Murphy won forty-nine of fifty-one races at Saratoga, New York. He became the first jockey to win the Kentucky Derby three times (in 1884, 1890, and 1891). In 1896, thirty-five and still young and full of life, he died of pneumonia.

Black
jockeys

In 1901 and 1902 Jimmie Winkfield was the last African American jockey to win the Kentucky Derby. By then most African American boys who wished to follow in his footsteps found their path blocked. As horse racing became big business, the whites who controlled the purse strings also insisted that only whites would hold the horses' reins. A proud tradition had ended.

"Deadwood Dick"

Ike Murphy

Nat Love, born in a Tennessee slave cabin in 1854, was one of many young people who found their opportunities crushed by the reign of white supremacy after the Civil War. Among the "destitute conditions" that convinced Love at fifteen to head west was the lack of schools for children of color.

In 1869 Love "struck out for Kansas" and the beginning of what he would later characterize with rare understatement as "an unusually adventurous life." He arrived in the bustling town of Dodge, "a typical frontier city, with a great many saloons, dance halls, and gambling houses, and very little of anything else." Its various dens of iniquity apparently drew no color line, so Love and others were accommodated "as long as our money lasted." He soon landed a $30-a-month job as a cowpuncher and was nicknamed "Red River Dick." For more than a generation he took part in the long drives from Texas to Kansas.

In 1907 Love wrote the only full-length autobiography by an African American cowhand. According to his narrative, he was captured by an Indian tribe and escaped by riding a hundred miles in twelve hours on an unsaddled horse. He was arrested when he tried to rope and steal a U.S. Army cannon, but his good friend Bat Masterson got him out of that scrape. He tried to rope a locomotive

Nat Love, known as "Deadwood Dick"

from his horse and both rider and mount landed hard. He rode his horse into a Mexican saloon and ordered two drinks – one for him, one for the horse. Should the reader find these tales hard to swallow, Love had a friend draw pictures that illustrated some of his most memorable moments.

Nat Love's story is filled with exciting and almost unbelievable instances of courage, and his yarns are spun with typical Western braggadocio. In his first Indian fight he initially "lost all courage," but after firing a few shots, he "lost all fear and fought like a veteran." As his tale becomes more boastful, more crowded with confrontations, he invariably stands tall, a confident gunslinger, proud and loud, sometimes sounding more like a dime novel hero than a flesh-and-blood cowpuncher.

Although some might prefer Love to be more restrained, this was neither his nature nor his style. With obvious relish and jaunty self-assurance,
he fought Indians, braved hailstorms, battled wild animals and men, and
lived to tell the vainglorious tale.

One has to be impressed by Love's miraculous invincibility. At one point
he writes, "I carry the marks of fourteen bullet wounds on different parts of
my body, most any one of which would be sufficient to kill an ordinary man,
but I am not even crippled." Another time, he relates, "Horses were shot
from under me, men killed around me, but always I escaped with a trifling
wound at the worst." Of harrowing experiences that would have sent a lesser
man back East, Love exclaims, "I gloried in the danger." He also provided his
twentieth century readers with the code of bygone era: "There a man's work
was to be done, and a man's life to be lived, and when death was to be met,
he met it like a man."

While Love's autobiography confirms the large-scale participation of
African Americans on the long drives, he provides little insight into racial
relationships, and he does not mention an instance of discrimination. To
hear him tell it, he was accepted by all – from the psychopathic Billy the Kid,
to the aristocratic Spanish maiden who was his first passion. He views Indians through white stereotypes – they are "terrorizing the settlers… defying
the Government" and Mexicans are "greasers." In each encounter with our
hero, foes fall before his unerring aim.

On July 4, 1876, Nat Love entered the rodeo at Deadwood City in the
Dakota Territory. He won the roping and shooting contests and reported:
"Right there the assembled crowd named me 'Deadwood Dick' and proclaimed me champion roper of the Western cattle country." This proud nickname he carried for the rest of his life, and into the subtitle of his book.

The wheels of progress finally caught up with Deadwood Dick and the
others. The iron horse galloped across the landscape and made the long cattle drives unnecessary. No longer did cattle lose weight and market value
with each mile up the Chisholm Trail; now powerful locomotives whisked
Texas beef to Eastern consumers.

Nat Love left the range for a job as a Pullman porter, one of the least
onerous positions of Jim Crow open to African American men. Now he
roared swiftly across the badlands he once had ridden as a cowpuncher. But

he never forgot those great days on the range, or his soulmates: Bat Masterson, Frank and Jesse James, and Billy the Kid.

Cherokee Bill

Billy the Kid, the psychopathic killer who murdered twenty-one men in cold blood before he was twenty and was shot by Sheriff Pat Garrett, had a handsome counterpart in Cherokee Bill. Born on the military reservation of Fort Concho, Texas, Cranford Goldsby or Cherokee Bill started life in an atmosphere of respect for the law. His father, Sergeant George Goldsby, served in the Tenth Cavalry. But when Bill was only two, his father led his men in a gun duel with white Texans, and fled to avoid trial.

Bill's mother, Ellen Lynch, remarried and suddenly there was no room for the boy, aged twelve, in her new marriage. He fell in with bad company, and at eighteen he shot and wounded Jake Lewis, a Black man who had beaten him fairly in a dance hall fistfight two days earlier.

Cherokee Bill fled to the hill country, joined the Cook brothers' outlaw gang, and soon scored his first notch, a pursuing posseman. Witty, virile, with long black hair touching his shoulders and a charming smile, he found a host of girlfriends who provided him with shelter and comfort as he eluded the law. Unlike white sheriffs and marshals, he was on good terms with Oklahoma's Creeks, Seminoles, and Cherokees, so he could ride across their land without challenge.

Cherokee Bill was noted for his skill with firearms and particularly his ability at rapid fire. He once told a friend that although his shooting was not always accurate, it would "rattle" his opponent "so he could not hit me."

Cherokee Bill

Cherokee Bill and his mother, Ellen Lynch, who advised him: "Stand up for your rights. Don't let anyone impose on you." This was not a problem for him.

This skill, and a murderous reputation, kept posses at a distance.

But posses could be persistent. When Cherokee Bill and Bill Cook tried to collect their $265.70 checks the U.S. government paid for confiscated Cherokee land, they found themselves in another gunfight. A month before his twentieth birthday, Cherokee Bill was captured and "Hanging Judge" Isaac Parker of Fort Smith, Arkansas, who in twenty-one years sent seventy-nine men to the gallows, sentenced him to death.

In his cell beneath the courthouse, someone – a rumor points to Ellen Lynch – smuggled Cherokee Bill a six-gun, which he used to break out, kill another deputy, and wound others before being subdued. This time Judge Parker thundered the young man was "the most ferocious monster," and referred to his "ferocity," "passion for crime," and capacity to "burn, pillage and destroy."

Surrounded by lawmen of both races, Cherokee Bill was brought to Fort Smith for trial before "Hanging Judge" Isaac Parker.

On a sunny day in 1896 Cherokee Bill awoke "at 6, singing and whistling," and strolled to the gallows accompanied by his mother. Asked if he had any last words for the crowd, tough to the end, he replied, "No, I came here to die, not make a speech."

The Rufus Buck Gang

The only photograph of the Rufus Buck gang, shows five slouching, smirking boys – some faces still showing a puffy baby fat – staring vacantly into a camera. None exhibit a demented or ferocious look, and they appear more muddled than evil. Do these faces reveal youths capable of the hideous crimes of rape, pillage, and murder against innocent men, women, and chil-

The Rufus Buck gang on their last day on earth. Left to right: Maoma July, Sam Sampson, Rufus Buck, Lucky Davis, and Lewis Davis.

dren? The handcuffs that join them are the only indication that this is their last day on earth.

When Rufus Buck, Sam Sampson, Maoma July, and Lewis and Luckey Davis first rolled up a series of minor juvenile crimes, Judge Isaac Parker placed them in jail for a while. That was kid's stuff. But in July 1895 they began a thirteen-day spree that took more lives than the infamous Dalton and Starr gangs combined.

Their wild rampage began with the murder of John Garrett, a Black Indian U.S. deputy marshal, near Okmulgee. They thought he was keeping too close an eye on them. Then they began to work in earnest, killing ranchers, small storekeepers, widows, farmers, and even a child. They took cash, gold watches, clothing, and boots, but theft was just an afterthought. They were enjoying themselves. The *Muskogee Phoenix* reported the gang's crime spree but insisted that "details are too revolting to publish."

The five outlaws voted three to two to let a white victim live, another time they shot a Black child in the back, and another time they raped and killed an Indian woman. At the Hassan family farm Rufus Buck announced "I'm Cherokee Bill's brother." Then, holding her husband at bay with Winchesters, they forced Mrs. Hassan to prepare a big meal, and after dinner, raped her.

On a warm summer day, reported the *Muskogee Phoenix*, a posse of "hundreds of men, whites, Indians and Negroes" turned out to hunt down the Rufus Buck gang. Trapped in a cave, they surrendered without a wound after a wild shootout.

The five were indicted for the rape of Mrs. Hassan and the murder of Marshall Garrett. Huge crowds assembled for a two-day trial that featured Mrs. Hassan's lurid testimony, which brought tears even to the eyes of stoic Judge Parker. After one of the gang's five defense attorneys told to the court, "You have heard the evidence. I have nothing to say," the jury reached a guilty verdict, and the young men were sentenced to die.

The prisoners spent a last night singing and praying. Each accepted baptism by Father Pius of the German Catholic Church. There was quiet at the gallows, except for Lucky Davis who, seeing his sister, shouted "Good bye, Martha." After the traps were sprung that July day, citizens of the Indian Territory agreed life was safer.

Mary Fields

Mary Fields, six feet tall, two hundred pounds, and carrying a .38 Smith and Wesson strapped under her apron, became a legend in Cascade, Montana. One of the most memorable characters to stride the Rocky Mountain trails, she was vividly remembered by actor Gary Cooper who knew (and adored) her from the time he was nine.

Born in a Tennessee slave cabin during Andrew Jackson's administration, Mary Fields began her Western career in 1884 hauling freight for Mother Amadeus and the Ursuline nuns at St. Peter Mission in Cascade. One night, while driving her wagon for the mission, wolves attacked. Her horses bolted, dumping Fields and her supplies on the prairie. She spent a lonely night surrounded by wolves, keeping them at bay with her rifle.

During her ten years at the convent, Fields proved a match for any who might try to trample her rights. When a hired hand crossed her, the two settled matters in a shootout. Though no one was wounded, the bishop, having heard complaints about her irascibility, ordered Mother Amadeus to fire her. In Cascade, Fields twice launched restaurants and twice went broke because she fed those who could only promise to pay.

In 1895, Mother Amadeus helped Mary Fields land a job with the U.S. postal service. For the next eight years she delivered letters regardless of terrain or subzero weather – "never missing a one," recalled Gary Cooper. In her sixties she drove a stagecoach and was known as "Stagecoach Mary."

At seventy, Mary Fields ran a laundry and spent time in the local saloon, drink-

"Stagecoach Mary" Fields of Cascade, Montana

ing and smoking cigars with card-playing male friends. She left the saloon one day to confront a customer who had failed to pay his $2 laundry bill. She knocked him down with one blow, said "His laundry bill is paid," and returned to her friends. When her laundry burned down in 1912, neighbors rebuilt it for her.

Gary Cooper remembered Mary Fields as a woman who helped "conquer and tame the Old Wild West." Years later he recalled: "The town mourned her passing and buried her at the foot of the mountains." Mary Fields was only the second American woman in history to drive a U.S. mail route.

Ben Hodges

In 1929 two noted Dodge City residents, Wyatt Earp and Ben Hodges, were laid to final rest. Both men earned their keep not at farm labor or cowpunching, but at cards. Historian Floyd Streeter has noted that Earp was "up to some dishonest trick every time he played," and so was Ben Hodges. But both died of natural causes, unlike the many desperadoes they befriended.

Two of the surviving photographs of Ben Hodges show him armed with his trusty shotgun and six-gun. But these convey a false impression. Hodges relied less on lethal weapons than gentle persuasion – he might be called "the fastest tongue in the West."

From the moment he arrived in Dodge City with a Texas trail crew and heard about an unclaimed Spanish land grant, he summoned wit and words to get ahead. Though his father was Black and his mother was Mexican, he claimed descent from an aristocratic Spanish family, galloped off to Texas and returned with "proof." He did not win his case, but he captivated friends and perfect strangers with his scam, and convinced Dodge City he was a fine showman.

Hodges persuaded the head of the Dodge City National Bank to lend him money, and got the head of the local railroad to give him a free pass. Brought to trial for rustling a herd of cattle, he argued his own case. His masterful two-hour dramatic summary mixed humor, pathos, and lies: "What me, the descendant of old grandees of Spain, the owner of a land grant embracing millions of acres, the owner of gold mines and villages and towns situated on that grant of which I am sole owner, to steal a miserable, miserly lot of old cows? Why, the idea is absurd. No, gentlemen, I think too much of the race of men from which I sprang, to disgrace their memory." Somewhat bewildering was his later claim that he was only a poor cowboy surrounded by personal enemies. Drama trumped consistency, however, and the jury acquitted him.

Despite his reputation as a forger, rustler, and card cheat, Hodges asked the governor of Kansas to appoint him a livestock inspector. After all, he pointed out, he had always been a loyal Republican. At this point Hodges's cattlemen buddies, seeing a wolf asking to guard the sheep pen, persuaded the governor to veto this dread possibility.

When Ben Hodges died, Dodge City residents decided to bury him in the Maple Grove Cemetery for

Ben Hodges, con man of Dodge City, Kansas

old-time cattlemen, cowboys, and other decent citizens. Why would you bury him among the best citizens? a pallbearer was asked. "We buried Ben there for a good reason," he said. "We wanted him where they could keep a good eye on him."

Matthew Bones Hooks

Born in 1867 in Orangeville, Texas, the eldest of eight children, to a formerly enslaved couple, Matthew Hooks learned to read, helped bring up his sisters and brothers, and developed a deep sense of personal responsibility. "They made me rock the cradle for my brothers," he said, "and I've been rockin' somebody's cradle ever since."

Thin and wiry as a boy, Hooks was nicknamed "Bones." At seven he could do a man's job, and by fourteen he came to love horses, learned how to break those who never quit bucking, and knew how to survive by outguessing their wildest moves.

When the young Hooks was told Clarendon in the Texas Panhandle "was the white spot of civilization," he decided to live there, since he was a good Christian who did not drink or curse. It took many years for the town to accept him. Hooks was also a keen observer who differentiated between good women and those men who enjoyed saloons and gambling: "Credit for the advancement on the Plains belongs to the pioneer mothers," he later wrote. "When the men brought their wives to the Plains the women demanded milk cows, chickens, schools, churches and all the attributes of civilization and culture."

More than a few times white women stepped forward on his behalf to confront white bigots. One woman pointedly answered a man who objected to eating with Hooks, "Everyone is treated alike at my table." His skills much in demand, Hooks was hired by leading ranchers in West Texas. Once, when

Matthew Bones Hooks (left) and other Texas cowhands in 1903

innocently found in the company of two white cattle rustlers, he was questioned and let off, but they were hanged.

Hooks joined many cattle drives from the Pecos country to railheads in the northern Panhandle. When he opened a store near Texarkana, night-riding Klansmen closed it down. However, in 1894, after he was granted land for a Black church in Clarendon, he brought a preacher from Fort Worth to begin an African American community. A conservative man by nature, he favored Republican presidential candidate William McKinley while most of his white friends favored William Jennings Bryan and the Populists.

In his early thirties, Hooks married Anna Crenshaw, "a good woman, a good cook and a wonderful housekeeper." In 1900 the couple worked at the Elmhurst Hotel in Amarillo, he as a porter and she washing and ironing the linens. Hooks became the first man of color chosen to serve on a jury and asked to join the Western Cowpunchers Association of Amarillo and the Western Cowboys Association of Montana.

At forty-three Hooks could still ride a horse described as "a thousand pounds of dynamite" to a standstill. He was still committed to building Black towns: "When I was a boy everywhere I went, folks would say, 'We're not goin' to let any Negroes live here.' But I said to myself, When I get grown I'm goin' to build a town right beside yours, and not let any white folks live there." Influenced by the militancy of Marcus Garvey and W.E.B. Du Bois, in 1930 he built North Heights, a twenty-eight-square-block town northwest of Amarillo, and it grew into a successful residential and business community with thirty-five families, four churches, an elementary school, a high school, and a general store. Town fathers planted a tree named after each child so they could watch them grow, named their park after Hooks, and later erected a statue to him.

Hooks went on to found Black historical societies, tutor underprivileged children, and donate money to those in need. In 1949, when he needed medical aid but had spent his money on others and had to leave the local hospital, his friends raised the money for a housekeeper.

Hooks gave many lectures and left important notebooks about his adventures in Texas. He liked to tell how he had arrived early in the Panhandle: "Folks talk about Judge Bean and the Law West of the Pecos, but there wasn't no law out here then." He died in 1951 at eighty-three.

Isom Dart

In 1900 Isom Dart, a tall, handsome cattle rustler, was only fifty-one when he was shot in the back and killed by Tom Horn, a notorious bounty hunter. Dart had tried to go straight many times but never succeeded, though some considered him a good man.

Born in slavery in Arkansas in 1849, Dart first developed his talents as a thief when Confederate officers sent him off to forage for them during the Civil War. He drifted into southern Texas and Mexico and worked as a rodeo clown, then he and a Mexican teamed up to steal cattle in Mexico and sell them in Texas.

Dart moved to Brown's Park, Colorado, a haven for cattle thieves. For a time he gave up rustling for prospecting and then broncobusting. "No man understood horses better," said one friend. Another added, "I have seen all the great riders, but for all around skill as a cowman, Isom Dart was unexcelled... He could outride any of them; but never entered a contest."

But in a few years Dart was back in a rustler's saddle, a member of the Tip Gault outlaw gang. One evening while he was burying a friend, the rest of the gang were ambushed and slain. Dart survived by spending the a night in the grave alongside his buddy.

Isom Dart, cattle rustler

Isom Dart and fellow cowhands at Brown's Park, Colorado

Dart tried time and again to flee his rustler past, but each time he slid back. Some people described him as "a laughing sort of guy" and "a good man, always helpful." "I remember Isom as a very kind man. He used to 'baby-sit' me and my brother when Mother was away or busy," wrote an elderly woman who still treasured her photograph of Dart, and insisted that people hear about his decent side.

Arrested many times for rustling, Dart was never convicted. In Sweetwater County, Wyoming, he probably made the best case of any criminal while being driven to jail by a deputy sheriff. The deputy's buckboard ran off the road, injuring the deputy but leaving Dart unhurt. Dart gave him first aid, calmed the horses, lifted the buckboard onto its wheels, and drove the lawman to the hospital at Rock Springs. Then Dart left the buckboard at the stable and turned himself in at the jail. In a land where cattle rustling was a capital offense, this was seen as proof of innocence and he was released.

Dart was both generous of heart and unlucky in love. When Tickup, a Shoshone woman with Mincy, her daughter of nine, fled Pony Beater, her abusive Ute husband, Dart rushed to help the two to safety and soon fell in love with Tickup. Pony Beater tracked the three down, tied up Dart, took his possessions and rode off with his prisoners. Dart freed himself and took off to find his new family, only to discover that life changes. Tickup had killed Pony Beater when he fell asleep, and took Mincy to Idaho. By the time Dart arrived to claim his love, Tickup had a new husband. An enraged Dart charged at the man, but Tickup, ever resourceful, used a stone ax to stun him. Nursing a badly cut ear, a heartsick Isom Dart rode back to Brown's Park and bounty hunter Tom Horn.

Bob Lemmons

In the 1500s domesticated horses, a mixture of North African barbs, Arabian steeds, and Andalusian horses, were brought to the New World by Spain's conquistadores. From Mexico they were led northward, where they bred with strays of Spanish origin to produce mustangs, noted for their endurance but almost impossible to control. In herds of twenty to three dozen, they grazed freely in ranges of twenty-five to fifty miles, a stallion in command.

For their long drives, which used as many as a hundred horses, cattlemen eagerly sought these mustangs. Considered more valuable than cattle, they were headstrong, resistant to restraints, and their leader stallions were cagey and hard to deceive. Cowmen developed techniques to seize or trap herds, but they required many men and resulted in more mustangs killed then corralled.

Then Bob Lemmons rode in. Born in Lockport, Texas, in 1848, to Cecilia, who was enslaved, and an unknown father, Lemmons's dark-skin, high cheekbones and straight, shoulder-length hair indicated his Indian and African ancestry. Freed at seventeen during the Civil War, by 1870 he had taught himself to read, and owned land, sheep, cattle, horses, and goats valued at $1,140.

Lemmons's "walk down" required him to become part of a herd and get it to follow him as they would a stallion. His singularly gentle technique meant becoming one with the herd, traveling with them, letting them get used to his smell, clothes, and body. It took limitless patience and many days. He explained: "It wasn't long before they wouldn't run from me, and then I got 'em to where they trusted me, because ever' time they'd scare, I'd scare and run as hard as they did. Sometimes I'd scare first and away we'd go, with me in the lead and them follerin' me. I soon have a whole bunch runnin' with me everywhere I went."

A humble man, Lemmons had a quick wit and a gift for storytelling, and he rejected violence. He married, his family grew to eight children, but only one survived him. When he died in 1947 he owned more than twelve hundred acres of land, and he had the admiration of his community. Folklorist J. Frank Dobie interviewed Lemmons and wrote: "What is it inside some individuals that makes horses untamable by others, submit to them gently?... The horses would follow him like mules magnetized by a bell mare." Bob Lemmons, Dobie concluded, "actually became the leader of a band of wild horses that followed him into a pen as fresh as they had been when he first sighted them."

Lemmons's gift was known far and wide in his own day, and today appreciation for his peaceful contribution is growing.

Daniel W. Wallace

Daniel Webster Wallace, born into slavery in Victoria County, Texas, was freed at twelve in 1860. He took a job that paid fifteen silver dollars and joined his first trail drive, riding point at the head of a herd. When he worked for a rancher who owned eight thousand roaming cattle, he learned his skills fast. Wallace raced after straying horses and cattle, learned to handle firearms, endured stampedes, battled rustlers, took part in range wars, survived ambushes, buried two young friends, and once punched a white man who tossed a racial insult his way.

At twenty-five, Wallace had saved two-thirds of his monthly salary and bought a homestead. Then he decided to return to high school to learn to read and write. He met Laura Owen, another student, and they married.

A white friend in Fort Worth gave Wallace a letter of credit for $10,000, which he used to buy Hereford cattle, invest in one of Loraine's first windmills, and pay his bills for twenty years. He and Laura owned 8,820 acres and an eleven-square-mile ranch. The Wallaces paid off their mortgages, built a modern home, and cross-fenced their land. They saw their four children educated.

Wallace had a reputation for feeding hungry Indians. He also lent money to poor friends and donated to educational projects, including a school in Colorado City later named after him. He was welcomed to the Texas and Southwest Cattle Raisers Association. The *Cattleman*, a newspaper, reported that he began to lecture about "the country as he first saw it more than half a century ago, unsullied by barbed wire and train smoke, a cowman's paradise of running water, grass covered hills, and wide fertile valley where the antelope played."

Bill Pickett (second row, third from right) and the 101 Ranch Wild West Show. His two assistants are Will Rogers (fifth from right) and Tom Mix (seventh from right).

Bill Pickett

Zack Miller, owner of the huge, sprawling 101 Ranch in Oklahoma, described Bill Pickett as "the greatest sweat and dirt cowhand that ever lived – bar none." But Pickett was far more. He invented bulldogging, the most famous rodeo sport and the only one of the eight rodeo sports credited to an individual.

Bill Pickett aboard "Spadley" at a rodeo

Bulldogging involves riding one's horse after a steer and then leaping out of the saddle to grab each of the steer's horns with a hand. Then with boot heels digging into the ground, Pickett would wrestle the giant beast into the dust by twisting its head back and its nose up. Like a ballet dancer, he then turned the animal over, and by slipping to one side he dragged it along until both came to a dusty stop. Pickett not only did this with relative ease, but also completed his daring act with a unique flourish: he sank his teeth into the steer's upper lip and raised his hands into the air to show his only grip was teeth to lip.

Pickett was born in 1870 to poor Black Cherokees, the second of thirteen children. Fascinated with animals, he left school after the fifth grade for a life in the out-of-doors. As he developed riding and roping skills, he noticed that a bulldog could leap up and bite a steer's lip and it would render the huge animal compliant. He used this to find his own path to fame. In 1890 he married Maggie Turner and they had nine children.

In 1907 Pickett signed a contract with the Miller Brothers' famous 101 Ranch Wild West Show, where at various times his assistants included Will Rogers and Tom Mix, both of whom later became successful in show business and Hollywood. The 101 Rodeo performed in Texas, Mexico, Argentina, and Canada. In 1912 alone the 101 gave more than four hundred performances in twenty-two states and three Canadian provinces, with Pickett as the chief box-office draw. In 1914, when the crew spent three months in Europe, Pickett learned to speak "a very high grade of German." The 101 also performed before King George and Queen Mary, who exclaimed "Most wonderful exhibition! Most wonderful exhibition!"

His muscular strength tightly focused, his slight, five-foot-seven, 145-pound frame gliding through the air like a ballet dancer, Pickett became the most significant practitioner of Western lore. He also survived harrowing experiences. In El Paso, Texas, he brought down a large male elk, avoiding his knifelike antlers, by riding his back until he tired. He is also credited with throwing a buffalo bull. The first night the 101 crew opened in New York City's Madison Square Garden, Pickett and Rogers had to gallop into the stands to corral a steer terrified by the bright lights. In Mexico City in 1908, Zack Miller bet $5000 Pickett could ride a bull for five minutes. Between the bottle-throwing audience and the bull, he was badly gashed, had three ribs broken, and barely survived his seven minutes on the bull's back.

In time, calculated rashness caught up with precision acrobatics and Pickett broke almost every bone in his body. He died in 1932 after he slipped in a barn and a stallion kicked him in the head. Will Rogers, by then a fa-

Riders of the 101 Ranch with Bill Pickett (first row, center, with white shirt)

mous actor, publicly mourned his mentor and told the *New York Times* how "Old Bill" thrilled millions with an act no other human being had ever done.

"Old Bill Is Dead"

He left a blank that's hard to fill
For there never will be another Bill.
Both black and white will mourn the day
That the "Biggest Boss" took Bill away.

Colonel Zack Miller, cited in Ellsworth Collings and Alma Miller England's *The 101 Ranch*, (Norman, Oklahoma), p. 172.

In 1971, two generations after his death, Pickett became the first African American voted into Oklahoma City's Cowboy Hall of Fame; in 1987, with African American movie star Woody Strode officiating, a bronze statue of Pickett bulldogging was unveiled at the Fort Worth Cowtown Coliseum.

Pickett mastered the ferocious in nature not with weapons of death, but with a craftsmanship rooted in respect for life. His enduring monument is a bulldogging act that never ceases to entertain millions. His act offered larger lessons: how an ordinary individual can summon the courage, stamina, and skill to overcome life's fearful beasts, and how one can live harmoniously with the untamed in nature.

Poster for a 1922 Bill Pickett movie

9
Exodus to Kansas

In 1865 chains and whips became relics of a barbaric past. From Virginia to Texas, people of color hugged each other, danced for joy, and set out to find children sold away during the long night of bondage. Hopes were high. In Texas, Felix Haywood recalled: "We thought we was goin' to be rich like the white folks. We thought we was goin' to be richer than the white folks, 'cause we was stronger and knowed how to work, and the whites didn't and they didn't have us to work for them anymore. But it didn't turn out that way. We soon found out that freedom could make folks proud but it didn't make 'em rich."

For almost a decade African American men and women could feel free to seek new jobs and adventures, a home of their own, and an education for their children. But soon former Confederates ruled the eleven states of the former Confederacy again, and imposed new forced labor systems called sharecropping system and convict-lease. Henry Adams, a former Georgia slave, told the U.S. Congress: "After they

An African American scout for a caravan heading west

told us we were free – even then they would not let us live as man and wife together. And when we would run away to be free from slavery, the white people would not let us come to their places to see our mothers, wives, sisters, or fathers. We was made to leave the place, or made to go back and live as slaves. To my own knowledge there was over two thousand colored people killed trying to get away, after the white people told us we were free, which was in 1865."

Adams told how this return of white supremacy spawned a major African American exodus to the West: "we lost all hopes... We said that the whole South – every State in the South – had got into the hands of the very men that held us as slaves." They were "holding the reins of government over our heads in every respect almost, even the constable up to the governor."

Saying "Ho for Kansas," thousands of Southern African Americans headed toward the land sanctified by John Brown's fight for freedom and the courage of the first Black recruits of the Civil War. Henry Adams became a leader of this new exodus.

Kansas, points out historian Quintard Taylor, was the nearest state to the South that permitted homesteading by people of color. And it was among the first Northern states to accept the Emancipation Proclamation and among the first to ratify the Thirteenth Amendment. A white supremacist Democratic Party dominated the South, but Lincoln Republicans governed Kansas.

Kansas had fertile, productive soil, good weather, and water for crops. Its Homestead Act offered 160 free acres to settlers who were willing to improve the land for five years or willing to buy a vast plot in six months for $1.25 an acre. Those who arrived in Kansas, however, found segregated schools and discrimination in hotels, restaurants, theaters, churches, hospitals, and the justice system. But they also found some schools and public facilities that did not discriminate, and both major parties and minor ones seeking their votes.

By 1875 almost ten thousand African Americans in Missouri, Tennessee, and Kentucky began to leave for Kansas towns and cities. Urged on by a thrilling convention in Nashville that year, this movement stimulated other migrations.

Nicodemus

In April 1877, Nicodemus, the first Black town in Kansas, was founded by W. R. Hill, a white man, its treasurer, and six Black men. Hill and the others considered it both a vision and business venture. The founders selected a site on good farmland on an open prairie, along the higher bank of the South Solomon River, in what would become Graham County. Hill filed in the Kirwin land office for a 160-acre townsite under the Nicodemus Town Company with an option to buy at $1.25 an acre.

When Hill emphasized African American pride and free farm acreage to an audience in Georgetown, Kentucky, he recruited 150 men, women, and children for a caravan of migrants. Most arrived at the Kansas site penniless, having spent their savings on transportation. An eyewitness reported that they "looked like a band of tattered refugees from *Uncle Tom's Cabin*! With all their worldly possessions tied in bundles balanced on top of the women's bandanna covered heads and in gunny sacks thrown over the shoulders of the men." Though some Nicodemus pioneers came with wagons, plows, and teams of horses, they arrived too late in the season to plant crops. Bad luck also dogged the new community. The abundance of wild game Hill promised had left for winter pasturage, and no one could capture the wild horses south of the town. No white Kansan was willing to survey

To the Colored Citizens of the United States

NICODEMUS, GRAHAM CO., KAN., July 2d, 1877.

We, the Nicodemus Town Company of Graham County Kan., are now in possession of our lands and the Town Site of Nicodemus, which is beautifully located on the N. W. quarter of Section 1, Town 8, Range 21, in Graham Co, Kansas, in the great Solomon Valley, 240 miles west of Topeka, and we are proud to say it is the finest country we ever saw. The soil is of rich, black, sandy loam. The country is rather rolling, and looks most pleasing to the human eye. The south fork of the Solomon river flows through Graham County, nearly directly east and west and has an abundance of excellent water, while there are numerous springs of living water abounding throughout the Valley. There is an abundance of fine Magnesian stone for building purposes, which is much easier handled than the rough sand or hard stone. There is also some timber; plenty for firs use, while we have no fear but what we will find plenty of coal.

Now is your time to secure your home on Government Land in the Great Solomon Valley of Western Kansas.

Remember, we have secured the service of W. R. Hill, man of energy and ability, to locate our Colony.

Not quite 90 days ago we secured our charter for locating the town site of Nicodemus. We then became an organized body, with only three dollars in the treasury and twelve members, but under the careful management of our officers, we have now nearly 300 good and reliable members, with several members permanently located on their claims—with plenty of provisions for the colony—while we are daily receiving letters from all parts of the country from parties desiring to locate in the great Solomon Valley of Western Kansas.

For Maps, Circulars, and Passenger rates, address our General Manager, W. R. HILL, North Topeka, Kansas, until August 1st, 1877, then at Hill City, Graham Co., via Trego.

The name of our post-office will be Nicodemus, and Mr. Z. T. Fletcher will be our "Nasby."

REV. S. P. ROUNDTREE, Sec'y.

NICODEMUS.

Nicodemus was a slave of African birth,
And was bought for a bag full of gold;
He was reckoned a part of the salt of the earth,
But he died years ago, very old.
Nicodemus was a prophet, at least he was as wise,
For he told of the battles to come;
How we trembled with fear, when he rolled up his eyes,
And we heeded the shake of his thumb.

CHORUS :   Good time coming, good time coming,
Long, long time on the way ;
Run and tell Elija to hurry up Pomp,
To meet us under the cottonwood tree,
In the Great Solomon Valley
At the first break of day.

An early Nicodemus poster inviting Black settlers

Preacher John Samuels and his wife,
Lee Anne Samuels, of Nicodemus,
Kansas

their plots until John Landers came along, but after he finished his work he was slain in an ambush.

Troubles mounted. Residents with money had to walk thirty miles to the nearest railroad for purchases. Hill, threatened with hanging by angry residents, fled to one white home, then another, and escaped by hiding in a hay wagon. The day after they reached the new Nicodemus townsite, sixty families from Lexington, Kentucky repacked and left for home.

By 1878 Nicodemus had a population of seven hundred and had largely turned to farming. People used milk cows to pull plows. Osage Indians

"Not at All Inviting": Nicodemus, March 1878

When we got in sight of Nicodemus the men shouted, "There is Nicodemus." Being very sick I hailed this news with gladness. I looked with all the eyes I had. I said, "Where is Nicodemus? I don't see it." My husband pointed out various smokes coming out of the ground and said "That is Nicodemus." The families lived in dug-outs. We landed and struck tents. The scenery to me was not at all inviting and I began to cry.

From there we went to our homestead fourteen miles west of Nicodemus...

Days, weeks, months, and years passed and I became reconciled to my home. We improved the farm and lived there nearly twenty years, making visits to Nicodemus to attend church, entertainments, and other celebrations. My three daughters were much loved school teachers in Nicodemus and vicinity.

Willianna Hickman, in the *Topeka Daily Capitol*, August 29, 1939

Nicodemus families and their wagons

brought the town's neediest families meat and a share of their government rations. Nearby whites offered charitable contributions, but Kansas governor George Anthony and U.S. officials refused to help.

In 1878 the energetic, knowledgeable Edwin P. McCabe, twenty-nine, arrived and was selected as secretary of the Nicodemus Town Company. Hardworking and ambitious, he threw himself into land sales, became a federal surveyor, and began his political career.

In 1879 McCabe and other leaders voted to reject further outside aid, rely on Nicodemus's harvest, and thus return to the original goal of a self-sufficient community. That year the ambitious Fletcher family added immeasurably to Nicodemus's community life. Z. T. Fletcher opened a retail business he had purchased from a white man, and his wife Frances Fletcher established the town's first school in the family's sod hotel. The school term of three to six months began after the fall harvest was in. On seats made of blocks and logs, she taught fifteen children arithmetic, literature, moral values, and hygiene. Pupils relied on a dozen books donated by a former slave. The poverty that first plagued the settlement had its impact on education. When a child was asked to comb his hair before coming to school the next day, he arrived with much of his hair cut off, explaining that his family did not own a comb.

Education in Nicodemus was taken seriously. In two years 39 percent of Nicodemus residents could read and 25 percent could write – at a time when the U.S. national average was under 10 percent and white frontier literacy rates were only marginally higher. After further efforts, reading levels for all citizens between fifteen and forty-five rose to 56 percent.

Nicodemus was different from other communities. It celebrated August 1, the date when England ended slavery in its West Indies colonies. It boasted 58 white residents and 258 African Americans, when Graham County's four thousand citizens were 88 percent white.

By 1880 Nicodemus boasted a school, three churches, a hotel, two stores, a livery stable, and a benevolent society. But few prosperous people were attracted to Nicodemus. Many residents, using town work as a step to owning farms, left for the countryside. Soon Nicodemus had annually elected township officers – a trustee, clerk, treasurer, road overseer, and two constables. Its justices of the peace were elected for two years. The school board had one white and two Black members. Its leaders heatedly promoted the town as the best choice for county seat, but the new governor, John St. John, picked Millbrook, a white town.

After four years of lean harvests, in 1884 crop yields and prosperity returned and spurred a new recruiting effort. White residents with capital

Four Nicodemus women pose before their clapboard home.

owned most of Nicodemus's fifteen stone and fourteen farm buildings, and a year later Nicodemus had a newspaper owned by whites, the *Western Cyclone*, which sought newcomers regardless of race. Whites also started the *Nicodemus Enterprise*. Both papers emphasized harmony and interracial cooperation.

In its first decade Nicodemus was peaceful, with only one shooting, one theft, one disorderly conduct incident, and three fist fights. By 1887 the town had four churches, two newspapers, two blacksmith shops, two barbers, a shoe store, a land company, literary societies, and baseball clubs; there were dances, parties, lecture, choruses, and festivals.

However, chances for growth ended when two railroad lines, after serious consideration of Nicodemus, decided to bypass it. Without a rail line, many residents began to leave.

The Great Exodus of 1879

As Nicodemus struggled to survive in 1879, a massive exodus of African Americans burst free from the Southern states, a people's response to the triumph of white supremacy. The Republican Party, in return for control of the White House after the contested 1876 election, struck a deal with the Democrats to withdraw the last federal troops from Southern states. In 1877 this handed the constitutional rights of former slaves back to their former masters.

From Virginia to Louisiana to Texas, people of color met to discuss what might be done, where they might go. A solution was slow in developing and passed through several stages. In 1870 a "Committee of 500" African American men formed in the South and over the next half dozen years dispatched a hundred or more investigators to report on labor conditions throughout the region. Agents worked alongside the people whose conditions they examined, and used their wages for their expenses. Their reports revealed patterns of unrelenting political, economic, and social persecution punctuated by violence that did not spare women and children. Free men and women, Henry Adams reported, were still "being whipped, some of them, by the old owners," and many were "being cheated out of their crops."

The Committee of 500 appealed to the president and the U.S. Senate, Adams said, "to help us out of our distress, or protect us in our rights and

Ho for Kansas!

Brethren, Friends, & Fellow Citizens:

I feel thankful to inform you that the

REAL ESTATE
AND
Homestead Association,

Will Leave Here the

15th of April, 1878,

In pursuit of Homes in the Southwestern Lands of America, at Transportation Rates, cheaper than ever was known before.

For full information inquire of

Benj. Singleton, better known as old Pap,

NO. 5 NORTH FRONT STREET.

Beware of Speculators and Adventurers, as it is a dangerous thing to fall in their hands.

Nashville, Tenn., March 18, 1878.

COME!

To the Colored People of the United States of America:

This is to lay before your minds a few sketches of what great advantages there are for the great mass of people of small means that are emigrating West to come and settle in the county of Hodgeman, in the State of Kansas—and more especially the Colored people, for they are the ones that want to find the best place for climate and for soil for the smallest capital. Hodgeman county is in Southwestern Kansas, on the line of the Atchison, Topeka & Santa Fe Railroad.

We, the undersigned, having examined the above county and found it best adapted to our people, have applied to the proper authority and have obtained a Charter, in the name and style of "THE DAVID CITY TOWN COMPANY," in the County of Hodgeman, State of Kansas.

TRUSTEES:

A. McCLURE.   STEPHEN ESSEX.
JOHN YATES.   THOMAS JACKSON.
THOMAS BIEZER.   JOHN GOTHARD.
HENRY BRILEE.

A. McCLURE, President.
J. WOODFORK, Secretary.

SEE
What Colored Citizens

ARE DOING FOR THEIR ELEVATION.

Having organized an Association, known as the

EDGEFIELD
Real Estate Association, No. 1.

We find that this is the greatest association we have ever organized since the emancipation. Therefore we earnestly solicit every colored citizen throughout the State of Tennessee, male or female, to save their money to invest in this great work. We pray that every minister of the gospel of Jesus Christ will be an active part in this work, as we feel it their duty, irrespective of their denomination.

The principal business office of the Association is at Main street, Edgefield, and persons desirous of learning more about this association can add the communications to A. McCLURE, MAIN ST., EDGEFIELD, who will take great pleasure in giving all information you desire to know. We have taken the following pledge:

We, the colored citizens of Edgefield, do solemnly pledge ourselves in good faith to carry out the object of the Association with true honesty. We will sustain this Association by the presence and money, such as the Constitution may require. We further pledge ourselves to be square-headed, honest men.

We meet at present at our hall in Edgefield every Friday night, and at the Second Baptist Church, Nashville, every Wednesday night, but we will give the time of meeting any time at the request of any club, and visit them.

A. McCLURE, President,
G. W. DEANE, Cor. Secretary,
W. ANTHONY, Jr., Rec. Secretary,
W. ANTHONY, Esq., Marshal.

COMMITTEE ON APPLICATION:
W. A. SIZEMORE, Esq.   REV. SINGLETON.

Three early Kansas posters issued by Benjamin "Pap" Singleton

privileges." When this plea went unheeded, they requested land in Western territories or "an appropriation of money to ship us all to Liberia, in Africa; somewhere where we could live in peace and quiet." With no response from Washington, committee members wanted to ask "other governments outside of the United States to help us get away from the United States and go there and live under their flag."

After all suggestions were ignored or rejected, Adams and his committee summoned conventions to consider their people's choices. Women were among the most outspoken advocates of emigration, some declaring they would leave even if their husbands refused. Many were widows whose

Exodus from Vicksburg, Mississippi, for Kansas in May 1879

husbands who had been slain by night-riding bands and who had to support large families. By 1875 women emerged as emigration's driving force.

In the spring of that year what some papers called "Kansas Fever" saw upwards of seven thousand penniless, ragged men, women, and children pack up and leave for Kansas. Some sailed up the Mississippi on riverboats and others walked up the Chisholm Trail. By early 1880 about fifteen thousand had settled in Kansas.

The "Great Exodus" was a spontaneous, leaderless movement largely of poor, bedraggled families, propelled by a faith and hope that peace and land awaited those who reached "the John Brown land." But as historian Nell Irvin Painter points out, these emigrants had a clear understanding of the cruel tyranny they sought to escape, particularly the relentless brutality it visited on women and children.

The white South reacted with a fury at the thought of losing a cheap labor supply. Leaders of the exodus were denounced as troublemakers and local agents were driven out of town or beaten. One man who came back to gather his family for the trip to Kansas was seized by whites, who cut off both his hands and threw him in his wife's lap, saying, "Now go to Kansas to work!" In May 1879, white Mississippians had closed the river and threatened to sink all vessels carrying migrants. General Thomas Conway reported to President Hayes: "Every river landing is blockaded by white enemies of the colored exodus; some of whom are mounted and armed, as if we are at war."

That December, Democrats in Congress ordered an investigation of the exodus, fearing it was a Republican plot to move voteless Black men into northern areas where they would vote Republican. In the spring of 1880 a Senate committee dominated by Democrats began to call witnesses. African Americans who testified told tales of violence and hatred in the "Solid South" and their hope for liberty and land in Kansas.

Black attorney John H. Johnson of St. Louis described how migrants he interviewed all agreed there was "no security for life, limb, or property" in the South. "We tried to get some of them to return and consulted with them on the subject, and they said they would rather go into the open prairie and starve there than go to the South and stand the impositions that were put upon them there." "It's no use," said one farm laborer, "I will go somewhere else and try to make headway like white workingmen." Women were adamant about not returning to a South that denied their children an education and violated their daughters with impunity. "What, go back!... I'd sooner starve here," said a mother.

One of the most interesting witnesses was Benjamin Singleton, a tall, lean Tennessee ex-slave who since 1870 had actively mobilized the migration. He insisted, "I am the whole cause of the Kansas migration!" Because of his exaggeration, some historians have credited Singleton with the Great Exodus.

Neither Southern violence, a congressional investigation, nor Northern resentment halted the Great Exodus. After seventeen hun-

Benjamin "Pap" Singleton, a leader of the famous exodus of 1879

Exodusters arriving in July 1879 at crowded relief facilities, as shown in *Harper's Weekly*, July 5, 1879

dred pages of testimony, senators had learned that the movement was not a Republican plot but a response to unrelenting racial oppression – and a people's vision of becoming landowners.

Leading Black political figures – called "representative colored men" – such as Frederick Douglass, opposed the exodus, fearing it meant abandoning the fight for justice in the South. Some critics, shocked by the emigrants' poverty and lack of skills, wondered how they would be able to support their families. The *Topeka Colored Citizen* welcomed the emigrants, editorializing, "It is better to starve to death in Kansas than be shot and killed in the South." But it sternly warned against laziness in Kansas: "everybody must work or starve."

Because they arrived in such large numbers, the "Exodusters" encountered immediate relief problems. Topeka's mayor, Michael Case, refused to spend taxpayers' money on the emigrants, but Governor John St. John and his wife personally welcomed the Exodusters and helped raise funds for their relief.

Later, as Kansas relief facilities became strained beyond capacity, Singleton, Adams, and other leaders of the migration advised people to choose other destinations. To provide relief for the newcomers, citizens of Kansas collected over $100,000. One-fourth of the aid came from English sym-

To the Great Exodus

The word it has been spoken;
The message has been sent:
The prison doors have opened,
and out the prisoners went.
To join the sable army of African descent,
for God is marching on.

Sojourner Truth, *St. Louis Globe-Democrat,* April 24, 1879

pathizers in the form of Staffordshire pottery. Philip D. Armour, after a personal tour of refugee facilities in Wyandotte, Kansas, collected $1,200 in donations from Chicago industrialists and, together with beef from his meat-packing plant, sent it to Kansas.

Some famous antislavery figures arrived to aid the migrants. In late 1879 Sojourner Truth, calling it "the greatest movement of all time," came

In May 1880, *Harper's Weekly* contrasted the 1879 exodus to Kansas with earlier escapes of slaves.

to help "her race in Kansas, waking, watching, waiting for the salvation of her people." Clara Brown left Colorado with donations and volunteered her labor. Laura Haviland, a white abolitionist, joined with African American Josephine St. Pierre Ruffin, director of the Kansas Relief Association, to raise money, collect food and clothing, and find work and homes for families.

In a few years, Haviland was able to report remarkable gains: "Comparatively few call for assistance who have been in the state for a year, and most of these are aged grandparents, the sick, and widows with large families of small children. Of those who came in the early Spring of 1879, many have raised from one hundred to four thousand bushels of corn each year, but divide with their friends and relatives who follow them."

Some fifteen thousand emigrants took jobs as farm laborers or worked for railroads, in mines, or as domestics and launderers. About a third of the newcomers moved to rural areas in the first year. Those with cash were able to purchase twenty thousand acres of land and built three hundred homes. In Graham County, people plowed a virgin prairie with spades. The pioneers soon accumulated property and cash totaling $40,000, hardly a fortune, but more than critics expected.

In 1886 a government survey found that about three-quarters of families owned homes, and because nearly all Black women worked, family income equaled that of white workingmen. The early years on the Kansas plains were also filled with heartbreak. Almost two thousand in Nebraska

In 1880 arriving migrants were welcomed to Kansas by Governor St. John and his wife (in back of right barrel).

Kansas homesteaders – the Taylor family – pose in their Sunday best at their home.

received a mixed welcome, and a group of 150 from Mississippi were driven out of Lincoln.

Those who reached Denver in the 1880s found, the *Denver Republican* reported, "that the owners of houses would not rent to them." This situation was alleviated when settlers of both races agreed "to build and sell these colored men small houses on the installment plan."

Life in Kansas continued to be a mixed blessing. In 1888 Frederick Douglass was turned away by a Leavenworth innkeeper, but he was received with honor at one of Topeka's best hotels. As the Black population headed toward 10 percent of the total, towns began to enforce residential segregation. In 1889 the editor of the *American Citizen* wrote of Topeka: "There are houses and lots and additions in and near this city where no negro can rent or buy at any price, let him be ever so talented, cultured or refined, and there are others where if he rents or buys, his life and property are in danger." Lynchings were not uncommon in Kansas, and more people of color than whites died at the hands of white mobs, but Black mobs also intervened to prevent lynchings.

Sons and daughters of the Great Exodus soon graduated from Nebraska high schools. Most large towns and many small ones had an integrated police force and integrated fire departments. Tom Cunningham became Lincoln's first African American policeman, and Topeka hired thirteen Black police

The Shores family of musicians settled in Custer County, Nebraska, and were photographed in 1887 displaying their new baby, dog, horses, wagon, and sod house.

and nine Black firemen. Dr. M. O. Ricketts, an ex-slave who graduated from the University of Nebraska's College of Medicine in 1884, was twice elected to the state legislature; five others followed in his footsteps. By the end of the century, African Americans in Kansas, better off than their sisters and brothers in the South, voted in elections, and were pleased they made the journey.

Edwin P. McCabe rode to political success with the Exodus. In 1882, when he was thirty-two, McCabe was called "the recognized leader of his race in the west." At that year's Republican State convention he was nominated for state auditor by acclamation as the cheers of 6 Black and 394 white delegates, reported a local paper, rent the air and hats flew in the smoke-filled hall.

Elected twice to this office, McCabe became the highest Black official in West. Then he was not renominated. He left to prospect for gold in California. Finally he headed to Oklahoma and dramatic new political adventures.

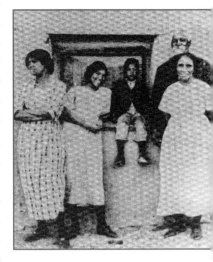

Nebraska homesteaders (left to right) Grace, Truth, Glen, Robert, and Hannah

Unknown Nebraska pioneer

Mrs. and Mrs. John Adams of Nebraska

At Marble Falls, Texas, prisoners in the 1880s worked at a quarry to obtain the rock used to build the Texas State Capitol.

Black Towns

In the decades after the Civil War, separate Black communities sprouted in the Western states. Historian James M. Smallwood has written, "At different times both during and after Reconstruction, blacks established at least 39 separate communities in fifteen Texas counties to escape white control." These included Kendleton in Fort Bend County, Shankleville in Newton County, Board House in Blanco County, and such settlements as Andy, Booker, Cologne, Mill City, Roberts, Union City, and Oldham. By 1870 more than five thousand former slaves attended four dozen Texas schools.

African Americans also created their own towns of Dora, Blackdom, and El Vado in New Mexico. In 1883 "Mr. Watkins," a Black Chicago firefighter, brought families to the Dakota Territory to settle. In Nebraska a number of African American farm colonies had taken root by 1889, one near Crete that used windmills, and another in Harland County begun by two hundred Tennesseans.

In 1908 Army Chaplain Allen Allensworth and Josephine Allensworth, believers in African American economic solidarity, persuaded investors to sponsor a town named after them in Tulare County in central California. By 1913 Allensworth boasted a library, school, church, civic center, and a park.

Oliver T. Jackson arrived in Colorado in 1887 and dreamed of starting a community based on Booker T. Washington's self-help philosophy and an urge to "get back to the land." A generation later, in 1911, Minerva and Oliver Jackson began Dearfield on 320 acres in Weld County, aided by seventy enthusiastic middle-aged pioneers from Denver. Though they lacked

A young Mrs. Boyer plows her field in Blackdom, New Mexico.

O. T. Jackson,
founder of
Dearfield,
Colorado,
holding child

Church
services at
Dearfield

both agricultural experience and capital, Eunice Norris, a resident, rhapsodized of Dearfield's benefits: "People got along well. It was a peaceful sort of situation: struggling people working hard; they didn't have time for trouble. There was a spirit of helpfulness."

The Jacksons advertised Dearfield as a "valley resort" complete with a gas station, barn pavilion for dances, and a variety of exciting food and drinks. Residents planted a dozen crops, reported one farmer, and "everything came up fine," only to be devastated by grasshoppers. The community prospered during World War I. Jackson looked forward to creating "the wealthiest Negro community in the world," but success finally eluded Dearfield's farmers after an agricultural depression struck in the early 1920s.

Residents of Dearfield, Colorado

Barney Ford

Despite fifty years of labor in behalf of a better Colorado, the only state monument to Barney Ford is a hill just southeast of Breckinridge's city limits called, until 1964, "Nigger Hill." Actually, white vigilantes drove Ford and five other companions off the place in 1860. Ford and other African American prospectors had begun digging for gold on the spot. They were prohibited from filing a claim by the Supreme Court's Dred Scott decision, so Ford asked a white lawyer to file the claim in his name. The lawyer complied and, as soon as they struck gold, dispatched the local sheriff with an order to the miners to vacate the land in twenty-four hours. That night, as the six prospectors pondered their choices, white riders galloped up to speed their departure and seize their gold. Ford and the others had to flee on foot without food or

Colorado pioneer Barney Ford

Pioneer H. O. Waggoner

blankets. Because they could not find any gold, the desperadoes began the legend that Ford had buried it somewhere on the mountainside, which they renamed "Nigger Hill." Many a man would try his luck on the land, but none struck it rich.

Both Ford and his good friend Henry O. Waggoner had begun their lives enslaved in the South, and once Ford and a gray mule were sold for $460. At seventeen Ford was told his mother had drowned while trying to locate an agent for the Underground Railroad who would help him escape. Both men taught themselves to read and write, and when Ford escaped from slavery, the two met for the first time, in Chicago. Waggoner was a correspondent for Frederick Douglass's newspaper and a local paper, and they became Underground Railroad conductors. Ford eventually married Julia, Waggoner's sister-in-law.

When gold was discovered in California, the Fords left for the West Coast. But when their ship docked in Nicaragua, they decided to open the "United States Hotel" there and returned to Chicago richer by five thousand dollars. Ford headed west again, this time alone, to try his luck as a prospector in Colorado. In Denver he was not allowed to board a stagecoach and had to take a job as barber in a wagon train heading west. At Mountain City he was refused a hotel room and had to board with Clara Brown. On more than one occasion before Waggoner joined him in Colorado, white outlaws jumped his claims.

Barney Ford's Inter-Ocean Hotel, Denver, Colorado

Ford and Waggoner opened various businesses – barbershops, restaurants, and hotels – in Denver. But in 1865 after Colorado's constitution prohibited equal male suffrage, a prosperous Ford took his family back to Chicago. His Colorado friends asked him to lobby in Washington against the Colorado statehood bill. Ford eagerly stepped into the fray and spoke with Senator Charles Sumner, who helped eliminate the provision. Ford then brought his family back to Denver.

Together with African American pioneers Ed Sanderlin and W. J. Hardin, Waggoner and Ford established Colorado's first adult education classes in Waggoner's home. They taught adults reading, writing, arithmetic, and the principles of democratic government.

INTER-OCEAN HOTEL, CHEYENNE, WYOMING.

Ford's Inter-Ocean Hotel, Cheyenne, Wyoming

Ford's business ventures were highly successful. He built and ran two fancy, prosperous Inter-Ocean hotels, one in Cheyenne and another in Denver, which catered to everyone from presidents to prospectors. Dinner at the hotel acquired a reputation as far east as Chicago for "the squarest meal between two oceans." Three times fires gutted his businesses, and each time he managed to rebuild.

Ford became the first African American man to serve on a Colorado grand jury; Waggoner became the first to serve as deputy sheriff of

Rocky Mountain News ad for Ford's restaurant, September 1, 1863

This Bonham, Texas, band took part in a fair around 1910.

Arapahoe County. In 1882 Barney Ford and Julia were the first people of color invited to a dinner of the Colorado Association of Pioneers.

The definitive *History of the State of Colorado*, published in 1895, allocated to Ford a two-and-a-half-page biography, larger than for territorial governors and other prominent whites. The author, however, did not mention Ford's race, and later editions of the book replaced his picture with that of a white man. But in 1964 local maps changed "Nigger Hill" to "Barney Ford Hill."

10
THE BUFFALO SOLDIERS

In the Civil War 178,958 African Americans had fought in a Union Army of one million, taken part in 449 engagements and 39 major battles, and been awarded twenty-two Medals of Honor. They earned the unstinting praise of their commanders in the field, and in 1864 their commander in chief in the White House admitted that without his Black troops "we would be compelled to abandon the war in three weeks."

Black men gained and quickly lost their right to vote, but in 1866 they won a permanent a right to serve in the U.S. armed forces when Congress authorized recruitment of African Americans to assist in the "pacification" of the West. By 1870 the goal of preserving peace with Native Americans – made impossible by Washington policy and the white appetite for Indian land – fell to 30,000 federal soldiers, including 2,700 former slaves.

Over the next two generations 25,000 African American men would pass through the ranks of the two Black caval-

In the Civil War, African Americans earned the right to serve in the U.S. Army.

The Twenty-Fourth Infantry test blanket rolls for the U.S. Army in 1893.

ry and two Black infantry regiments. The average recruit was about twenty-three, an illiterate laborer or farmer seeking a stable job, steady income, and higher status. Soldiers were paid $13 a month with small annual increases. For African American units the army provided a chaplain to oversee education. "I felt I wasn't learning enough, so I joined," recalled soldier Mazique Sancho. Men who had not learned to read and write leaped at the

This 1893 photo shows Twenty-Fourth Infantry men using 1884 model 45/70 Springfield rifles with bayonets.

The Twenty-Fifth Infantry band, Fort Missoula, Montana, around 1900

opportunity, and despite a shortage of trained teachers, they made remark-able progress. In 1875 Chaplain George C. Mullins reported: "For the most part the soldiers seem to have an enthusiastic interest in the school. They are prompt in attendance, very orderly and cheerful. In learning to read and write many of them make astonishing progress."

The African American regiments, the Ninth and Tenth Cavalry and the Twenty-Fourth and Twenty-Fifth Infantry, were mired in painful irony. Recruits were commanded by whites and denied the right to be commissioned officers. And they contributed to the final defeat of Native Americans, the first victims of racism in the Americas. Native Americans named them "buffalo soldiers" after an animal that provided them with clothing, food, and shelter.

The Twenty-fourth Infantry at Los Angeles County, around 1898

Mounted buffalo soldiers, around 1898

In an age that increasingly viewed Black men as either comic or dangerous and denied them decent jobs, army life offered reliable, dignified, and rewarding labor. It also provided those symbols by which man has traditionally cushioned a lowly status – pride in country, discipline, decent clothes, and faith in authority.

Soldiers follow orders and these men were no different. But some vehemently opposed Washington's policies toward Native Americans and expressed their views. For example, George Washington Williams, sergeant major in the Tenth Cavalry, recalled he and his men felt "it is wrong to persecute the poor Indian" and that "white people would have to answer for their wickedness in the Day of Judgment." When his company left for the frontier, he reported: "We felt that if there was an Indian near we would run and fall upon his neck and weep." Appalled by a white officer who was "thirsting for Indian blood," Williams decided "killing people isn't a job for a Christian," and he left the service. In 1881 he wrote a two-volume *History of the Negro Race in America*, the century's most important Black historical study in this field.

George W. Williams, historian

Camping out
on the frontier

Some assignments had buffalo soldiers guarding Indians from white soldiers, lawmen, or civilians. In 1879 Texas Rangers were about to engage in a scalp-hunting foray against a Kiowa village when Tenth Cavalrymen blocked their path. In 1887 the Ninth Cavalry kept Colorado militiamen from charging into a Ute reservation. Buffalo soldiers also protected the Indian Territory from aggressive white intruders.

The men of the Ninth and Tenth Cavalry Regiments comprised 20 percent of the U.S. Cavalry in the West and rolled up an outstanding record. They patrolled from the Mississippi to the Rockies, from the Canadian border to the Rio Grande, and occasionally were ordered into Mexico in pur-

Black soldiers guarding a stagecoach

"The Friendship of the Negro Race"

People may think it isn't true, but the Indians never shot a colored man unless it was necessary. They always wanted to win the friendship of the Negro race, and obtain their aid in campaigns against the white man."

Caleb Benson, Tenth Cavalry, 1875–1908, cited in *Northeast Nebraska News*, November 9, 1934 (*Nebraska History*, summer 1993)

suit of outlaws or Indians. Their white scouts included Kit Carson and Wild Bill Hickok.

Officers such as George Armstrong Custer rejected service in the regiments, as did many West Point graduates. On the other hand, General John J. Pershing was proud to earn the nickname "Black Jack" leading a company of the Tenth Cavalry against bandits and Indians in Montana, against Spaniards at San Juan Hill, and against Pancho Villa in Mexico. In 1921 Pershing wrote: "It has been an honor which I am proud to claim to have been at one time a member of that intrepid organization of the Army which has always added glory to the military history of America – the 10th Cavalry."

Black Jack Pershing and his Tenth Cavalry men

Troopers of the Ninth and Tenth Cavalry participated in almost two hundred engagements and won the respect of every military friend or foe they encountered. They suppressed civil disorders, chased Indians who left their reservations, arrested rustlers, guarded stagecoaches, built roads, protected survey parties, shielded mail carriers, mapped uncharted regions, and rescued settlers and other soldiers. In 1892 they ended a cattle war in Wyoming and two years later they preserved order when jobless citizens marched on Washington to demand economic relief.

A wounded Tenth Cavalryman, sketched by Frederic Remington

Particularly in East Texas, buffalo soldiers faced hostility from the people they defended, often former Confederate soldiers contemptuous of armed, blue-coated men. Jacksboro, Texas, had twenty-seven saloons for its two hundred white residents – tough cow-punchers and prostitutes who enjoyed baiting Black soldiers. One Texas citizen murdered a Black soldier and then killed the two African American cavalrymen who came to arrest him. A jury of his white peers found him not guilty.

The Ninth Cavalry at Fort Robinson, Nebraska

Black troops line up in 1899.

In 1867, when vigilantes lynched three Black infantrymen in Kansas, other Black soldiers returned to the town center and a blazing gunfight. In February 1878 a Black company from Fort Concho, Texas, armed with carbines, shot it out in a San Angelo saloon with local cowboys, gamblers, and pimps, leaving two men dead and several wounded. In 1900 in El Paso, Texas, after police arrested two Black infantrymen, others used their rifles to raid the jail. In the ensuing gun duel, each side lost a man.

At times soldiers of both races united against their tormentors. On February 3, 1881, in San Angelo, after a Black private was killed by a gambler and a white soldier was also slain, white and Black soldiers posted a handbill:

> We, the soldiers of the United States Army, do hereby warn cowboys, etc., of San Angelo and vicinity, to recognize our rights of way as just and peaceable men. If we do not receive justice and fair play, which we must have, someone will suffer; if not the guilty, the innocent. It has gone too far; justice or death.
>
> U.S. SOLDIERS, ONE AND ALL.

Two companies of enlisted men, one Black and one white, then marched into San Angelo, arrested the sheriff, and demanded he surrender the murderer in his jail. At that point a white colonel ordered the troopers back to Fort Concho.

Cannon firing at
Fort Robinson,
Nebraska

The Army brass consistently took a dim view of its buffalo soldiers. In Texas, General Edward Ord called them "with few exceptions, liars and thieves," and General William T. Sherman told Congress he preferred to enter a battle with "5,000 white men." The army high command also dealt buffalo soldiers an unfair hand. Captain Louis Carpenter, one of several white officers to earn the Medal of Honor leading Black troopers, complained that "this regiment has received nothing but broken-down horses and repaired equipment" – usually castoffs from George Custer's favored Seventh Cavalry. Even the Tenth's regimental banner was homemade, faded, and worn

A buffalo soldier band

– unlike the silk-embroidered standard supplied by headquarters to white regiments. Not until 1891 were African American soldiers assigned to guard the national capital.

Buffalo soldiers, scholar William H. Leckie has shown, were consistently assigned to the most dreary forts: "Their stations were among the most lonely and isolated to be found anywhere in the country and mere service at such posts would seem to have called for honorable mention. Discipline was severe, food usually poor, recreation difficult, and violent death always near at hand. Prejudice robbed them of recognition and often of simple justice."

From a remote Texas post, the white commander of the Twenty-Fifth Infantry described "everything saturated with rain, the dirt floor four inches deep of mud, and the men sitting at meals with their feet in more than an inch of water, while their head and back were being defiled with ooze from the dripping dirt roof."

Punishments of African Americans, Leckie found, exceeded those of white soldiers. However, Black cavalrymen had fewer courts-martial for drunkenness, and boasted the lowest desertion rate in the frontier army. In 1876, the Ninth had 6 and the Tenth had 18 deserters – compared to 170 for the Third, 72 for the Seventh and 224 for the Fifth.

Black deserters found more places to hide than whites, including among Native Americans, Mexican Americans, and other people of color. Frustrated in his hunt for deserters among the ninety African American residents of Las Vagas, New Mexico, Lieutenant Matthias Day grumbled, "The whole

Interior of barracks at Fort Shaw, Montana

colored population here seem to be in league with" his Black escapees, "and spy around to find out everything I do."

Despite discriminatory conditions, morale among Buffalo Soldiers remained high, and a dozen men earned the nation's highest military decoration, the Medal of Honor. The first recipient, Emanuel Stance, a sergeant in Company F, Ninth Cavalry, in two years had five encounters with Plains Indians and accounted himself so well that his captain was unstinting in his praise.

Others followed. Sergeant George Jordan of the Ninth earned his medal for two engagements. In one he commanded twenty-five troopers who "repulsed a force of more than 100 Indians," read the official report. A few years later, in 1881, he and nineteen Buffalo Soldiers "forced back a much superior number of the enemy, preventing them from surrounding the command." That same year another sergeant in the Ninth, Moses Williams, received his Medal of Honor with this citation: "Rallied a detachment, skillfully conducted a running fight of three or four hours, and by his coolness, bravery and unflinching devotion to duty in standing by his commanding officer in an exposed position under heavy fire from a large party of Indians, saved the lives of at least three of his comrades." The heroism of other troopers is forever buried in terse military phrases such as "bravery in action," "gallantry

Fighting off an ambush

in hand-to-hand fight," and "saved the lives of his comrades and citizens of the detachment."

On June 25, 1876, Isaiah Dorman, a Sioux with African American ancestry, a friend of Chief Sitting Bull, and a highly trusted War Department courier and scout in the Dakota Territory, rode into history with General Custer. With Custer and 264 Seventh cavalrymen, he fell mortally wounded at the Little Big Horn. Sitting Bull reportedly approached the fallen Dorman and said, "Don't kill that man, he's a friend of mine." After he gave Dorman a drink from his buffalo horn, he died. A Cheyenne later wrote: "I went riding over the ground where we had fought the first soldiers during the morning of the day before. I saw by the river, on the west side, a dead black man. He was a big man. All of his clothing was gone when I saw him, but he had not been scalped nor cut up like the white men had been. Some Sioux told me he belonged to their people but was with the soldiers."

Neither extraordinary competence, courage, nor sacrifice led to an easing of Army discrimination. African American soldiers found it difficult to advance beyond sergeant, and were denied opportunities granted white recruits. Asked if he would form an artillery unit a Black man could join, Captain Henry Wright of the Ninth Cavalry answered, "He lacks the brains."

Captain Dodge's Colored Troopers to the Rescue is the title Frederic Remington gave this famous picture. For bravely leading buffalo soldiers against the Ute Indians at Milk River, a white officer received the Medal of Honor.

The Ninth
Cavalry
dining room

The last decades of the nineteenth century have been characterized by scholar Rayford Logan as "the nadir" of African American life. Citizens of color had little to sustain their spirits, he pointed out – except for the buffalo soldiers. Many Black homes proudly displayed photographs of these intrepid fighters.

The Ninth Cavalry

The Ninth Regiment Cavalry, United States Colored Troops, was organized in New Orleans in 1866 under Colonel Edward Hatch and under the fifteen-year command of Major Albert P. Morrow. It became a tough, hard-hit-

The Ninth
Cavalry Band
in Santa Fe
Plaza, 1885

The Ninth Cavalry amusement room

ting unit. Lieutenant Colonel Wesley Merritt, who with six companies of the Ninth rebuilt Fort Davis in Texas, called his troopers "brave in battle, easily disciplined, and most efficient in the care of their horses, arms and equipment." The Ninth served in Texas, New Mexico, Kansas, Oklahoma, Nebraska, Utah, and Montana.

The Ninth earned a reputation for always arriving in the nick of time to rescue settlers or troopers pinned down by outlaws or Indians. In Texas their fiercest foes included Mescalero Apaches, Kickapoos, and Mexican and U.S. bandits – all of whom crossed the Mexican border at will, something the troopers could not do. The Ninth's duties included scouting for cattle thieves and marauders, providing escort duty for survey parties, picket and patrol

The Ninth Cavalry machine gun platoon

Trumpeters of the Tenth Cavalry

duty, protecting river crossings, acting as couriers, guarding the Rio Grande, providing escort to cattle herds, securing prisoners, chasing Indians, and defending trains and wagons.

During the Ghost Dance rebellion of the 1890s, a company of the Ninth rode one hundred miles and took part in two fights in thirty hours to relieve the Seventh Cavalry. The company commander, Captain Dodge, earned the Medal of Honor, and his action was immortalized in a Frederic Remington drawing.

The Tenth Cavalry

Mobilized at Fort Leavenworth, Kansas, in 1866, the Tenth Cavalry Regiment became a legend on the frontier. Their first commander, Colonel Benjamin Grierson, was a former music teacher famous for his spectacular six-hundred-mile cavalry raid into Confederate territory. Devoted to his job and his men, Grierson helped them form a regimental band. He and his fellow white officers contributed to the fund for musical instruments. Grierson's wife

Colonel Benjamin Grierson

The Tenth Cavalry at Diamond Creek, 1891

wrote letters home for soldiers who could not write, and served as an informal volunteer lawyer for those in trouble with their officers.

For a time the Tenth Cavalry constituted the only U.S. military presence in West Texas. They also made the first thorough exploration of Texas's Staked Plains, a trackless wasteland, riding for days in temperatures of over 100 degrees. They discovered several good springs and found land with excellent

The Tenth Cavalry Band at Crawford, 1906

Sgt. Vance Marchbanks: Brownsville, Texas, 1899

The majority of the inhabitants of that section, are a class that think a colored man is not good enough to wear the uniform of a United States soldier – near not good enough even to wear the skin of a dog.

They sneer at a colored soldier on the sidewalk and bar him from their saloons, resorts, and places of amusement. Why, when I was down there, one Sunday I thought I would go down to Point Isabella, on the Bay, to spend the day. So in company with a young lady I went down to the depot and purchased two tickets (taking advantage of the excursion rates then offered), boarded the train (which was only a little better than walking), went into the car and took a seat. When the train started, one of the so-called "Texas Rangers" came up to me and told me I was in the wrong place. I said "No, I guess not, I just read your law, and it says the Negro and white passengers will not ride in the same coach except on excursions." He replied, "Don't make any difference, you get out of here; you are too smart any way; I will break this gun over your head if you say much," the meantime menacing me with a six-shooter, of the most improved villainous pattern and caliber. Well I obeyed his orders because I was alone and could not help myself. I knew that I was being treated wrong, but he held a "Royal flush," and I only had a "four-card bob," and I knew I could not "bluff" him.

A colored man who has the disposition of a toad frog (I mean one who can stand to be beaten on the back and puff up and take it) is all right; he can stay in that country. But those who feel hot blood running through their veins, and who are proudly and creditably wearing the uniform of a United States soldier; standing ready to protect and defend the American flag, against any enemy whomsoever, to obey the orders of the President of the United States and the orders of the officer appointed over them (which they have always done with pride and honor), cannot stay down there in peace with honor. The people do not want them either because they will probably not be able to carry out their favorite sport, hanging a colored man to a limb, or tarring and feathering him and burning him at the stake without trial, while the colored soldiers are stationed there.

Sergeant Vance Marchbanks in *The Voice*, December 1906, p. 549

The Twenty-Fifth Infantry at Missoula, Montana, around 1900

grass. The report on their foray stimulated a migration by cattlemen, sheep-men, and homesteaders, but failed to mention the gallant horsemen who first crossed this land.

The Tenth patrolled Kansas, Oklahoma, New Mexico, and Arizona, bat-tled Sioux, Apaches, and Comanches, and helped capture Geronimo and Billy the Kid. One of their most frustrating assignments was to keep the peace between angry settlers and cattlemen after barbed wire drew a steel line between the two.

The Twenty-Fifth Infantry at Fort Snelling, Minnesota, 1883

The Twenty-
fifth Infantry
Fort Missoula
baseball team,
1902

The Twenty-Fourth and
Twenty-Fifth Infantry Regiments

The Twenty-Fourth and Twenty-Fifth Infantry Regiments also served on the
Western plains. The Twenty-Fourth was organized in 1869 from two units
scattered from Louisiana to Texas and New Mexico. Lieutenant Colonel Wil-
liam R. Shafter, an obese and lackluster officer, was its first commander. The
Twenty-Fifth was organized in New Orleans in 1869 from remnants of the
Thirty-Ninth regiment from North Carolina and the Fortieth in Louisiana.

Both regiments were dispatched to desolate Western garrisons and
directed to defend the frontier from violence. In 1889 a small detachment

Soldiers from the Twenty-Fifth Infantry leave Missoula, Montana, in the first U.S.
Army test of a bicycle corps, riding to St. Louis and back in 1899.

from the Twenty-Fourth Infantry and the Ninth Cavalry were ambushed by bandits in Arizona as they guarded an army payroll wagon and its driver. Firing from a promontory, a band of outlaws pinned the soldiers down, wounded several, and made off with the strongbox. Paymaster J. W. Wham, who fought in sixteen Civil War battles under General Grant, found their bravery exceptional: "I never witnessed better courage or better fighting than shown by these colored soldiers, on May 11, 1889, as the bullet marks on the robber positions to-day abundantly attest." For their courage under fire and fighting on despite severe wounds, Sergeant Benjamin Brown and Corporal Isaiah Mays were awarded Medals of Honor.

Black Officers at West Point

One of the most disgraceful chapters in U.S. military history is West Point's refusal to protect its earliest African American cadets. Of the twenty Black candidates who entered West Point in the nineteenth century, only three graduated. The first cadet, James W. Smith of South Carolina, was harassed and then ousted from the academy for striking back at his tormentors by hitting one on the head with a coconut dipper.

West Pointer James Smith

Your kind letter should have been answered long ere this, but really I have been so harassed with examinations and insults and ill treatment of these cadets that I could not write or do anything else scarcely. I passed the examination all right, and got in, but my companion Howard failed and was rejected. Since he went away I have been lonely indeed. And now these fellows appear to be trying their utmost to run me off, and I fear they will succeed if they continue as they have begun. We went into camp yesterday, and not a moment has passed since then but some one of them has been cursing and abusing me... It is just the same at the table, and what I get to eat I must snatch for like a dog. I don't wish to resign if I can get along at all; but I don't think it will be best for me to stay and take all the abuses and insults that are heaped upon me.

James Smith, in *The New Era*, July 14, 1870

A court-martial hearing in the case of Black West Point cadet Johnson C. Whittaker

In 1880, Cadet Johnson C. Whittaker, after two years of academic success at the academy, was found tied to his bed, his ears slashed and his hair
cut. He was charged with inflicting the wounds on himself and falsely accus-
ing others; a court-martial found him guilty. In 1882 President Chester A.
Arthur reviewed the case and found the evidence insufficient, but the Academy's board again ruled against Whittaker,
and he was dismissed.

The first African American graduate of
West Point, Henry O. Flipper, was the son
of a Georgia slave. He endured the rage of
other cadets and instructors who would not
speak to him, and in June 1877 graduated
fiftieth in a class of seventy-six. Assigned to
the Tenth Cavalry, he hoped to find better
times. In 1881, Lieutenant Flipper was tried
for "embezzling public funds and conduct
unbecoming an officer." He was acquitted
on the first charge but found guilty on the

Second Lieutenant Henry Flipper

In 1880 *Puck* magazine published this cartoon on its cover.

second. For years after his discharge he wondered if the fact that he had gone riding with a young white woman while serving at Fort Concho had led to his conviction.

Despite Lieutenant Flipper's discharge, his extraordinary skills as a civil engineer led to his being hired by federal, state, and local governments. His work and incorruptibility resulted in the return of large portions of land to the public domain. Flipper served as a translator for the Senate Committee on Foreign Relations, helped build a railroad in Alaska, and worked for the U.S. secretary of the interior. Many decades after his death Flipper was exonerated.

After his graduation from West Point in 1887, Lieutenant John Alexander, served seven years as an officer with the Ninth Cavalry in Nebraska,

Wyoming, and Utah, earning the respect and trust of his men. He died suddenly in 1894 while on active duty. In 1918 the U.S. Army belatedly honored this "man of ability, attainments and energy – who was a credit to himself, to his race and to the service," when it named a post in Virginia "Camp Alexander."

Charles Young, the last African American West Point graduate of the nineteenth century, was assigned to the Tenth Cavalry in 1889

Second Lieutenant Charles Young in 1889

and began an illustrious career that would span more than three decades, the longest of the three graduates.

As a commander of Black Ohio volunteers during the Spanish-American War, Young took part in the charge at San Juan Hill. During Mexican border battles against Pancho Villa, he served with John J. Pershing in the Tenth Cavalry. In 1903 Young, speaking at Stanford University, rejected the accommodationist views of educator Booker T. Washington and said his people should assert their citizenship rights. He asked his audience: "All the Negro wants is a white man's chance. Will you give it?"

At the outset of World War I, Colonel Young received his answer. He was suddenly dropped from active duty. Although the official explanation was "high blood pressure," Young knew many wanted to prevent his assuming command of U.S. troops in the war to "make the world safe for democracy." To prove his fitness, Young rode his horse from Ohio to Washington and back. But not until three days before the Armistice was he placed back on active duty.

Assigned to diplomatic duty in Africa, Young died there in 1922, and was buried with full military honors at Arlington National Cemetery. By the time of his death Young had mastered six foreign languages, written books of poetry, and composed music for violin and piano. Not until 1936 would another African American man graduate from the U.S. Military Academy.

Frederic Remington's Black West

Frederic Remington sketched this dismounted Tenth Cavalryman.

Born in New York and educated at the Yale School of Fine Arts and at the Art Students League, Frederic Remington became the great artist of the last frontier. Among his twenty-seven hundred drawings and paintings, sketchbooks, reports, and short stories are preserved rare glimpses of buffalo soldiers in action.

In the summer of 1888 Remington accompanied a unit of the Tenth Cavalry in Arizona. He brought the trained eye of a journalist, the hands of an artist, and a rare ability to rise above the era's coarse stereotypes. "They are charming men with whom to serve," Remington wrote. He addressed another issue: "As to their bravery, I am often asked, 'Will they fight?' This is easily answered. They have fought many, many times. The old sergeant sitting near me, as calm of feature as a bronze statue, once deliberately walked over to a Cheyenne rifle-pit and killed his man. One little fellow near him once took charge of a lot of stampeded cavalry-horses when

Frederic Remington sketched this mounted Tenth Cavalryman.

Frederic
Remington,
second in
line, sketched
*Marching in
the Desert* in
Arizona with the
Tenth Cavalry,
in 1888.

Apache bullets were flying loose and no one knew from what point to expect them next. These little episodes prove the sometimes doubted self-reliance of the negro."

A decade later Remington again rode with the Tenth Cavalry. He revealed that this outfit "never had a 'soft detail' since it was organized, and it is full of old soldiers who know what it is all about, this soldiering." The media of the day treated Black men as brutes or buffoons, but Remington's images were natural and genuine: "The physique of the black soldiers must be admired – great chests, broad-shouldered, upstanding fellows..."

A Frederic
Remington sketch

A Remington sketch of the Tenth Cavalry on a Montana mountain pass in 1888

In a short story in *Collier's* in 1901, "How the Worm Turned," Remington responded to an early confrontation between troopers from Fort Concho and white criminals in San Angelo. His Black narrator reports how white Texans shot at Black soldiers "on sight." After some whites brutalized a Tenth Cavalry sergeant, he and his men rode in to settle matters. They entered the culprits' saloon, ordered a drink, then spun and opened fire. "When the great epic of the West is written," wrote Remington, "this is one of the wild notes that must sound in it."

A Remington party of buffalo soldiers from Fort Concho, Texas, shooting up Bill Powell's saloon to revenge a wounded comrade shot by one of its patrons

Seminoles at Fort Clark, Texas

The Seminole Negro Indian Scouts

On July 4, 1870, more than two hundred Black Seminole men, women, and children crossed the Rio Grande to settle at Fort Duncan, Texas. For the only time in history an African people and its reigning monarch, John Horse, had negotiated their admission to the United States by formal treaty and arrived intact as a nation. In a treaty initiated by U.S. General Zenas A. Bliss, the nation agreed to have its young men serve as army scouts in return for family rations and eventually some land. Their desert skills would even the army's odds against the cattle rustlers and desperadoes who kept the Rio Grande region in turmoil.

Charles Daniels; his wife, Mary; and daughter Tina

Seminole
Negro Indian
Scouts, 1889

The freedom-fighting record and many triumphs of these Seminole Negro Indian Scouts had begun in Florida before the Declaration of Independence. From 1850 until their return a generation later, they had served in Mexico as "military colonists." Their unmatched desert skills had brought down a host of border scorpions and pacified Mexico's turbulent Rio Grande border.

Men who could fire with pinpoint accuracy from the saddle were handed U.S. Sharps carbines, which allowed for faster, easier loading and action than any they had known. Civil War veteran Lieutenant John Bullis, their commander, was a diminutive, wiry, red-faced Quaker who gave them high fitness ratings except for "military appearance," which he rated "very poor" – his response to their Indian dress and feathered war bonnets.

Bullis and the Scouts survived the Texas desert on canned peaches and rattlesnakes. And they rolled up an unequaled military record. In twelve major engagements and twenty-six skirmishes, they never lost a man in battle or had one seriously wounded.

Scout Joseph Phillips described their relationship with Bullis: "The Scouts thought a lot of Bullis. Lieutenant Bullis was the only officer ever did stay the longest with us. That fella suffer just like we-all did out in de woods. He was a good man. He was a Injun fighter. He was tuff.

Lieutenant John L. Bullis, commander of the Seminole Scouts

He didn't care how big a bunch dey was, he went into 'em every time, but he look for his men. His men was on equality, too. He didn't stand and say, 'Go yonder'; he would say 'Come on boys, lets go get 'em.'"

Bullis could count on his men in an emergency, and on April 25, 1875, he had an emergency. Bullis, Sergeant John Ward, trumpeter Isaac Payne, and Private Pompey Factor attacked twenty-five Comanche rustlers who were guiding stolen horses across the Pecos River at Eagles' Nest. After the scouts twice separated the Comanches from their horses, the Indians regrouped and bore down on Bullis, who had fallen from his horse. "We can't leave the lieutenant, boys," shouted Sergeant Ward, and the three raced back. "I... just saved my hair by jumping on my Sergeant's horse, back of him," Bullis

Private Pompey Factor

Mary and
Fay July at
Brackettville,
Texas

A Seminole family outside their home in Brackettville, Texas

later wrote. Bullets whizzing around them, the four miraculously escaped unscathed. Bullis saw that Payne, Ward, and Factor were awarded Medals of Honor.

By this time Chief Horse and his Seminole Nation had found that U.S. government promises of land and food were would not be kept. Rations to families were sharply reduced. U.S. agencies denied responsibility for the treaty that brought the Seminoles to Texas. Generals Augur, Bliss, and Sheridan and Lieutenant Bullis supported Seminole petitions for relief, land, and fair treatment, but to no avail. Federal indifference and stark hunger soon turned families into scavengers and thieves.

The notorious King Fisher outlaw gang, furious at armed Black soldiers in Texas, tried to assassinate Chief Horse and drive his people off. For safety, the Seminoles were moved to Fort Clark, but Fisher's outlaws were unrelenting. In 1876 John Horse narrowly escaped death in an ambush that killed scout Titus Payne. The Seminole Nation suffered a near fatal blow during their New Year's Eve dance in 1877, when a Texas sheriff and his deputy arrived to arrest Adam Paine, the fourth Medal of Honor recipient. Instead of arresting him, the sheriff blasted Payne from behind with his shotgun at such close range that his clothes caught fire. At this point Pompey Factor led four other scouts to the Rio Grande, where they washed the dust of Texas from their horses' hooves and rode back to Mexico.

In 1882 Chief Horse, still seeking a home, land, and refuge for his people, left for Mexico, where he died in a hospital. The scouting unit began to

A 1914 picture of the Seminole Negro Indian Scouts

disintegrate and finally was disbanded in 1914. The Seminole Negro Indian Scouts could survive ferocious desert warfare and many enemies but not the unyielding racism of Texas.

Cathay Williams, Buffalo Soldier

In 1842 Martha Williams, an enslaved woman married to a free man of color, gave birth to their daughter Cathay near Independence, Missouri. Cathay Williams, destined for action, was compelled to work for Union troops during the Civil War, and witnessed a land battle and another at sea.

On November 15, 1866, Cathay Williams was seeking excitement. "I wanted to make my own living and not be dependent on relations with friends." She dressed in men's clothing and enlisted as William Cathay in Captain Charles E. Clarke's Company A, Thirty-Eighth Infantry, U.S. Colored Troops. The army conducted no medical examinations, so her military records describe a five-foot-nine-inch man. Her uniform was loose enough to hide her identity; two men in the company – a cousin and a good friend – knew and kept her secret.

Williams's fellow soldiers included many criminals. "About half of them had been in the penitentiary," a court investigation later found. Though she had to be treated for smallpox in an East St. Louis hospital, Williams returned to her company in New Mexico, and later served in Kansas. "I was never put in the guard house, no bayonet was ever put to my back. I carried my musket and did guard duty, and other duties while in the army," she proudly told the *St. Louis Daily Times* on January 2, 1876.

After two years of service Williams was ready to return to civilian life. "I played sick, complained of pains in my side, and rheumatism in my knees. The post surgeon found out I was a woman and I got my discharge. The men all wanted to get rid of me after they found out I was a woman."

Williams' discharge papers also carried an odd and unsupported evaluation but did not mention that she was a woman and being discharged for that reason: "He was then, and has been since, feeble both physically and mentally, and much of the time is unfit for duty."

The evidence about Cathay Williams is undisputed on one salient point: a courageous Texas African American woman had blazed a new path in the annals of the U.S. Army. A century ahead of her time, she emerged from the buffalo soldiers to tell her tale.

Cathy Williams tills her own Texas farm. (Only known photograph of Williams)

11
OKLAHOMA

At noon on April 22, 1889, an agitated mob of 100,000 men, women, and children, including an estimated 10,000 African Americans, braced themselves for the gunshot that would open two million acres of Indian land to settlement. Overheated claim seekers made a frenetic stampede by foot, horse, bicycle, and cart that flooded the area. Some ten thousand people turned Oklahoma City into a tent city, and fifteen thousand did the same in Guthrie. By the following morning businesses opened in both cities.

A Black family and their dugout home in Guthrie

Exodus to Oklahoma

Each time Congress opened additional Indian lands for settlement in 1891, 1892, and 1893, African Americans were at the starting line. In 1907 Oklahoma became a state, and its African American population stood at 137,000.

Most of these newcomers were fleeing white violence in the Southern states. In his letter of July 22, 1891, to the American Colonization Society, A. G. Belton captured a people's desperation in one run-on sentence: "We as a people are oppressed and disfranchised we are still working hard and our rights taken from us times are hard and getting harder every year we as a people believe that Africa is the place but to get from under bondage we are thinking of Oklahoma as this is our nearest place of safety."

To the oppressed, Oklahoma offered hope and a haven. Edwin P. McCabe, a former state auditor of Kansas, arrived in early 1890 with a wider vision. "I expect to have a Negro population of over 100,000 within two years in Oklahoma." From Langston City, which he founded in October 1890, McCabe dispatched agents into the South armed with railroad tickets and brochures. His was a mission that mixed rescue, commerce, and nation-building: "We will have a Negro state governed by Negroes."

In many instances, a hundred or more people from a single Southern community traveled to Oklahoma together. This provided benefits during and beyond the journey. Loved ones and neighbors united in a common purpose marched across the prairies. Upon arrival, familiar faces assured a minimum of friction. Further, with

Oklahoma pioneers – the Sutton family – pose for a studio portrait.

Langston City's Roman Catholic Church

merchants, skilled workers, professionals, and other key workers in their party, community life could start within days. This unified approach also surrounded women with strong family and support networks during the voyage and at the trail's end.

Between 1890 and 1910, thirty-two self-governing African American towns sprouted in Oklahoma. Their most common building was a "shot-gun house," traceable to seventeenth-century West Africa. One room wide, two

Music class in early Oklahoma

or three rooms deep, its oblong shape meant a shotgun fired through the front door would pass through without hitting anything and exit the back door. It did not look like much, but it was a better home than people had left in the South.

Langston City

Langston City, Oklahoma's first Black town, was founded by Edwin McCabe in October 1890 and reached out to hardworking families imbued with middle-class values. Its *Herald* newspaper reached four thousand readers, its town fathers outlawed prostitution and gambling, and residents could boast their community had no serious crimes. Its streets were named after Black political heroes of the Reconstruction era, and its main avenues were Commercial and Lincoln. The *Herald* began 1892 by estimating the total value of Black-owned property in Oklahoma at between $250,000 and $400,000.

That year Langston's mothers and fathers decided their civic priority would be to turn their community of two thousand into the educational heart of Black Oklahoma. They started a tax-supported public school for elementary grades, then a high school for all "regardless of race, color or number."

School scene in early Oklahoma

A Resident Recalls Langston City

For some time, every few days the Santa Fe train from Texas would pull in a couple of coaches of some southern railroad loaded to the roof with Negro immigrants, Langston bound. They brought their families and their household goods. It was really something to see. Some even came in wagons and lots on foot. Lots of people who came here were so disappointed that they went back home. It took real enterprising folks to stick it out. There wasn't but one building in town so most of the families lived in tents while houses were being built for them.

Quoted in Mozell C. Hill,
Journal of Negro History, vol. 21 (July 1946)

Mozell C. Hill, who grew up in Langston City, wrote of his town: "The titles to these lots could never pass to any white man, and upon them no white man could ever reside or conduct a business according to the literature of the promoting company."

Langston's fascinating story is preserved in copies of the *Langston City Herald*, which McCabe and its editors used to promote their economic investment and political dream. Though desperate to attract settlers, each edition cautioned "COME PREPARED OR NOT AT ALL." Each issue reprinted the government rules for filing land claims. On its front page headlines blared

FREEDOM!
PEACE, HAPPINESS AND PROSPERITY
DO YOU WANT ALL THESE?
THEN CAST YOUR LOT WITH US &
MAKE YOUR HOME IN LANGSTON CITY

The *Herald* was inspirational, gossipy, and opinionated, and it carried the motto "Without fear, favor, or prejudice, we are for the right, and ask no quarter save justice." It strenuously opposed "lynch law," Democratic Party candidates, and discrimination. It praised crusading journalist Ida B. Wells, who visited the town and was favorably impressed, and published a letter from Frederick Douglass who called McCabe a "brave and much needed pioneer."

The Prairie Center School in Oklahoma and teacher M. E. Porter (right)

By 1897 Oklahoma's territorial legislature voted the town a grant of forty acres for Langston College. The new college stabilized the community. In 1957 it had 1,250 students.

By 1900 Langston City boasted one of the highest literacy rate on the frontier: 72 percent of its residents could read and 70 percent could write. For Langston's women between fifteen and forty-five, these figures soared to 96 percent and 95 percent.

Boley's town council with mayor (front row, fourth from left) and sheriff (back row, left)

A Boley
bank

Boley

Boley, like most African American towns in Oklahoma, was carved out of the Indian Territory around Muskogee. Founded in 1904 by Abigail Barnett, a young Black Choctaw woman, on eighty acres, its four thousand residents made it the largest Black town in the West. Boley's boosters had a lot to be proud of: it had the tallest building between Oklahoma City and Okmulgee, half of its high school students went on to college, and Black men ran the government.

Boley began with a breach of the peace. Dick Shaver, its first city marshal, rode out to arrest Dick Simmons, a white horse thief with a $500 reward on his head. Simmons, who had threated to kill the marshal, fired two shots from his Winchester and one ripped into Shaver's stomach. As he tumbled from his horse, Shaver fired three shots and each bullet hit Simmons. Both men died. The Boley town council selected another Black man as marshal. Since only Black people ruled the town, they had no intention of turning over the vital matter of law and order to someone who did not care about their lives. For the next two years the new marshal did not have to fire his gun or make an arrest. Peace reigned in Boley.

Though early pioneers arrived to primitive living conditions and dusty streets, Boley grew quickly. In a few years it had 150 children in school, four church congregations with their own buildings, a women's club, the Union Literary Society, the Odd Fellows Hall, a grocery, a drugstore, a hardware store, a hotel, a sawmill, and a cotton gin. When Oklahoma was admitted

The Creek Seminole College in Boley

to the Union, Boley boasted eight hundred residents and another two thousand lived on nearby farms.

Citizens of Boley often struck an independent note. For example, when its Union Literary Society debated whether residents should "celebrate George Washington's birthday," the negative carried. *The Boley Progress* exhorted prospective migrants to strive for the best: "What are you waiting for? If we do not look out for our own welfare, who is going to do so for us? Are you always going to depend upon the white race to control your affairs for you? Some of our people have had their affairs looked after by the white man for the past thirty years and where are they today? They are on the farms and plantations of the white men... with everything mortgaged so that they cannot get away and forever will be so long as they are working upon their farms and trading in their stores."

Boley's resident poet, Uncle Jesse, strummed an old guitar and sang of his noble town:

Say, have you heard the story,
Of a little colored town,
Way over in the Nation
On such a lovely sloping ground?
With as pretty little houses
As you ever chanced to meet,

With not a thing but colored folks
A-standing in the streets?
Oh, 'tis a pretty country
With not a single white man here
To tell us what to do – in Boley.

U.S. deputy marshals serving Judge Isaac Parker at Fort Smith. Left to right: Amos Maytubey, Luke Miller, Neely Factor, and Bob L. Fortune.

The Struggle for Oklahoma

The forces of white supremacy mobilized to end McCabe's dream. In 1891 mobs ordered African Americans at gunpoint out of several Oklahoma communities. Even as Black families poured into Oklahoma, earlier residents formed Africa Societies and prepared to leave.

Responding to the speeches and writings of Bishop Turner, who advocated an exodus to Africa, and the American Colonization Society, some

Street scene in Muskogee when the U.S. Dawes Commission came to settle Indian claims

African American families left Arkansas and Oklahoma for New York and ships that would take them to Liberia. Refugees rest in a Brooklyn baptist church. (*Leslie's Illustrated Newspaper,* October 24, 1880)

Black Oklahoma families sold their land for a fraction of its value and camped in vigils near railroad stations for trains that would carry them to New York City and ships bound for Africa. Some two hundred penniless Oklahomans were housed at a Methodist Mission in Brooklyn. They were joined by another contingent of men, women, and children from Arkansas. Under the sharecropping system, explained one, "We jest make enough to keep in debt." In 1895 Bishop Turner probably spoke for many of his people in Oklahoma and elsewhere: "There is no manhood future in the United

"We Saw Colored Merchants and Lawyers"

There [Guthrie] we saw more colored people than we have ever seen in a northern city. It seems as if a third of the people were colored. We saw colored merchants and lawyers and in almost every capacity, except banking... Every train brought a number of new ones while very few were going back...

[In Langston City] we saw the largest school house in the territory, 6 businesses, mill and gin in course construction, and two churches. There seemed to be about 200 children in attendance at the schools...

I would say to every colored man who has no home try and get one in this country...

Now in order to show sincerity in what I have written, I shall practice what I preach and will locate in the beautiful Oklahoma.

W. A. Price in the *Langston City Herald,* March 19, 1892

In the 1890s African Americans were among those who laid railroad tracks across Oklahoma.

States for the Negro. He may eke out an existence for generations to come, but he can never be a man – full, symmetrical and undwarfed."

As Oklahoma moved toward statehood, African Americans, mobilized in the Suffrage League, Equal Rights League, and Negro Protective League, hoped to send their representatives to the U.S. Congress and influence new state government. But African Americans were outnumbered, enjoyed little white support, and did not build alliances with disfranchised Native American residents.

Creek council

Choctaw friends in Oklahoma

Indians of Oklahoma, including thousands of African Americans, also struggled to survive. Former slaves in each nation had gained their freedom, but fought to win political equality and education for their children. However, few African Americans left their ancestral homes, for they were aware of what awaited them in white society. Many African Americans who came to Oklahoma also chose to live among Native American people.

As Oklahoma lurched toward statehood, Native Americans and newly arrived African Americans inhabited different worlds. Indian communities in Oklahoma derisively referred to the newcomers as "state Negroes." The *Herald* did not print negative references to Indians, but neither did it build bridges. When the U.S. Dawes Commission agreed to pay Native Americans for their lands, those members of African descent hired African American attorney James Milton Turner to defend their interests, and after

At Hayden, Oklahoma Black Cherokees met to receive their awards from the U.S. government.

Enrollment
of Choctaws
around 1899

years of legal wrangling he helped them gain $75,000. Turner represented a
rare instance of multicultural cooperation in Oklahoma.

As Oklahoma edged toward statehood, the Western Negro Press Association, convening in Muskogee, asked President Theodore Roosevelt to
hold off admission until the new state agreed not to pass Jim Crow laws. The
president did not respond.

Store at Fort Gibson around 1899

The last Native American uprising – the Crazy Smoke War of 1909 – included Black and Native members.

Oklahoma entered the Union in 1907 as another bastion of white supremacy. It became the first to segregate telephone booths. In 1910 its all-white legislature enacted a "grandfather clause" that disfranchised African Americans because their grandfathers, as slaves, had not voted. Where legality failed, election fraud and night-riding terrorists succeeded in nullifying the African American vote. A refuge and a dream became another Southern nightmare.

At the end of World War II Oklahoma had only nineteen Black towns, and in 1990 the number fell to 13. Only Boley had become a National Historic Landmark.

Edwin P. McCabe

One of the most enigmatic and shadowy figures in U.S. Western history is Edwin P. McCabe, who first achieved fame when he was twice elected Kansas state auditor. In 1890 he planned to make Oklahoma a home for African Americans, and build a Black state, perhaps with him as governor. He was shot at for his audacity, but he did not relent, risking his life and spending his money to advance his vision.

In 1889 in Guthrie, during the first stampede of settlers, McCabe found a white man who sold him 160 acres forty miles northeast of Oklahoma City.

He purchased another 160 acres, set up the
McCabe Town Company, and sent agents
to recruit settlers in the South. McCabe
named Langston City after John Mercer
Langston, a Howard University scholar recently elected to Congress from Virginia.

McCabe's broad plan was to settle a
majority of African American voters in
each election district so they could shape
the new state. Because his goal offered a
rare opportunity for African Americans
to demonstrate citizenship rights and economic skills, the African American press
gave it full coverage.

Edwin P. McCabe, Kansas state
auditor, 1883–1887

Attired in his impeccable three-piece
suit, McCabe was confident and optimis-
tic. His successful Kansas career had been
based on persuasiveness with white political figures. In Oklahoma, he started with an African American population of more than 100,000 as a base to

African Americans in the first parade to celebrate the 1889 opening of
Oklahoma land to non-Indian settlement

Four Black cowhands join others in an Oklahoma saloon around 1900. Behind outstretched white hand in center are two puppets, one white and one Black.

forge political coalitions. Oklahoma would prove African Americans adept at managing economic affairs and a progressive, republican government.

Named deputy auditor of the Oklahoma Territory, McCabe quickly became a lightning rod for white fury. The *Kansas City Star* described white people who "almost foam at the mouth when McCabe's name is suggested for Governor." The *New York Times* reported from Oklahoma that McCabe

Teachers and their male principal at Guthrie, Oklahoma

Cherokee Teachers Institute, 1890

might be "assassinated within a week" and quoted a white man who said, "I would not give five cents for his life." When McCabe mobilized Black citizens for a September 1891 land rush, he was fired on by three whites, and had to be rescued by African Americans armed with Winchesters.

Once the icy hand of white supremacy gripped the new state of Oklahoma, McCabe sold his house and left for the East. But he was not finished. Three months after statehood he initiated a lawsuit to challenge Oklahoma's right to segregate railroad passengers. Perhaps he believed a court victory would end segregation in the state or in the country. For seven years his case wound through the judicial system, but he lost again and again. In 1914 the U.S. Supreme Court ruled against McCabe and reaffirmed that segregation was legal in Oklahoma and the nation.

McCabe and his wife lived in Chicago, where at seventy he died in poverty. Despite uncommon business and political acumen and a tenacious courage, he ultimately failed to rescue his people or become governor. But to a people only a generation from slavery, he helped bring the imperishable gifts of pride, self-reliance, and educational opportunity.

BLACK WOMEN OF THE LAST FRONTIER

Though the West often meant unknown dangers, isolation, and loneliness for African American women, they eagerly embraced its promises and opportunities. On many frontiers African American women became the moving force and apex of community solidarity. "The mountains were free and we loved them," recalled Dr. Ruth Flowers, born in 1902 in Boulder, Colo-

rado. "Black women," said Dr. Flowers, "were the backbone of the church, the backbone of the family, they were the backbone of the social life, everything." They were zealous in efforts to educate the young, advance the race, and develop churches and self-help societies that would sustain community. At times they did not hesitate to contest racial restrictions and the rules of male society. They often saw themselves as an elite breed.

In the U.S. Southwest, the Smaulding family stare intently into the camera. (Date unknown)

Women were at the center of the major African American migrations from the South.

But after the Civil War, Black women first had to eradicate the legacy of slavery and restore family. Laura Pearson had been purchased by Richard Pearson in North Carolina and brought to Utah, where he married a white woman. After he divorced his wife, in 1853 Richard and Laura had a

These representatives of the Montana Federation of Colored Women's Clubs met in Bozeman, Montana, in July 1924.

Pioneer named Chloe in a studio portrait

child and then sanctified their love in a marriage ceremony that freed her according to Utah law. Two years later the Pearson family settled down as farmers in sparsely settled Colusa County, California. By 1865 they had five children. After Richard died, the first Mrs. Pearson sued for his possessions, arguing that since Laura had been enslaved, she lacked a claim to his estate. A determined Laura Pearson appeared in court, defended her family's inheritance, and won.

Some women realized they had to make good on family and life's promises. Clara Brown left her Denver real estate investments and laundry business for Gallitan, Kentucky, to search for family members lost during slavery. In California, Mary Pleasant, who had helped escaped slaves, sued a segregated San Francisco street car company for rude treatment and won her case and $600. Her legal precedent helped desegregate the city's street cars. Former slave Biddy Mason used the money she saved as a midwife to found the first Los Angeles African Methodist Episcopal Church.

In California, Mary Ward, a talented and spirited twelve-year-old in search of her education, faced an old fight. Denied admission to San Fran-

A typical Creek family home in Oklahoma

cisco's Broadway Grammar school, Mary and her family mobilized the community behind her effort. In 1871 men and women convened at an African American convention in Stockton and agreed to support Ward, publicize her case, and pay her legal fees. By 1875 Mary Ward was admitted to a public school, and her campaign forced the Board of Education to end segregation.

Other African American women, such as Diana Fletcher, who had long lived with the Kiowas, continued to cast their lot with Native Americans, affirming a fellowship that began when Africans first met the original inhabitants of the Americas.

Kiowa Diana Fletcher

BLACK PIONEER WOMEN

In the West, African American woman had to face and tame the wild in nature and man. But, recalled Sarah Fountain of Dearfield, Colorado, "they were that kind of women. To make a life you endure most anything, women do." They proved as tough, spirited, and resilient as the wilderness around them.

Some Black women began to write their own future. Melissa Bulware and her husband Silas Smith bought 160 acres in Wyoming when it was a territory, and then a 1,700-acre ranch in 1892, two years after Wyoming became a state. Later, she saw her son Nolle win election to the territorial legislature of Hawaii. In 1875 Sarah Miner, a widow in Virginia City, Nevada, turned her husband's hauling business into a $6,000 enterprise, lost it in a fire, and rebuilt it the next year. In 1898 May Mason of Seattle journeyed to

A Sunday congregation in front of Mt. Pilgrim Baptist Church in Raton, New Mexico

the Yukon and returned with $5,000 in gold dust. She turned down a $6,000 bid for her claim. When she appeared at her fancy wedding, "her ears and fingers sparkled with diamonds."

Few women – or men – were as tough as Henrietta Foster, born into slavery in Mississippi in 1827 and one of six sisters who grew up on the Texas Coastal Bend. "Aunt Rittie," as she was called, was outspoken, "knew a lot about herb medicines," and "worked cattle bareback with the men." Some remember her for her skill with livestock and others recall her eagerness to defy a male society. Some said "Aunt Rittie" once split a man's skull with a hammer over a land dispute, and others claim that she killed a man who tried to rape her. "She was ready for any trouble and the men were afraid of her. She would put a club on you if you didn't act right," recalled a male rela-

Sarah Montgomery was a maid during the day, folklorist on her own time.

In 1870 Luticia Parson Butler served as a nurse for the buffalo soldiers.

Famous chef Katie Rose, who founded a church in the Southwest, shown with her adopted son. She lived to be 106.

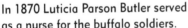

tive. She lived to be about a hundred, and in the 1990s was still remembered by relatives and friends as a small, dark, obstinate women who carried a knife.

Some women nailed down elusive dreams. Mrs. Hattie Rothwell and her husband bought a home in Denver in the 1880s, then borrowed $500 on it to homestead in Dearfield, where their son Charles helped lay out the town. In Yankton, Dakota Territory, in 1888, when Kate Chapman, nineteen, the only Black student in her high school class, had her poem

Black Indian Mamie Conners, a New Mexico homesteader who brought up a large family

Reverend John Turner (back, center) of Grant Chapel with some of his Southwest congregation

published in an Indianapolis paper, she was thrilled: "my work as a writer has but barely begun." In 1908 Mrs. Daisy O'Brien Rudisell gave birth to William, the first African American child born in the Yukon, as winds howled and temperatures plunged to 52 degrees below zero outside the tent hospital.

From Kansas to California, African American women raised and educated families, then went on to run hotels, hairdressing parlors, restaurants, businesses, and boarding houses. They built churches, orphanages, schools, and literary societies. In 1867 African American men and women in Helena, Montana, started an Episcopal congregation, and in 1889, when Montana became a state, the African American Episcopal congregation had a building. Three women, two of whom owned their own businesses, served on the eight-member managing board of Helena's "Afro-American Building Association." In 1874 African American women in Nevada organized a Dumas Society and Literary Club in Virginia City, and three years later other women began a literary club in Carson City. That same year Mrs. Anna Graham's hairdressing estab-

Bessie McCoy married Thomas Jones, who served with the buffalo soldiers and was a miner in Colorado, Wyoming, Arizona, and New Mexico. Bessie was born to a pioneer New Mexican family from Missouri.

Unidentified musical
family at their Colorado
home

lishment in Virginia City faced competition from three other hairdressing parlors run by Black women on C Street.

Historian Nell Irvin Painter wrote that "Black women were more likely than their white counterparts to be active on the grass roots level in the late nineteenth century, yet we learn little about them. Not only was there a long tradition of black women working alongside men, but in addition, the generations maturing after the Civil War acquired their Western education in coeducational institutions." By the late nineteenth century, African American author Francis Ellen Watkins Harper, who had become a national speaker for the Women's Christian Temperance Union, wrote, "The coloured women have not been backward in promoting charities for their own race and sex." As the nineteenth century turned into the twentieth, Lena Ma-

De Marge Duesse was the first African American child born in the Wyoming Territory.

son stepped before huge audiences in St. Paul, Minnesota, to deliver electrifying evangelistic lectures.

Westward Ho!

The West was known as a fine place for men and horses, but hard on women, children, and good manners. For women of color, the West could be lonely, forbidding, and unpleasant. In 1879, a generation after William and Sarah Grose arrived in Seattle, there were only nine African American women. A decade later little had changed. In 1889 one recalled, "There were few of our own people in Seattle when we came and at times I got very lonely."

African American women who traveled westward often had little in common with their white counterparts. White women tended to be younger than Black women pioneers, who were largely in the 20 to 40 age range and more likely to be married. They also had a lower child-bearing rate than white women and were more likely to be educated. Half of Black teenagers

Unidentified Nebraska women and baby

in the West attended high schools. For white women work served as a transition between their arrival in a frontier community and early marriage, while Black women, five times as likely to have jobs, generally were employed throughout their lives.

African American women, having associated rural life with slavery, preferred to live and work in urban areas, even though this often meant taking jobs as house servants, cleaners, or midwives. By the 1900 Census Black women outnumbered their men in Los Angeles and Denver.

A sparse population made community mobilization difficult but not impossible. In 1892, when

Howard Kerr, a former Tenth Cavalryman, and his wife in the Southwest

In 1899 Mrs. Sara Elizabeth Heights Maunder arrived in Seattle, Washington, and raised her family in a large home at 59th and Kensington.

only 24 Black women lived in Seattle, a bartender told two of them, "I don't wait on niggers." In the ensuing fracas one woman was scratched, the other broke her parasol, and both were arrested for heaving rocks that shattered the saloon's large window.

Seattle grew quickly. In 1896 Horace Cayton and Susan Revels arrived, got married, and began a family. With their fancy home and Japanese servant, and as editors of their own newspaper, the *Republican*, they initiated a Black upper class. "There was something going on all the time. Balls, barbecues, picnics, excursions. There was always a place to go," remembered Elizabeth Oxindine. By 1901 Seattle boasted an Evergreen Literary Society and a Music Club.

Mrs. Anderson of Leadville, Colorado

Black women, such as these members of the Seattle Francis Harper branch, were active in the Women's Christian Temperance Union and other reform associations. When denied admission to white WCTU branches, they formed their own.

In 1876 Thomas Detter and Emily Brinson of Eureka, Nevada, were married in a ceremony the local paper reported as "attended by nearly all of the colored folk in town, besides some twenty-five or thirty white people, including some of our most prominent citizens and their wives."

In rural regions Black women were vastly outnumbered by men. However, this meant they were more able to find marriage-minded suitors than their sisters in the East. In some places Black men waited for incoming stages and trains hoping to find a partner for life. This imbalance helped Black women, as it did white women, chip away or directly challenge male Victorian codes and habits.

Primitive rural conditions also brought perils. Mrs. Tilghman, wife of a barber, riding in the back seat of the Marysville-Comptonville stage, was caught in the crossfire of California's first stagecoach robbery. The Tom Bell Gang blazed away, passengers returned fire, and Mrs. Tilghman was the only fatality.

Unidentified Reno, Nevada, pioneers

Some women grew used to rural life. In Colorado Eunice Russell Norris was so helpful in building the family log cabin and sawing wood for the stove that her father and grandfather affectionately called her "son." In Brighton, Colorado, Marguerite Gomez, sixteen, married farmer James Thomas, thirty-two, father of seven children, and learned to herd, break horses, and pour medicine down the throats of ailing animals. Doris Collins of Rock Springs taught herself to become a better rider – even bareback – than her two brothers, and despite her mother's disapproval.

The West was a safer place than the East. African American pioneer women were less likely to suffer white rape, police brutality, and violence than their sisters in the East. They were more likely to find a good education, a decent job, and a greater measure of white hospitality. Most were glad they made the trip.

Women of the Exodus of 1879

Women who massed for the Great Exodus to Kansas often felt white violence left them no alternative. "A poor woman might as well be killed and done with it," said one victim. "We can do nothing to protect the virtue of our wives and daughters," bemoaned a Mississippian. "There are forty widows in our band. The white men here take our wives and daughters and serve them as they please and we are shot if we say anything about it," wrote a Mississippi leader to Kansas governor John St. John.

Family and women's issues dominated the long debates over leaving. Emigrants repeatedly decried "the want of education and protection" for women, as historian Paula Giddings notes, and sought in Kansas "to rear their children up – their girls – to lead a virtuous and industrious life." R. J. Cromwell, Louisiana president of the Negro Union Coop-

Lena Mason, famous Evangelist preacher, around 1900

Arizona Miners and Mail-Order Brides

The abundance of single males contributed to the unsettled life in the 19th century mining camps, so married Black women began vigorous efforts through churches to locate possible brides. Letters were sent back east promising suitable females a secure marriage to an upstanding worker, and a good home.

Young mail-order brides on their wedding day in Arizona

Many ventured forth to leave poverty and oppressive conditions behind in search of love, family life and a fulfilling marriage. Some jumped at the free trip. Since older, experienced miners controlled the camps, they demanded and won first choice in brides. Many men lived through several wives and were left with large families as repeated child births under unsanitary conditions took a high death toll among frontier women. Men old enough to be their choice's father or grandfather picked the youngest mail-order candidates, hoping that decent instincts, strength and small miracles would produce surviving wives and successful families.

Arizona mail-order bride

The Black mail-order brides had to labor dawn to dusk in field and home, and work at making their marriage successful with a man not of their own choosing. Often they had to rear children from previous marriages as well as their own. There was work aplenty and a wealth of children, but they were used to making something out of nothing whether it was homes, food, clothes or scraps for bedding. Their pioneer grit deserves celebration.

Arizona bride on her wedding day

Dr. Barbara Richardson, historian, Tucson, Arizona

Arizona's "Busy Bee Club," which arranged to bring brides to Arizona

erative Aid Association, complained to President Hayes of "churches burned, ignorant defenseless negroes killed, innocent women, that were pregnant had the child rifled from the womb, of a living mother – Our young women subjected to treatment too horrible to mention."

In December 1875, at an emigration convention in New Orleans, women delegates, many widows of husbands slain in Mississippi, Alabama, Texas, Arkansas, Louisiana, and Georgia, assumed leadership. A leading proponent of emigration, Henry Adams, recalled the crucial vote to depart for Kansas "in a unanimous voice... echoed by all; and we all agreed to it, both women and men that were assembled at the conference." Women stated, Giddings noted, "that even if their husbands did not leave, they would."

The Great Exodus produced some small miracles. Mr. and Mrs. Henry Carter walked from Tennessee to Kansas, she carrying bedclothes and he the tools. In a year they secured jobs with sheep ranchers, bought and cleared forty acres, built a sixteen-foot stone home, and acquired a horse and two cows.

In Texas, teachers and students of San Antonio's Riverside School pose in the 1890s

Education and Progress

In every frontier community, African American women spearheaded efforts at education, moral piety, and economic uplift. They built Western churches, school systems, and other cultural and social institutions. By 1860 frontier African American women boasted a literacy rate of 74 percent, which not only soared above their sisters in every other part of the country, but surpassed white Western women. The percentages in the West rose each generation. Black women in California and the Mountain states had a literacy rate of 73 percent in 1890 and 92.4 percent in 1910. In Oregon the rate was 83 percent in 1890 and 96 percent in 1910.

In 1864, when Nevada became a state, its new government denied "Indians, Negroes and Mongolians" a public education. But two years of protests by African American women and men compelled one school to admit sixteen children of color. By 1874 Nevada, with fewer than four hundred African Americans, had Black cultural and educational societies. In Virginia City the Dumas Society enrolled twenty-two "ladies and gentlemen," and lecturer Andrew Hall told members that education will "fit us for positions where caste would be obliterated forever by the brilliancy of our intellectual attainments." Also in Virginia City, women organized a Calico Ball that

In 1898 this San Antonio sewing class at St. Philip's College posed with
Reverend Marshall (right) and teacher Alice Cowan (behind him).

extended invitations to all the men and women of color in western Nevada.
Carson City's Literary and Religious Association of Colored Citizens was
formed to promote the idea that "we value our black babies."

U.S. Census figures on Western school attendance in 1890 for six months
or more a year show African American girls ahead of white girls. When
segregation ended in the 1880s, many African American teachers were not
hired to teach in integrated schools, and this added to the sense of isolation
felt by Black students. In Glenwood Springs, Colorado, Mrs. Russell brought
her daughter Eunice to class on the first day of school only to have a white
teacher scoff, "I don't know if it can learn." The furious mother reassured her.

In Seattle's Pacific School in 1900, Theresa Flowers suffered "great prej-
udices" and recalled "They'd call you names." Mattie Harris and her brother
attended the city's Warren Avenue school, where white pupils accepted her
brother, "but I had no chance." The first teenager of color to graduate from
a San Francisco high school was alone in a class of 1,500. Her daughter became the only African American graduate in a class of several hundred.

Black children, often alone in an all-white class or school, experienced disturbing isolation. This 1904 photo shows an eighth-grade class in Denver's Longfellow School on 16th Street.

In many places Black women bearing the banners of education, uplift, and progress registered significant victories. In 1893 Colorado became the second state to extend voting rights to women, and a Colored Women's Republican Club of Denver started in 1901. By 1906 it proudly announced that a larger percentage of women of color had voted in that year's election than white women. When the Montana Federation of Black Women's Clubs met in Bozeman in 1924, its more than thirty delegates represented clubs scattered all over the state.

Even imprisoned women of color in the West proved to be exceptional. Historian Anne Butler's study found that in Texas and other frontier states African American women were more likely than white women to be arrested, convicted, and jailed for minor crimes. They also served longer sentences and were less likely to be granted early parole. Butler found that in the forty-one years after 1865, three-fourths of those jailed were women of color. And she also found they had an astounding 87 percent literacy rate.

Lucy Parsons, Texas Rebel

Born a slave in Texas in 1853, Lucy Gonzales was not the kind of hero history texts ask us to celebrate. She had four strikes against her: she was African American, a woman, a worker, and a lifelong radical. She grew to womanhood during an age of Klan terror and may have been a victim.

Her biographer describes Lucy as "stunningly beautiful": "Her dark skin and vibrant personality radiated with the Texas sun. She was passionate in her loves and in her hatreds. There was nothing lukewarm about Lucy. Her skin was golden brown, that of a mulatto or quadroon. She had soft sensuous lips, a broad nose, curly black hair, and the high cheekbones of her Indian ancestors."

In Albert Parsons, a former Confederate soldier, Lucy chose to marry a white man dedicated to fighting inequality. He was editor of a Waco paper that championed justice for ex-slaves and denounced the Klan. Driven from the state in 1873, the Parsonses settled in Chicago, where they had two boys and Albert became a radical labor leader. In 1886, in the aftermath of the Haymarket Riot, in which a bomb killed seven policemen, Albert and seven other union leaders were framed for the crime, and he was among the three executed.

Crusader Lucy Gonzales Parsons

Lucy Parsons brought up their two children, and continued to write against injustice and for the downtrodden and march in picket lines. Her militant participation in demonstrations landed her in jail dozens of times, but never slowed her effort.

In 1905, at the founding convention of the Industrial Workers of the World (IWW), Lucy Parson was one of two women delegates – the other was "Mother" Mary Jones – and gave several speeches. In one she insisted dues for "women who get such poor pay should not be assessed as much as the men who get higher pay." In a longer speech, she introduced the concept of passive resistance, which would become the philosophical cornerstone of many non-violent radical movements. "Do not strike and go out and starve, but strike and remain in and take possession of the necessary property of production," she advised. From Ghandi in India to Martin Luther King, Jr. in the United States, from the sit-down strikes of the 1930s to the antiwar and civil rights movements of the 1960s, she provided food for thought and action.

Lucy Parsons died in 1942, when a mysterious fire swept through her Chicago home. Friends arrived hoping to salvage her large collection of books and writings, only to find the FBI had confiscated them. Even in death, Lucy Parsons was a danger to the state.

Lucy Gonzales Parson: "Organize the Women"

We, the women of this country, have no ballot even if we wished to use it, and the only way that we can be represented is to take a man to represent us. You men have made such a mess of it in representing us that we have not much confidence in asking you...

We are the slaves of slaves. We are exploited more ruthlessly than men. Whenever wages are to be reduced the capitalist class use women to reduce them, and if there is anything that you men should do in the future it is to organize the women...

Let us sink such differences as nationality, religion, politics, and set our eyes eternally and forever toward the rising star of the industrial republic of labor; remembering that we have left the old behind and have set our faces toward the future. There is no power on earth that can stop men and women who are determined to be free at all hazards. There is no power on earth so great as the power of intellect. It moves the world and it moves the earth...

Lucy Parsons, quoted in *The Constitutional Convention of the Industrial Workers of the World*, Chicago, 1905

Oklahoma's Black Towns

Unidentified Reno, Nevada, woman

African American women played a vital role in the thirty-two Black towns that sprouted in the Indian Territory and Oklahoma after 1890. Langston City promoted Victorian values, told men to give their church seats to women, and boasted of its "homes, churches and schools, where you can raise your family in good and respectable society." Its officials outlawed gambling and prostitution within its limits. "How do you expect other races to respect our ladies when you fail to do so yourselves," the *Langston City Herald* lectured. This was typical of the dedication of Black Oklahoma communities to protect and respect their women.

Victorian values flourished in Boley, whose Boley Progress warned Black women "against meeting white men at the trains, under any pretext," and told white men to stay away from its women. The paper also advised women to assist in community uplift and to "manage your husbands and see the results." Men were told to marry soon, buy a home, and raise a family; men and women who lived out of wedlock were scolded. One Boley club debated such questions as whether a boy had more of a right to education than a girl, and whether laziness was more an issue for boys or girls. In Clearview a woman teacher suggested the formation of a literary society to train the mind, overcome timidity, and encourage women and men to speak in public.

School attendance percentages for girls in many Oklahoma towns exceeded that of boys, and some families said they were more concerned their daughters complete their education than their sons.

Though women could not vote in Oklahoma, African American women were welcomed at lectures and debates and spoke at political meetings. They turned out in large numbers to hear antilynching crusader Ida B. Wells and Populist orator Mary Ellen Lease. They enthusiastically approved when Boley attorney Moses J. Jones said "our boys and girls" should become "business men and women."

When James Thompson formed the Patriarchs of America, both sexes were invited, participated in meetings, read papers, and led discussion groups. But Neva Thompson felt the women still lacked enough creative outlets, so she started a Sisters of Ethiopia, an Alpha Club, and a Thompson Literary Society.

More than talk took place. In Boley, the "United Brotherhood of Friends and Sisters Mysterious 10" built a home for elderly people and orphans. Another club collected money for a poor woman. In Langston, women sold needlework and raised funds that paid for fifteen gas lamps that lighted the main street at night. In 1909 Boley women urged mothers and fathers to order dolls from The National Negro Doll Company in Nashville, Tennessee.

Black women in these communities achieved a level of equality that had to be the envy of their sisters elsewhere. They scaled heights of independence and accomplishment that their sisters in the East had only dreamed about.

Elvira Conley

Ex-slave Elvira Conley, tall and as proudly straight-backed as a forest pine, was destined for adventure. Emancipated at age nineteen in 1864, she married an educated retired soldier. When she discovered his infidelity, she issued a few choice words, left for the West, and never looked back.

By 1868 Conley reached Sheridan, Kansas, where, wrote an eyewitness, "the reckless spirit and lawlessness of the frontier town reached its acme." Undaunted by threats from assorted "reprobates, gamblers, horse thieves, murderers and

Early residents of Reno, Nevada

disreputable women," Conley started a laundry business. Barbara Storke, who met her years later, provides clues: "She was black, black as ebony, and she was proud of it. She knew who she was. The majesty of her bearing, her great pride always commanded respect."

Conley's laundry lured the town's leading gunslingers, Wild Bill Hickok and Buffalo Bill. Decades later she remembered how they walked into her store in their broad-brimmed hats bringing "shirts which were made of a fine dark blue flannel and needed special care." The three became friends, shared stories, and Conley "always had a high opinion of them." For an unattached woman in a wild railroad town, such friends were strong insurance.

In Sheridan, Conley also met the wealthy Sellar-Bullard family, which supplied dry goods to railroads, and by 1870 they hired her as the family governess. For the next sixty years – during four generations of Sellars and Bullards – she traveled to Kit Carson, New Mexico, San Francisco, and Naples, Italy, where the family vacationed in style.

Awed by her bold assertiveness and towering pride, the Sellar and Bullard children believed Conley was descended from African royalty. At eighty-three, the regal governess could still take a stand. In 1927 Barbara Storke was fourteen and remembered this incident at a fancy restaurant in Evanston, Illinois: "We settled ourselves at a table when the head waitress came over and said that 'the restaurant does not serve negroes!' With no hesitation Conley stood up with great dignity and said, 'Come, children, we will go to the Blackstone.' We all swept after her."

13
Empire:
Buffalo Soldiers Abroad

In 1898 the United States defeated Spain in what Secretary of State John Hay called "a splendid little war" of ten weeks. Though the announced goal was to "free Cuba," President McKinley later admitted to wider goals: "We must keep all we get; when the war is over we must keep all we want." The United States began not to free but to occupy Spain's former possessions from Puerto Rico in the Caribbean to the Philippines in the Pacific. By 1902 it

This 1899 photo from the Library of Congress bore the caption "Some of our brave colored boys who helped face Cuba."

governed a vast empire of dark-skinned people, and each step of the way to the new colonial empire, buffalo soldiers and other African Americans played crucial roles.

From the outset, the U.S. march into the twentieth century was marked by bigotry at home and abroad. The day Congress declared war, Missouri Congressman David A. De Armond called African Americans "almost too ignorant to eat, scarcely wise enough to breathe, mere existing human machines." Senator Albert Beveridge, imperialism's leading U.S. advocate, justified U.S. overseas rule by referring to those in the new colonies as "children... not capable of self-government." Beveridge and McKinley promised to bring "Christianity" and "civilization" to these new children.

When an explosion sunk the U.S. battleship *Maine* in Havana Harbor on February 15, 1898, 22 African American sailors were among the 250 men who lost their lives. U.S. troop mobili-

Sergeant Horace Bivins wrote of African American military heroism in Cuba in his *Under Fire with the Tenth U.S. Cavalry.*

zation included the Ninth Cavalry from the Department of the Platte; the Tenth from Fort Assiniboine, Montana; the Twenty-Fourth Infantry from Fort Douglas, Salt Lake City, Utah; and the Twenty-Fifth from Missoula, Montana. As the Twenty-fifth rolled across the continent by rail toward Tampa, Florida, Sergeant Frank W. Pullen reported: "At every station there was a throng of people who cheered as we passed. Everywhere the Stars and Stripes could be seen. Everybody had caught the war fever."

Then the Twenty-Fifth entered the Southern states. "There was no enthusiasm nor Stars and Stripes in Georgia," reported Pullen.

The Twenty-
Fourth Infantry in
Cuba, 1898

In Tampa, Florida, local lawmen and civilians attacked buffalo soldiers. *The Richmond Planet* commented, "It would have been far better [for Black soldiers] to have been sent to the guardhouse than to Cuba. If colored men cannot live for their country, let white men die for it."

Before they left for Cuba, aboard the U.S. government transport ship *Concho* docked at Tampa, the Twenty-Fifth Infantry Regiment was segregated from the white Fourteenth Infantry, who "came and went as they pleased," reported Pullen. Men of the Twenty-Fifth were confined to the lower deck, "where there was no light, except the small portholes," and the heat "was almost unendurable." When the *Concho* sailed, he noted, "orders were issued providing that black and white troops should not mix."

The highlight of the short war was the successful U.S. assault at San Juan Hill, Cuba, which propelled Rough Rider Teddy Roosevelt to the White House. Walter Millis's classic account of the war, *The Martial Spirit*, described the dramatic moment when "Mr. Roosevelt, with his followers at his back, swept down, splashed through the lagoon and gained the opposite height." They found, Millis noted, "some of the Tenth Cavalry who had got up before them." Roosevelt's version was unstinting in its praise for the buffalo soldiers: "We went up absolutely intermingled, so that no one could tell whether it was the Rough Riders or the men of the 9th who came forward with greater cour-

"If the Government Cannot Protect Its Troops..."

The action of the white police officer at Key West, Florida, in ordering Sergeant Williams of the 25th United States Infantry to put up his revolver, is without a parallel in the history of any nation...

We noted with undisguised admiration and satisfaction the action of the twenty-five colored soldiers who repaired to the City Hall and demanded the surrender of their officer at the point of the bayonet, and gave the sheriff just five minutes in which to comply with this demand...

We trust to see colored men assert their rights. If the government cannot protect its troops against insult and false imprisonment, let the troops decline to protect the government against insult and foreign invasion.

Editorial, *Richmond Planet*, April 30, 1898

age to offer their lives in the service of their country... I don't think any rough rider will ever forget the tie that binds us to the Ninth and Tenth Cavalry."

Rough Rider Frank Knox, later secretary of war during World War II, joined a unit of the Tenth that day, and recalled, "in justice to the colored race I must say that I never saw braver men anywhere. Some of these who rushed up the hill will live in my memory forever." The tough, unemotional, Lieutenant John J. Pershing of the Tenth wrote: "We officers of the Tenth Cavalry could have taken our black heroes in our arms."

Colonial Resistance and U.S. Occupation

As the brief war to save Cuba became a long battle to seize and control overseas colonies, most African Americans viewed imperialism through their own experience. Bishop Henry M. Turner scoffed at U.S. claims of humanitarianism as "too ridiculous," and predicted that "all the deviltry of this country would be carried into Cuba the moment the United States got there." "I don't think there is a single colored man, out of office or out of the insane asylum, who favors the so-called expansion policy," said Howard University professor Kelley Miller.

Troup C, Ninth Cavalry, charges San Juan Hill. Painting by Fletcher C. Ransome

In the Philippines the U.S. first supported independence and General Emilio Aguinaldo, who had been leading his freedom-fighting army of 40,000 against Spain for years. Then McKinley ordered 70,000 troops, including 6,000 African Americans, to occupy the islands. After they kept Aguinaldo from marching into Manila, a full-scale war began. Almost the entire African American press favored Aguinaldo's Insurrectos. "Maybe the Filipinos have caught wind of the way Indians and Negroes have been Christianized and civilized," wrote Salt Lake City's *Broad Ax*.

To pacify the Philippines, U.S. troops were issued orders to destroy civilian villages and turn the islands, in the words of Marine Brigadier General Jacob Smith, into "a howling wilderness." General Robert Hughes, commander in Manila, told the U.S. Senate: "The women and children are part of the family and where you wish to inflict punishment you can punish the man

Ninth Cavalrymen come ashore in Hawaii as part of the first U.S. overseas empire.

probably worse in that way than in any other." Asked if this was "civilized warfare," he responded, "these people are not civilized."

This was the first war, historian Gail Buckley has pointed out, in which "American officers and troops were officially charged with what we would now call war crimes." In forty-four military trials, all of which ended in convictions, "sentences, almost invariably, were light." A leading voice opposing the war was Mark Twain, who suggested a new Philippine flag: "We can have our usual flag, with the white stripes painted black and the stars replaced by the skull and crossbones." Bishop Henry Turner, speaking for rising African American opposition to imperialism, said of the African American soldiers "fighting to subjugate a people of their own color," " I can scarcely keep from saying that I hope the Filipinos will wipe such soldiers from the face of the earth."

Buffalo soldiers arrived in the Philippines to find people who were not hostile. General Robert Hughes reported: "The darkey troops... sent to Samar mixed with the natives at once. Whenever they came together they became great friends. When I withdrew the darkey company from Santa Rita I was told that the natives even shed tears or their going away."

But Black soldiers had entered another conflict rich in ironies. They heard white officers instruct their soldiers, "the Filipinos were 'niggers,' no better than the Indians, and were to be treated as such." A white private wrote home: "The weather is intensely hot, and we are all tired, dirty and

The first Spanish prisoners of the war were captured by the Black Twenty-fifth Infantry regiment, who are shown guarding them in Miami, Florida, in a rare photograph taken on May 4, 1898.

hungry, so we have to kill niggers whenever we have a chance, to get even for all our trouble."

Black soldiers, ordered into battle against a foe whose cause they believed just, wrote home to African American newspapers. Trooper Robert L. Campbell insisted "these people are right and we are wrong and terribly wrong," and said he would not serve as a soldier because no man "who has any humanity about him at all would desire to fight against such a cause as this." Private William Fullbright said the United States was conducting "a gigantic scheme of robbery and oppression." "The whites have begun to establish their diabolical race hatred in all its home rancor... even endeavoring to propagate the phobia among the Spaniards and Filipinos so as to be sure of the foundation of their supremacy when the civil rule is established," wrote soldier John Galloway.

Words soon led to action. A larger percentage of buffalo soldiers defected and joined the insurgents than white troops. Half a dozen members of the famed Ninth Cavalry and six other African Americans were among the twenty U.S. soldiers who joined Aguinaldo. Washington officials saw David Fagen as the most notorious, though he had been a model solider who had served with the Twenty-Fourth Infantry in Idaho and had won promotion to corporal.

Soon after Fagen's arrival on the islands in July 1899, he witnessed U.S. atrocities against civilians and was discriminated against by his white officers. A Black noncommissioned officer from his company reported, "From the treatment he got I don't blame him for clearing out."

When Fagen marched with General Lawton's army into Northern Luzon, he probably read Aguinaldo's famous broadside appeal to African Americans in the army of occupation:

To the Colored American Soldier:
It is without honor that you are spilling your costly blood. Your masters have thrown you into the most iniquitous fight with double purpose to make you instrument of their ambition and also your hard work will soon make the extinction of your race. Your friends, the Filipinos, give you this good warning. You must consider your situation and your history...

On November 17, 1899, Fagen defected with the help of a rebel officer. Historian Frank Schubert has concluded: "He was exposed and probably influenced by the indignation expressed by Negro journalists and fellow Negro soldiers over America's imperialistic adventures in the Philippines."

Granted a commission by rebel General Lacuna, Fagen was warmly referred to by the Filipinos he led as "General." With the slogan "This is our struggle," he also urged fellow African Americans to join the Insurrectos. U.S. General Frederick Funston considered him a wily foe and offered a $600 reward for him dead or alive. *The Manila Times* condemned Fagen as "a vile traitor" deserving "the most severe punishment."

In the next year and a half David Fagen deftly hurled his troops eight times against U.S. forces, not relenting until the spring of 1901, when Filipino resistance collapsed. By then he had married a Filipino woman, and the couple disappeared. The U.S. Army once announced Fagen had been slain by a Filipino hunter, but the army's internal records cast grave doubts on this claim. More than a few people reported seeing Fagen and his wife living peacefully in a remote village.

A few months after Rough Rider Teddy Roosevelt returned from the war, he rode to victory as governor of New York. Two days later, in Wilmington, North Carolina, white mobs attacked African Americans, including war

The Broad Ax Swings At Imperialism

March 25, 1899

And we do not blame Aguinaldo and his forces for resisting every effort to be subjugated by the American troops or forces.

...this government has launched upon a career of murder and robbery; and every native who is shot down in cold blood, like common dogs, is conclusive proof that the only object in waging the war against Spain was to acquire new territory by unlawful means.

...What right has it to foully murder innocent women and children? Is this civilization? ...This war is simply being waged to satisfy the robbers, murderers, and unscrupulous monopolists who are ever crying for more blood!

May 16, 1899

The chief reasons why we are opposed to the war which is being waged upon the inhabitants of those islands are that whenever the soldiers send letters home to their relatives and parents they all breathe an utter contempt "for the niggers which they are engaged in slaying"...

In view of these facts, no negro possessing any race pride can enter heartily into the prosecution of the war against the Filipinos, and all enlightened negroes must necessarily arrive at the conclusion that the war is being waged solely for greed and gold and not in the interest of suffering humanity.

The Broad Ax, Salt Lake City, Utah

veterans, in a violent effort to drive Black voters and office-holders from the city. The "Wilmington Riot" became the first in a quarter century of coordinated daylight mob assaults on African American neighborhoods.

Senator "Pitchfork" Ben Tillman, who often justified lynchings before his Senate colleagues, now rose to speak about the war being conducted in the Philippines: "No Republican leader, not even Governor Roosevelt, will now dare wave the bloody shirt and preach a crusade against the South's treatment of the Negro. The North has a bloody shirt of its own. Many thousands of them have been made into shrouds for murdered Filipinos, done to death because they were fighting for liberty."

In 1901 Roosevelt was sworn in as vice president of the United States. Two weeks later the capture of Aguinaldo ended armed Filipino resistance. Less than six months later the assassination of President McKinley brought the brash young Rough Rider to the White House.

General Pershing (left) and his expedition to Mexico included Colonel Charles Young (right).

A WAR AT HOME

In 1899 buffalo soldiers returned to the United States to find their sacrifice meant little in peacetime. Tenth Cavalry troops on a train bringing war veterans from Alabama to Texas were fired on in Meridian, Mississippi, and in Harlem, Texas. In Rio Grande City, Texas, whites brandished guns and taunted Ninth Cavalrymen until the troopers opened fire and drove them off. The Twenty-Fourth Infantry Regiment returned from Cuba to its base near Salt Lake City, Utah. They were changed men. When their Douglass

Memorial Literary Society debated the topic, "Resolved, that there is no future for the negro in the United States," the affirmative won.

As racist violence intensified for African American citizens, Roosevelt changed his mind about the Black heroism he saw at San Juan Hill. Now he said the buffalo soldiers were "peculiarly dependent upon their white officers." He now claimed they "began to get a little uneasy and to drift to the rear" so he had to draw his revolver to prevent their flight.

President Roosevelt entered the war over race at home. In 1906, members of the Twenty-Fifth Infantry returned to Brownsville, Texas, to find signs barring them from parks, stores, and bars. When shots were fired in town one night, the infantrymen seized arms and prepared to defend themselves. Though none of their weapons had been fired, and none of the bullets recovered in town came from Aarmy rifles, 167 soldiers in three companies of the Twenty-Fifth were charged with a violent assault on whites. When each soldier denied knowledge of any attack, the 167 were accused of shielding the guilty and dishonorably discharged. President Roosevelt even insisted that at least some were "bloody butchers." In 1972 a congressional investigation exonerated the 167 men, changed their discharges to honorable, and awarded the sole survivor, eighty-seven-year-old Dorsie Willis, $25,000.

November 1917 trial of 64 members of the Twenty-Fourth U.S. Infantry for murder

In 1917, four months after the nation entered World War I to "make the world safe for democracy," Houston, Texas, exploded in violence after soldiers of the Twenty-Fourth Infantry were repeatedly harassed by civilians and beaten and jailed by lawmen. Shouting "To hell with going to France, get to work right here," they surged into town and opened fire. Sixteen whites, including five policemen, and four Black soldiers died in the gunfight. One Army court-martial sentenced thirteen men to death and forty-one to prison for life, and another sentenced sixteen to death and twelve to life in prison.

War Department officials used the Houston riot to inflict a mortal blow on the four buffalo soldier regiments: it forever removed them from combat duty and assigned them to menial tasks. Until World War II, men who had repeatedly shed their blood and demonstrated their patriotism were put to drilling, grooming, and training horses. Never again would distinctive buffalo soldier units fight on a U.S. battlefield.

14
A Black West in
White America

The story of pioneers of African descent is one of new paths taken, alternative frontiers opened, and untiring efforts to extend the democratic promise of the Founding Fathers. Some of these early pathfinders fled bondage, and, often with Native Americans, became our first freedom fighters. Still others arrived in the West to find restrictions imposed by white settlers; their re-

Beauty parade in Bonham, Texas, around 1910

sistance also turned them into freedom fighters. It is hardly surprising that Native Americans, the first to be enslaved and stung by racial oppression in the New World, often greeted men and women of African descent as allies, and the two peoples soon became family.

"America never was America to me," wrote Langston Hughes. He lived in a country infected with an ideology that declared the natural inferiority of people of color. Originally conceived to justify those who traded in or profited from the forced labor of men, women, and children of color, this belief soon affected more than slave-ship captains and owners, Indian-hunting armies and slave-hunting posses, plantation masters and overseers. As bondage became entrenched, its rationale became the sine qua non of Southern life, taught to eight million whites from pulpit, schoolroom, newspapers, books, lecture halls, and legal codes. This racist ideology drew its arguments from a spurious science, a twisted history, and selected quotations from the Bible. Its acceptance rested on popularly held European notions about race and a circular reasoning that claimed the enslavement of Africans as proof of

Workers on the Central Pacific Railroad are identified as Chinese – but look at them again.

Bessie Russell holds her baby sister, Lucille, in Floresville, Texas, around 1910.

inferior status. With its self-serving rhetoric elevating whites over other people, its impact was assured. Whites who dared to challenge the creed of white supremacy risked their reputations, livelihoods, and sometimes life and limb – and stood little chance of influencing others.

To expect so fundamental a conviction to be left behind when families gathered their belongings for the voyage westward is to expect too much. White pioneer fears were further inflamed by Indians, who beginning with Columbus had been classified as "primitive." This became the excuse to seize their lands, enslave their women and children, and burn their villages. Those who announced "The only good Indian is a dead Indian" also dealt with people of African descent.

Whether the European newcomers silently or loudly proclaimed their racial beliefs was a personal matter. But that they chose to carry them into the wilderness, plant them in virgin soil, and cloak them with the majesty of law has been a historical development of the highest consequence. At the moment when slavery lost its foothold in the North and appeared barred from the West, the intolerance it spawned marched westward. The slaveholders who commanded the new federal government breathed new life into their system as the frontier expanded.

The frontier experience furnishes ample proof of the nationalization of racial animosity. The intrepid men and women who crossed the Western plains carried the virus with them, as much a part of their psyche as their great fears and heralded courage. Once established in frontier communities, these hearty souls erected the barriers their forefathers had constructed in the East. As ax-wielding men and women cleared the land; built homes, schools,

Students and their teachers at a Black school in the early twentieth century

and churches, and planted crops, their ancient ideas took root. The death of slavery and the final subjugation of Native Americans did not diminish but appeared to elevate national acceptance of white superiority. The hardy pioneers and their children tenaciously clung to the creed of their ancestors.

Black pathfinders soon found they had no hiding place from European racial attitudes and edicts. Even the West's vaunted antislavery convictions did not stem from moral repulsion to an evil institution, or even calculated white self-interest, but rather from fear of and revulsion toward people of color. By overwhelming majorities, white settlers voted to keep African Americans from voting in elections, testifying in court, serving on juries, and exercising their rights of citizenship. Those who had united to seize Native American lands also agreed to keep people of color from settling in their communities, entering their churches and schools, and receiving justice in their courts.

There were intrepid white pioneers who spoke up for a prospector denied the right to protect claims, a violated woman who had no right to bring her transgressor to justice, or a merchant who was robbed and was kept from testifying against the criminals. Some registered their disgust at the ballot box, or on petitions, or by donating to African American church and school projects. From Ohio to California, white attorneys stepped forward

to aid African Americans ensnared in legal nets. Untold numbers of ordinary white men and women pursued a higher law to aid fugitives.

But white officeholders in the West captalized in the white fright that
escalated geometrically to arithmetical increases on the Black population.
Legislatures passed punitive and restrictive laws against less than a doz-
en families of color. This reaction to the infinitesimal indicates how racial
anxiety and suspicion had outdistanced both reason and simple economic
self-interest. It also indicates how deeply psychological an originally economic problem had become. An Underground Railroad ditty composed by
fugitive slaves, "Ohio's Not the Place for Me," summarized Black reactions
to frontier hostility.

Black settlers in the West, few in number, lacking in political power,
and helped by few allies, mobilized as best they could. They provided aid
and comfort to sisters, brothers, and perfect strangers who fled slavery. They
sent representatives to assemble in state and national conventions to air
grievances, discuss protest strategies, and petition for their rights. Though
short-lived due to lack of readers and capital, crusading pre–Civil War Black
papers such as *Voice of the Fugitive, The Aliened American, Herald of Freedom, Palladium of Liberty*, and *Mirror of the Times* broadcast community
grievances and mobilized support for justice and equality.

Denied basic rights of citizenship, African Americans lacked the civic
strength white politicians would heed. A handful of judges acted out of con-

A large Texas crowd assembles for a baptism at the San Antonio River
in 1914.

science, but officeholders knew it was safe to ignore people who could not vote. At election time white candidates found more was to be gained by denouncing rather than listening to people of color.

During the crisis of the 1850s, Black separatist sentiment became pronounced in the West. In 1854 the country's largest emigrationist convention assembled in Cleveland, Ohio, its president from Michigan, its first vice president from Indiana, and leading voices from states in the Ohio Valley.

In the age of lynch law that followed the Civil War, the annihilation of Native Americans was not a lesson lost on African Americans. When Ku Klux Klan murders of African Americans mounted in Georgia in 1869 and some advised retaliation, Reverend Charles Ennis sounded this warning: "the whole south would then come against us and kill us off, as the Indians have been killed off." He knew his enemy.

John Q. Adams served as editor of *The Western Appeal* in Minnesota from 1887 until his death in 1922.

President Bill Clinton honors surviving buffalo soldiers at the White House.

Between 1880 and 1915, Black Westerners published 43 newspapers, including 16 in Colorado, 15 in California, and 4 in Montana. Begun by highly literate editors with bristling energy and commitment, they sought to educate and advocate for their constituents and advance the battle for equality. A tribute to rising literacy, pride, and sense of community, they sought to unite people, promote community development, and demand respect from white citizens. *The Colorado Statesman* spoke as the "organ of the colored people of Colorado, Wyoming, Montana, Utah, and New Mexico." In 1906 Joseph Bass began the *Montana Plaindealer* in Helena with a mission of standing up for the right and denouncing the wrong. Bass increasingly exposed prejudice among local and state officials until his paper lost its white advertisers and folded in 1911.

The frontier that beckoned to Black migrants after the Civil War did not become their El Dorado. The "Exodusters of 1879" sought land and opportunity in Kansas and found a respite from Southern violence and a partial freedom. The solitary symbol of their state power, Kansas auditor Edwin P. McCabe, was dropped from his post after two terms. His plan to build a sanctuary and power base for his people in Oklahoma was also overwhelmed.

By the 1890s Black emigrationist sentiment reappeared among Western African Americans as a clear barometer of rising suffering, discontent, and frustration. Hundreds of Black pioneer families from Arkansas and Oklahoma said they were ready to board the first ship to Africa. If the frontier

"An Equal Chance in the Race for Life"

With a homogeneous population pouring into the country from Europe, we must secure an equal chance in the race for life now. If this opportunity be lost, all is lost. We must learn to conform to the conditions that surround us. We must learn many new things and forget many old ones... Our boys and girls must be trained to be more ambitious and aspiring and self-dependent. We must be menials and pariahs no longer. We must get an education...

C. L. de Randemie, *The Colored Patriot*,
Topeka, Kansas, April 27, 1882

LES « LYNCHAGES » AUX ÉTATS-UNIS
Massacre de nègres à Atlanta (Georgie)

As the frontier West came to a close, a quarter century of white invasions of African American neighborhoods – called "race riots" by the U.S. media – disrupted major Eastern cities, the earliest in Wilmington, North Carolina, in 1898. Atlanta, Georgia, experienced several days of a massive mob murder and mayhem in 1906 – similar to European pogroms that drove Jews to leave for the Americas. For people of color in the West, these riots were a stark reminder of the violence they fled. An artist for a popular French newspaper showed how Black people in Atlanta, some with guns and knives, tried to defend their neighborhoods.

proved a "safety valve" for white discontents, as historian Frederick Jackson Turner claimed, it rarely proved so for people of color. It provided an escape from systematic violence and a respite from the more intense forms of hatred, but hardly a new America.

However, frontier life emphasized the need for cooperation. Marked by social fluidity, a blurring of class and caste distinctions, and the sharply defined Victorian roles accorded men and women, the frontier offered rare opportunities. North of Oklahoma and west of Texas in particular, and in cowboy trail crews generally, African Americans found few barriers. Frontier dangers called forth interdependence and informal living and working arrangements that undermined divisiveness and challenged segregation.

Kenneth Wiggins Porter's study finds that while multiracial trail crews endured violence, few shootouts had a racial component. Some cowpunchers – often Confederate veterans – did target people of color, more often Indians and Mexican Americans than Black fellow cowhands. Several Black Indian bands in Oklahoma – the Creek Lighthorsemen (police) in 1878 and the Dick Glass outlaw crew in the early 1880s – raised their rifles, as would

Leavenworth's first electric railway in 1902 drew children of both races.

California's latter-day Black Panthers, against those who perpetuated white violence.

Racial hatred crossed the bumpy post–Civil War trails in prairie schooners and was dusted off for use in growing frontier towns, particularly after the arrival of white women. The closer Black cowboys rode to town and to its white families and institutions, the more likely they would encounter hostility. Discriminatory patterns sharpened in Western communities with the delivery of Sears Roebuck catalogs, the beginning of public schools, and early meetings of white religious congregations.

Slavery's sharpest legacy after ingrained racism was a financially devastated community. Though unpaid Black labor nationwide had produced the capital for factories, farms, and ranches, four million people left bondage penniless, unable to buy the extensive farms or sprawling ranches that made economic survival likely. Cowhands rode out their lives as landless horsemen, and only a handful eventually owned a ranch.

Rodeo doors were often closed to Black cowpunchers with extraordinary skills. Many also lacked the cash required by sponsoring associations, or the sociable contacts with rodeo officials that had opened the way for white performers. Until his success with the 101 Ranch Rodeo made him a legend, Bill Pickett had to perform as a "Mexican toreador."

Women and men in the West resisted oppression in every way they could. Black women swung their umbrellas and men raised their fists at belligerent laws and neighbors. A white man in Texas accused Bill Pickett of stealing a horse and said, "You better hand him over," shoving him and raising his fist for a haymaker. A Pickett punch sent him rolling and groaning on the ground.

Was the West "A Better Deal"?

Your west is giving the Negro a better deal than any other section of the country. I cannot attempt to analyze the reasons for this, but the fact remains that there is more opportunity for my race, and less prejudice against it in this section of the country than anywhere else in the United States.

James Weldon Johnson, secretary of the NAACP,
Denver Post, June 24, 1925

Some Black residents sued for justice in courts, and others pounded away in letters, petitions, picket lines, and delegations. And there were occasional successes. Petitions, entreaties, and lobbying by determined African Americans in Colorado, led by William J. Hardin, convinced the U.S. Congress in 1868 to extend voting rights to all adult Black males in western territories.

The 1890s – which saw the close of the frontier – was an era of agonizing change in the United States. During the next generation each Southern state, including Texas and Oklahoma, codified segregation, often into state constitutions. In 1896 the U.S. Supreme Court in the Plessy case ruled by eight to one that segregation was constitutional. The Populist movement briefly united Southern Black and white farmers against Eastern bankers and merchants, but ended in a bitter defeat that led to more lynchings and an explosion of white violence north and south.

During this low point in the fortunes and power of African Americans, their suppressed rage rested close to the surface. The only African American to dedicate a book to a Western state also delivered a highly inflammatory condemnation of his country. Sut-

Sutton E. Griggs, crusading writer

ton E. Griggs, born in 1872 in Texas and graduated from Bishop College in Marshall, dearly loved both his people and his state. To "Texas soil which fed me, to Texas air which fanned my cheeks, to Texas skies which smiled upon me, to Texas stars which searched my soul, chased out the germs of slumber," Griggs dedicated a book of essays on race relations. Rarely a man to slumber, Griggs devoted his life to examining the painful world whites created for his people and evaluating different solutions. A Baptist minister who played a prominent part in the national affairs of his church, Griggs, though barely known today, was probably the most widely read novelist among his people, surpassing white favorites Paul Lawrence Dunbar and Charles W. Chesnutt.

In 1899 Griggs published his first novel, *Imperium in Imperio*, in which conspiratorial Victorian characters engage in a raging revolutionary melodrama. Griggs describes an African American society, the Imperium, that meets underground in Waco, Texas, and plans to unite with foreign enemies of the United States during a war (the Spanish-American War), and seize Texas and Louisiana. A Griggs character states: "Louisiana we will cede to our foreign allies" but "Texas we will retain... Thus will the Negro have an empire of his own." For more than half a century no one reviewed Grigg's *Imperium in Imperio*. Perhaps it was too subversive. That this flaming banner could be unfurled by so loving a son of Texas is a measure of the West's failure to provide people of color their share of America's promise.

Frederick L. McGhee around 1891

Along with other civil rights proponents, Sutton Griggs joined the Niagara Movement of Dr. W.E.B. Du Bois, which demanded full and immediate citizenship rights. Its legal director was Frederick L. McGhee, a former Mississippi slave. According to Du Bois, "the honor of founding the organization belongs to F. L. McGhee, who first suggested it." An early settler in St. Paul, McGhee was the first Black American admitted to the Minnesota bar. He handled civil rights cases, served Booker T. Washington as a lobbyist with Congress, and became his emissary to Catholic prelates.

Following the war with Spain in 1898, the United States ruled millions of aboriginal peoples on islands from the Caribbean to the Pacific. McGhee's anguish grew. America might have crushed the Filipino drive for independence but failed to halt racial violence and lynchings at home. McGhee denounced "the spirit of mob rule, the prevalence of lynch law, in all parts of our country." He linked it to his country's effort overseas "to rule earth's inferior races, and if they object make war upon them." African Americans "should be the loudest in the protestations against the oppression of others." He concluded: "The Negro cannot, if he would, God forbid that he would if he could, support the present administration in its war on the Filipino."

"The Same Thing Cropping Out at Home"

Our soldiers wrote home of what fun it was to shoot the "niggers" and see them keel over and die. Then came the famous order, "Take no prisoners," followed by the shameful account of the fiendish slaughter of forty-six Tagals, because one had killed an American soldier. Of the number of women and children killed in attacks upon villages defended by men armed with bamboo spears, this with the profoundly and oft-repeated assertion, of late so prevalent, that the proud Anglo-Saxon, the Republican party, by divine foreordination, is destined to rule earth's inferior races, and if they object make war on them, furnishes an all-sufficient cause. Is it to be wondered then that so little value is placed upon the life, liberty, freedom and rights of the American Negro? Is he not also one of the inferior races which Divine Providence has commissioned the Republican party to care for? These things cannot go on with impunity abroad without the same thing cropping out at home...

Frederick L. McGhee, *Howard's American Magazine*, October 1900

In 1916 buffalo soldiers leave Mexican soil.

A highly informed understanding undergirded the impatient fury of Sutton E. Griggs of Texas and Frederick L. McGhee of Minnesota – both successful Western professional men, respected community and religious figures. They measured their government in language as broad and clear as the land that stretched from McGhee's Minnesota to Griggs's Texas.

Afterword

While most of this book is focused on the past, since writing it, I'm regularly reminded that the Black West is still a vital and ever-influential part of our national fabric. Take, for example, the tale of J. B. Keeylocko, and the town he built in Arizona after the Vietnam War.

One of the first invitations I received to launch the first edition of *The Black West* brought me to the University of Arizona at Tuscon. When I landed at the airport, Mr. J. B. Keeylocko was there to greet me. One of the first African American cowboys to own a ranch, he spent years publicizing the story of cowboys who looked like him, and he was there to make sure we would take a photo.

Born in 1931 to Alice Long and a white father, J. B. (sometimes called Ed), was brought up by Esther Brooks, a family friend. He joined the U.S. Army at nineteen, and served in Korea and Vietnam. Stationed in Arizona, he decided to remain there when discharged.

"When you're a little boy, you dream of all kinds of things," J. B. told me. "You dream of things that never were, and then you try and do them. People say, 'How do you dream all these things up?' I guess it's just part of my life when you grow up alone."

And J. B. never stopped dreaming. He enrolled in Pima Community College and at the University of Arizona to study agriculture. Then, in 1976, he bought forty acres of land, with a $1,660 down payment for the $15,800 property. This property, bought to be a ranch, became the basis of something much greater: a town.

In describing how he founded Cowtown Keeylocko, J. B., said, "Two old fellas, tobacco juice running down their lips ... One said, 'You ought to build your own town, and sell your cows in your own town.' I drove a little

My first meeting with J.B. Keeylocko, at the Tucson airport.

bit away, and then I said, 'What did you say?' 'I said, you ought to build your own town, then you wouldn't have to come up here and complain about nothin'.' I said, 'You know that's a good idea, I'll do that. I'll build my own town.'" He recalled how the two men "laughed right up their sleeves. But nobody laughs today."

The directions to his town were almost as freewheeling as his decision to build it. To get to Cowtown Keeylocko, J. B. said, "Head west. Watch Kitt Peak, and follow the signs to milepost 146. Cowtown Keeylocko. You see a sign that says three hoops and a holla, then two hoops and a holla, then one hoop and a holla, and then you'll be right in the town of Keeylocko. We have the coldest beer in Arizona, so cold you have to open the beer with your overcoat on."

Longtime friend David Beaubien recalled J. B.'s goal. "He wanted to make this basically an open oasis where everyone was welcome." His Keeylocko Land Feed and Cattle Co., "soon had dozens of cattle, horses, and hogs roaming his land."

This goal matched J. B.'s desire to live according to Martin Luther King, Jr.'s creed, "I look to a day when people will not be judged by the color of their skin, but by the content of their character."

Another friend described how he acted on this belief: "The amount of respect and kindness he gave to everyone who came around, it was just amazing." Most important, his friend McDowell recalled, J. B. wanted the people of Arizona to know that Black cowboys were commonplace in the old West.

In the end, it was always about staying true to the dream. J. B. always dreamed that the best outcome was possible. "You dream and think. Believe the impossible. Because you can do the impossible. Always stay the course, no matter how hard. Dream of things that never were and ask why not."

In 2014, nearing the end of his life, he told a documentary filmmaker, "The difficult, I'll do right away. The impossible, it might take me a few days longer." He added, "Cowtown Keeylocko is the real, real West. We are the way the West really was."

In March 2019, J. B. "Ed" Keeylocko died, in the town he built as a living, thriving tribute to the Black West.

Acknowledgments

Since its first issue by Doubleday in 1971, *The Black West* has remained almost constantly in print. Now in its sixth incarnation, it has made many friends and incurred many debts of gratitude to staunch allies. These include, first of all, Dr. Sara Dunlop Jackson of the National Archives, who over a dozen years provided documents, advice, and numerous leads; author Esther Mumford of Seattle; Bertha Calloway of the Great Plains Black History Museum; Jack D. Haley of the University of Oklahoma; Dr. Barbara Richardson of Tucson, Arizona, who provided documents and dozens of photographs from her incomparable collection; Dr. Ivan Van Sertima, who warmly shared information, photographs, and his experiences in the field; researcher Kevin Mulroy of the Gene Autry Western Heritage Museum, who is an authority on the African Seminoles; Susan Robeson, who offered her collection of Native American photographs; the Fort Smith National Historic Site; and Carol Storke and Tonsie Whelan of the Bullard-Sellar-Storke family of California, who remembered the governess Elvira Conley.

This project benefited enormously from several unpublished or rare manuscripts. A historian of the Plains soldiers, Don Rickey, Jr., generously volunteered two valuable manuscripts on Black troopers on the last frontier. The Pentagon's James C. Evans provided a copy of *M-5*, a history of Black soldiers written for the U.S. Army by Ulysses Lee of Morgan State College. Mr. Evans also volunteered a copy of the mimeographed *History of the Negro in the Armed Forces*, a documented study "of uncertain vintage" made available in 1964 by the U.S. Civil Rights Commission. Mrs. Dorothy A. King of Denver, Colorado, whose father served at San Juan in the Ninth Cavalry, kindly offered her father's keepsake volume, "Ninth Cavalry, United

States Army, an Illustrated Review," from which she also furnished copies of rare photographs. Joseph P. Doherty of the Kansan Commission on Civil Rights sent along a paper on Black coal miners in his state and included some original photographs. Professor Kenneth Wiggins Porter generously commented on portions of this volume; I appreciated his candor, scholarship, and criticism. Cary P. Stiff, whose "Black Colorado" articles appeared in the 1969 Sunday editions of the *Denver Post*, volunteered copies of manuscripts and newspaper articles he dug out of the Denver newspaper files; he also commented on my conclusions. Sara Dunlop Jackson of the National Archives provided valuable documents on Henry O. Flipper, the first Black West Point graduate, and read and critiqued the chapter on African American soldiers, troopers, and scouts. Ann Eskridge sent along a video showing scenes of Oklahoma's Black towns of the early twentieth century.

A number of scholars responded to my letters and questions with valuable insights, evaluations, and bibliographical suggestions: the late Ulysses Lee, James M. McPherson, John Hope Franklin, Roland C. McConnell, Eugene H. Berwanger, Sara Dunlop Jackson, Ernest Kaiser, Robin Kelley, Edwin S. Redkey, George P. Marks III, James T. Abajian, Sidney Kaplan, Cherill Wilson, Theodore Vincent, Benjamin Quarles, Glenda Riley, Ann Butler, Herb Boyd, Howard H. Bell, Herbert Aptheker, John J. Appel, Franklin Folsom, Dorothy Sterling, Thomas Phillips, Dudley T. Cornish, William H. Leckie, Philip Durham, and Kenneth Wiggins Porter. I only regret that Langston Hughes did not see the book.

Although the pictures and photographs came from many sources across the nation, several individual archivists and librarians went beyond any call of duty to scour their resources. Among these were Dorothy Gimmestad of the Minnesota Historical Society, Myrtle D. Berry and Louise Small of the Nebraska State Historical Society, Sara Dunlop Jackson of the National Archives, Russell E. Belous of the Los Angeles County Museum, Maxine Benson of the State Historical Society of Colorado, Jack D. Haley of the Western History Collection of the University of Oklahoma, Robert Richmond of the Kansas State Historical Society, and Bobby Crisman of Fort Davis National Historic Site. Mrs. Katherine O. Krutsch of San Diego, California, and Mrs. Elizabeth Stanton of Manila, Utah, kindly sent unique personal photographs.

For their untiring help, I am indebted to my family, particularly my father, Ben Katz, for his support and leads. He read the manuscript, lustily offering his criticism and gently his help. His nineteenth-century picture collection early aimed this project toward a picture history.

Let it be understood that any errors of fact or judgment are mine, not those of my helpers. I decided and wrote.

Initially a cause of pain and often a hindrance, it is now a matter of pride that since its origins this project has not received a penny of private, university, or government funding.

Bibliography

When *The Black West* first appeared in 1971, its annotated bibliography was introduced by this sentence: "Kenneth Wiggin Porter (ed.), *The Negro on the American Frontier* (New York: Arno Press, 1971), a pioneer collection of essays, reprinted with new bibliographical material, is probably the best starting place in black western history." If Professor Porter were alive today – he died in 1981 – he would agree that this statement has an antique ring. He would have been delighted with the enormous scholarly attention that has followed his pioneering efforts.

The leading bibliographical sources today are: W. Sherman Savage's *Blacks in the West* (Westport, Conn.: Greenwood Press, 1976); Roger D. Hardaway's "The African American Frontier: A Bibliographic Essay" in Monroe Lee Billington and Roger D. Hardaway, eds., *African Americans on the Western Frontier* (Niwot: University Press of Colorado, 1998); and James de T. Abajian's *Blacks and their Contribution to the American West: A Bibliography* (Boston: G. K. Hall, 1974).

Today's most up-to-date bibliography appears in Quintard Taylor's *In Search of the Racial Frontier: African Americans in the American West, 1528–1990* (New York: Norton, 1998), which, with its fourteen maps, two dozen tables, and footnoted text, is the current definitive history of African Americans in the West ("West" being west of the 98th meridian). This volume extends from the pioneer period of the 1600s to life in the 1990s.

In addition to those outstanding bibliographies, the following sources were highly useful in researching this volume of *The Black West*. This list also includes some books designed for young readers.

Aptheker, Herbert, ed. *A Documentary History of the Negro People in the United States* (New York: Citadel, 1951).

―――. *Abolitionism: A Revolutionary Movement* (Boston: Twayne Publishers, 1989).

Armitage, Susan, Theresa Banfield, and Sarah Jacobus. "Black Women and Their Communities in Colorado," *Frontiers*, vol. II, no. 2.

―――, and Deborah G. Wilbert. "Black Women in the Pacific Northwest, A Survey and Research Project," in Karen Blair, ed., *Pacific Northwest Women* (Seattle: University of Washington Press, 1987).

Asbaugh, Carolyn. *Lucy Parsons: American Revolutionary* (Chicago: Kerr, 1976).

Barr, Alwyn. *Black Texans: A History of African Americans in Texas, 1528–1995* (Norman: University of Oklahoma Press, 1996).

Beasley, Delilah L. *The Negro Trail Blazers of California* (Los Angeles, 1919).

Belous, Russell E., ed. *America's Black Heritage* (Los Angeles: Los Angeles County Museum of Natural History, 1969).

Berlin, Ira. *Many Thousand Gone: The First Two Centuries of Slavery in North America* (Cambridge, Mass: Belknap Press, 1998).

Berwanger, Eugene H. *The Frontier Against Slavery* (Urbana: University of Illinois Press, 1967).

Bittle, William E., and Gilbert L. Geis. "Racial Self-Fulfillment and the Rise of an All-Negro Community in Oklahoma" in August Meier and Elliot M. Rudwick, eds., *The Negro in the Making of Black America*, vol. I (New York: Atheneum, 1969).

Blockson, Charles L. *The Underground Railroad* (New York: Prentice Hall, 1987).

Bolton, Hubert Eugene, ed. *Original Narratives of Early American History, Spanish Explorations in the South West, 1542–1706* (New York: Charles Scribner, 1925).

Bonner, T. D., ed. *The Life and Adventures of James P. Beckwourth* (New York: Arno Press, 1969), a reprint of the Beckwourth "autobiography."

Bontemps, Arna, and Jack Conroy. *Anyplace But Here* (New York: Hill and Wang, 1966).

Brice, Henry C. *The New Man: Twenty-Nine Years a Slave, Twenty-Nine Years a Free Man* (Lincoln: University of Nebraska Press, 1996).

Bringhurst, Newell G. *Saints, Slaves, and Blacks: The Changing Place of Black People Within Mormonism* (Westport, Conn.: Greenwood Press, 1981).

Browne, John Ross. *Report of the Debates in the Convention of California, on the Formation of the State Constitution in September and October, 1849* (New York: Arno Press reprint, 1973).

Bruyn, Kathleen. *"Aunt" Clara Brown* (Boulder, Colo.: Pruett Publishing Co., 1970).

Buckley, Gail. *American Patriots: The Story of Blacks in the Military from the Revolution to Desert Storm* (New York: Random House, 2001).

Bunch, Lonnie, III. *Black Angelenos: The Afro-American in Los Angeles, 1850–1950* (Los Angeles: California Afro-American Museum, 1988).

Burton, Art. *Black, Red, and Deadly: Black and Indian Gunfighters of the Indian Territories* (Austin, Tex.: Eackin Press, 1991).

Butler, Ann M. "'Still in Chains': Black Women in Western Prisons, 1865–1910," *Western Historical Quarterly*, vol. 20 (February 1989).

Carroll, John M. *The Black Military Experience in the West* (New York: Liveright, 1972).

Carroll, Joseph C. "William Trail: An Indiana Pioneer," *Journal of Negro History*, vol. XXIII (October 1938).

Cashin, Herschel V., et al. *Under Fire with the Tenth Cavalry* (New York, 1899; reprinted, New York: Arno Press, 1969).

Christiansen, James B. "Negro Slavery in the Utah Territory," *Phylon*, vol. XVIII, no. 3.

Coffin, Levi. *Reminiscences* (1878; reprinted, New York: W. W. Norton, 1966).

Cox, Clinton. *The Forgotten Heroes: The Story of the Buffalo Soldiers* (New York: Scholastic, 1993).

Crane, R. C., ed. "D. W. Wallace ('80 John'): A Negro Cattleman on the Texas Frontier," *West Texas Historical Society Yearbook* (1952).

Crimmins, Colonel M. L. "Captain Nolan's Lost Troop on the Staked Plains," *West Texas Historical Association Yearbook*, vol. III (July 1928).

Crockett, Norman L. *The Black Towns* (Lawrence: University of Kansas, 1979).

Daniels, Douglass Henry. *Pioneer Urbanites: A Social and Cultural History of Black San Francisco* (Philidelphia: Temple University Press, 1980).

Davis, Harry E. "John Malvin, A Western Reserve Pioneer," *Journal of Negro History*, vol. XXIII (October 1938).

Debo, Angie. *A History of the Indians of the United States* (Norman: University of Oklahoma Press, 1984).

DeGraff, Lawrence B. "Race, Sex and Regions: Black Women in the American West," *Pacific Historical Review* (May 1980).

———, Kevin Mulroy, and Quintard Taylor, eds. *Seeking Eldorado: African Americans in California* (Seattle: University of Washington Press, 2001).

Downey, Fairfax. *The Buffalo Soldiers in the Indian Wars* (New York: McGraw-Hill, 1969).

Drinnon, Richard. *Facing West: The Metaphysics of Indian-Hating and Empire Building* (New York: Meridian, 1980).

Du Bois, W.E.B. "The Mcgees of St. Paul," *The Crisis*, vol. XL (New York: NAACP, 1933).

———, ed. *The Atlanta University Publications* (Arno Press reprint, 1968).

———. *John Brown* (1909; reprinted, New York: International Publishers, 1963).

Durham, Philip, and Everett L. Jones. *The Negro Cowboys* (New York, Dodd, Mead, 1965).

———. *The Adventures of the Negro Cowboys* (New York: Dodd, Mead, 1966).

Dykstra, Robert B. *Bright Radical Star: Black Freedom and White Supremacy in the Hawkeye Frontier* (Cambridge, Mass.: Harvard University Press, 1993).

Flipper, Henry Ossian. *The Colored Cadet at West Point* (1878; reprinted, New York: Arno Press, 1968).

Foner, Jock D. *Blacks and the Military in American History* (New York: Praeger, 1974).

Forbes, Jack D. *Afro-Americans in the Far West: A Handbook for Educational Research* (Berkeley, 1969).

———. *Africans and Native Americans: The Language of Race and the Evolution of the Red-Black Peoples* (Chicago: University of Illinois Press, 1993).

Franklin, Jimmie Lewis. *Journey Toward Hope: A History of Blacks in Oklahoma* (Norman: University of Oklahoma Press, 1982).

Franklin, John Hope. *From Slavery to Freedom* (New York: Knopf, 1967).

Franklin, William E. "The Archy Case: The California Supreme Court Refuses to Free a Slave," *Pacific Historical Review*, vol. XXXII (1963).

Garrison, Wendell P., Jr., ed. *"Smoked Yankees" and the Struggle for Empire: Letters from Negro Soldiers, 1898–1902* (Urbana: University of Illinois Press, 1971).

———. *Black Americans and the White Man's Burden, 1898–1903* (Chicago: University of Illinois Press, 1975).

George, Lynell. *No Crystal Stair: African Americans in the City of Angels* (London: Verso Press, 1992).

Gerber, David A. *Black Ohio and the Color Line, 1860–1915* (Chicago: University of Chicago Press, 1976).

Gibbs, C. R. *Black Explorers: 2300 BC to the Present* (Silver Spring, Md: Three Dimensional Publishing, 2003).

Gibbs, Mifflin Wister. *Shadow and Light* (Washington, D.C.: n.p., 1902; reprinted, New York: Arno Press, 1968).

Goode, Kenneth G. *California's Black Pioneers* (Santa Barbara, Cal.: McNally & Lofton, 1974).

Greene, Lorenzo Johnston. *The Negro in Colonial New England* (New York: Atheneum, 1968).

Griggs, Sutton E. *Imperium in Imperio* (1899; reprinted, New York: Arno Press, 1969).

Haley, James Evetts. *Charles Goodnight: Cowman and Plainsman* (Norman: University of Oklahoma Press, 1936).

Hamilton, Kenneth Marvin. *Black Towns and Profit* (Chicago: University of Illinois Press, 1991).

Harris, Richard E. *The First Hundred Years: A History of Arizona Blacks* (Apache Junction, Ariz.: Relmo Publishers, 1983).

Hill, Mozell C. "The All-Negro Communities of Oklahoma: The Natural History of a Social Movement," *Journal of Negro History*, vol. XXXI (July 1946).

Hine, Darlene Clark, et al., eds. *Black Women in America: An Historical Encyclopedia* (Brooklyn: Carlson, 1992).

Horse, Gerald. *Black and Brown: African Americans in the Mexican Revolution, 1910–1920* (New York: New York University Press, 2005).

Hughes, Langston. *Famous Negro Heroes of America* (New York: Dodd, Mead, 1985).

Kaplan, Sidney, and Emma N. Kaplan. *The Black Presence in the Era of the American Revolution* (Amherst: University of Massachusetts, 1989, revised edition).

Katz, William Loren. *Black Indians: A Hidden Heritage* (New York: Atheneum, 1986).

———. *Black People Who Made the Old West* (New York: Africa World Press, 1992).

———. *Eyewitness: A Living Documentary of the African American Contribution to American History* (New York: Touchstone, 1995).

———. "Elvira Conley: A Black Frontier Business Woman," paper delivered October 19, 1984, at the annual meeting of the Association for the Study of Afro-American Life and History in Washington, D.C.

———. *Black Women of the Old West* (New York: Atheneum Publishers, 1995).

———. *Black Pioneers: An Untold Story* (New York: Atheneum, 1999).

Kremer, Gary R. *James Milton Turner and the Promise of America* (Columbia: University of Missouri Press, 1996).

Lapp, Rudolph M. *Blacks in Gold Rush California* (New Haven, Conn.: Yale University Press, 1977).

Leckie, William H. *The Buffalo Soldiers* (Norman: University of Oklahoma Press, 1967).

Lee, Irvin H. *Negro Medal of Honor Men* (New York: Dodd, Mead, 1967).

Limerick, Patricia Nelson. *The Legacy of Conquest* (New York: W. W. Norton, 1987).

Littlefield, Daniel F., Jr. *Africans and Creeks: From the Colonial Period to the Civil War* (Westport, Conn.: Greenwood Press, 1979).

————. *Africans and Seminoles: From Removal to Emancipation* (Westport, Conn.: Greenwood Press, 1993).

Logan, Rayford W., and Michael R. Winston, eds. *Dictionary of American Negro Biography* (New York: Norton, 1982).

Love, Nat. *The Life and Adventures of Nat Love, Better Known in the Cattle Country as "Deadwood Dick" by Himself* (Los Angeles, 1907; reprinted, New York: Arno Press, 1968).

MacLaughlin, Colin M., and Jaime E. Rodriguez. *The Forging of the Cosmic Race: A Reinterpretation of Colonial Mexico* (Los Angeles: University of California Press, 1990).

Marks, George P., ed. *Black Cowboys of Texas* (College Station: Texas A&M Press, 2000).

McConnell, Roland C. *Negro Troops in Antebellum Louisiana* (Baton Rouge: Louisiana State University Press, 1968).

McLogan, Esther. *A Peculiar Paradise: A History of Black Oregon* (Portland: Georgian Press, 1980).

McPherson, James M. *The Negro's Civil War* (New York: Pantheon Books, 1956).

Millis, Walter. *The Martial Spirit* (Boston: Little, Brown, 1931).

Mulroy, Kevin. *Freedom on the Border* (Lubbock: Texas Tech University Press, 1993).

Mumford, Esther Hall. *Seattle's Black Victorians, 1852–1901* (Seattle: Ananse Press, 1980).

————, ed. *Seven Stars & Orion* (Seattle: Ananse Press, 1986).

Painter, Nell Irvin. *Exodusters* (New York: W. W. Norton, 1976).

Penn, I. Garland. *The Afro-American Press and its Editors* (Springfield, Ill., 1981; reprinted, New York: Arno Press, 1969).

Porter, Kenneth W. *The Negro on the American Frontier* (New York: Arno Press, 1971).

Price, Armistead S., and Clint Wilson. *A History of the Black Press* (Washington, D.C.: Howard University Press, 1996).

Price, Richard, ed. *Maroon Societies* (Baltimore: Johns Hopkins University Press, 1969).

Proceedings of the State Convention of the Colored Citizens of the State of California, first held at Sacramento, November 20, 21, and 22, 1855, in the Colored Methodist Church in Sacramento (*Democratic State Journal*, San Francisco, 1856).

Quarles, Benjamin. *Black Abolitionists* (New York: Oxford University Press, 1969).

Rawick, George P., ed. *The American Slave: A Composite Autobiography* (Westport, Conn.: Greenwood Publishing Co., 1972).

Redkey, Edwin S. *Black Exodus* (New Haven, Conn.: Yale University Press, 1969).

Richardson, Barbara. "Research on Black Women in the Early Southwest U.S.," unpublished handwritten manuscript (1987) provided by the author.

Roberson, Jere W. "Edwin P. McCabe and the Langston Experiment," *Chronicles of Oklahoma*, vol. 51, no. 3 (October 1971).

Rout, Leslie B., Jr. *The African Experience in Spanish America: 1502 to the Present Day* (London: Cambridge University Press, 1977).

Rusco, Elmer R. *"Good Time Coming?" Black Nevadans in the Nineteenth Century* (Westport, Conn.: Greenwood Press, 1975).

Schomburg, Arthur A. "Two Negro Missionaries to the American Indians," *Journal of Negro History*, vol. XXI (October 1936).

Sertima, Ivan Van, ed. *African Presence in Early America* (New Brunswick, N.J.: Transaction Press, 1992).

Sherman, General W. T. "Old Times in California," *North American Review* (March 1889).

———. "Old Shady, With a Moral," *North American Review* (October 1888).

Siebert, Wilbur Henry. *The Mysteries of Ohio's Underground Railroad* (Columbus, Ohio: Long's College Book Company, 1951).

———. *The Underground Railroad from Slavery to Freedom* (New York: Macmillan, 1898; reprinted, New York: Arno Press, 1970).

Sprague, John T. *The Origin, Progress, and Conclusion of the Florida War* (1848; reissued 1964 by the State of Florida).

Steward, T. G. *The Colored Regulars in the United States Army* (Philadelphia, 1904; reprinted, New York: Arno Press, 1969).

Stewart, Paul W., and Wallace Y. Ponce. *Black Cowboys* (Broomfield: Phillips Publishing, 1986).

Strode, Woody. *Goal Dust* (New York: Macmillan Books, 1990).

Takaki, Ronald T. *Iron Cages: Race and Culture in 19th Century America* (New York: Knopf, 1979).

Taylor, Quintard. "Blacks in the West: An Overview," *Western Journal of Black Studies* (March 1977).

———, and Shirley Ann Wilson Moore, eds. *African American Women Confront the West, 1600–2000* (Norman: University of Oklahoma Press, 2003).

Teall, Kaye M., ed. *Black History in Oklahoma: A Resource Book* (Oklahoma City Public Schools, 1971).

Thompson, Erwin N. "The Negro Soldiers on the Frontier: A Fort Davis Case Study," *Journal of the West*, vol. VII (April 1968).

Thornbrough, Emma Lou. *The Negro in Indiana* (Bloomington: Indiana Historical Bureau, 1957).

Thurman, Sue Bailey. *Pioneers of Negro Origin in California* (San Francisco: Acme Publishers, 1952).

Tucker, Phillip Thomas. *Cathy Williams: From Slave to Female Buffalo Soldier* (Mechanicsburg, Pa.: Stackpole Books, 2003).

U.S. Bureau of the Census. *Negro Populations in the United States, 1790–1915* (Washington, D.C.: Government Printing Office, 1918; reprinted, New York: Arno Press, 1968).

Vincent, Ted. "Afromestizos in Mexican Politics 1810–1937," 1997 manuscript in author's possession.

Voegli, V. Jacque. *Free but Not Equal* (Chicago: University of Chicago Press, 1967).

Wallace, Edward S. "General John Lapham Bullis, Thunderbolt of Texas Frontier," *Southwestern Historical Quarterly*, vol. LV (July 1951).

Williams, George Washington. *History of the Negro Race in America from 1619 to 1880* (1883; reprinted, New York: Arno Press, 1968).

Winegarten, Ruthe. *Black Texas Women: 150 Years of Trial and Triumph* (Austin: University of Texas Press, 1996).

Woodson, Carter G. "The Negroes of Cincinnati Prior to the Civil War," *Journal of Negro History*, vol. 1, no. 1 (1915).

Woodward, Elon A. *The Negro in the Military Service of the United States*, vols. I–III (National Archives manuscript, 1888).

Wright, Richard R. "Negro Companions of the Spanish Explorers" in August Meier and Elliot M. Rudwick, eds., *The Making of Black America*, vol. I (New York: Atheneum, 1969).

Photo Credits

Page xiii   William Loren Katz Collection
Page xv   William Loren Katz Collection
Page xvi   William Loren Katz Collection
Page 2   William Loren Katz Collection
Page 3 (top) William Loren Katz Collection
Page 3 (bottom) British Museum, London
Page 4   William Loren Katz Collection
Page 5   Bibliothèque Nationale, Paris
Page 7   William Loren Katz Collection
Page 8   William Loren Katz Collection
Page 9   William Loren Katz Collection
Page 10 (top) Susan Robeson Collection
Page 10 (bottom) William Loren Katz
   Collection
Page 11   William Loren Katz Collection
Page 12   William Loren Katz Collection
Page 13   William Loren Katz Collection
Page 14   William Loren Katz Collection
Page 17   William Loren Katz Collection
Page 18   William Loren Katz Collection
Page 19   William Loren Katz Collection
Page 20 (top) William Loren Katz Collection
Page 20 (bottom) William Loren Katz
   Collection
Page 21   William Loren Katz Collection
Page 22   William Loren Katz Collection
Page 24   William Loren Katz Collection
Page 29   William Loren Katz Collection
Page 32   William Loren Katz Collection
Page 33   U.S. Postal Service
Page 34   Library of Congress
Page 35   William Loren Katz Collection
Page 38   Nevada State Historical Society
Page 39   William Loren Katz Collection
Page 40   Minnesota Historical Society
Page 41   Minnesota Historical Society
Page 45   Minnesota Historical Society
Page 47   William Loren Katz Collection
Page 48   William Loren Katz Collection

Page 54 (top) William Loren Katz Collection
Page 54 (bottom) William Loren Katz
   Collection
Page 58 (left) Illinois Historical Society
Page 58 (right) Illinois Historical Society
Page 59   Chicago Historical Society
Page 60   Oregon Historical Society
Page 61   William Loren Katz Collection
Page 62   Esther Mumford Collection
Page 63   Esther Mumford Collection
Page 65   Oregon Historical Society
Page 66   Barbara Richardson Collection
Page 67   William Loren Katz Collection
Page 70   William Loren Katz Collection
Page 71   Detroit Public Library
Page 73   Institute of Texan Cultures
Page 74   John P. Bailey Collection, Gaines-
   ville, Texas
Page 75   William Loren Katz Collection
Page 76   William Loren Katz Collection
Page 78   William Loren Katz Collection
Page 81 (top) William Loren Katz Collection
Page 81 (bottom) William Loren Katz
   Collection
Page 82   William Loren Katz Collection
Page 84   Detroit Public Library
Page 85   William Loren Katz Collection
Page 86   William Loren Katz Collection
Page 89   William Loren Katz Collection
Page 90 (top) William Loren Katz Collection
Page 90 (bottom) William Loren Katz
   Collection
Page 91   Library of Congress
Page 92   William Loren Katz Collection
Page 95   William Loren Katz Collection
Page 96 (top) Minnesota Historical Society
Page 96 (bottom) William Loren Katz
   Collection
Page 98   William Loren Katz Collection

Page 100 William Loren Katz Collection
Page 101 William Loren Katz Collection
Page 102 William Loren Katz Collection
Page 105 William Loren Katz Collection
Page 106 William Loren Katz Collection
Page 107 William Loren Katz Collection
Page 108 William Loren Katz Collection
Page 109 William Loren Katz Collection
Page 110 William Loren Katz Collection
Page 111 William Loren Katz Collection
Page 112 (left) William Loren Katz Collection
Page 112 (right) William Loren Katz Collection
Page 113 William Loren Katz Collection
Page 114 William Loren Katz Collection
Page 115 William Loren Katz Collection
Page 116 William Loren Katz Collection
Page 118 (top) William Loren Katz Collection
Page 118 (bottom) African American Museum, Oakland
Page 119 William Loren Katz Collection
Page 120 (top) William Loren Katz Collection
Page 120 (bottom) William Loren Katz Collection
Page 122 African American Museum, Oakland
Page 123 William Loren Katz Collection
Page 124 California State Library
Page 125 William Loren Katz Collection
Page 127 African American Museum, Oakland
Page 128 William Loren Katz Collection
Page 129 (top) William Loren Katz Collection
Page 129 (bottom) William Loren Katz Collection
Page 130 (top) William Loren Katz Collection
Page 130 (bottom) William Loren Katz Collection
Page 133 (left) African American Museum, Oakland
Page 133 (right) British Columbia Archives
Page 134 William Loren Katz Collection
Page 135 William Loren Katz Collection
Page 136 William Loren Katz Collection
Page 138 William Loren Katz Collection
Page 141 William Loren Katz Collection
Page 142 William Loren Katz Collection

Page 145 Library of Congress
Page 146 Denver Public Library
Page 147 Institute of Texan Cultures
Page 148 (top) Library of Congress
Page 148 (bottom) William Loren Katz Collection
Page 149 (top) Denver Public Library
Page 149 (bottom) Denver Public Library
Page 150 (top) William Loren Katz Collection
Page 150 (bottom) William Loren Katz Collection
Page 151 (top) William Loren Katz Collection
Page 151 (bottom) William Loren Katz Collection
Page 152 Library of Congress
Page 153 (top) William Loren Katz Collection
Page 153 (bottom) William Loren Katz Collection
Page 154 William Loren Katz Collection
Page 155 (top) William Loren Katz Collection
Page 155 (bottom) William Loren Katz Collection
Page 156 William Loren Katz Collection
Page 157 (top) William Loren Katz Collection
Page 157 (bottom) Library of Congress
Page 158 Library of Congress
Page 160 William Loren Katz Collection
Page 161 (top) William Loren Katz Collection
Page 161 (bottom) Denver Public Library
Page 162 William Loren Katz Collection
Page 164 William Loren Katz Collection
Page 166 Denver Public Library
Page 167 Institute of Texan Cultures
Page 169 Denver Public Library
Page 170 Denver Public Library
Page 173 William Loren Katz Collection
Page 174 William Loren Katz Collection
Page 175 William Loren Katz Collection
Page 177 William Loren Katz Collection
Page 178 William Loren Katz Collection
Page 181 William Loren Katz Collection
Page 182 University of Kansas Library
Page 183 William Loren Katz Collection
Page 185 (top) William Loren Katz Collection
Page 185 (right) William Loren Katz Collection
Page 185 (bottom) William Loren Katz Collection
Page 186 William Loren Katz Collection
Page 187 William Loren Katz Collection

Page 188 University of Kansas Library
Page 189 William Loren Katz Collection
Page 190 University of Kansas Library
Page 191 Barbara Richardson Collection
Page 192 (top) Nebraska State Historical
Society
Page 192 (bottom) Nebraska State Historical
Society
Page 193 (top left) Nebraska State Historical
Society
Page 193 (top right) Nebraska State Histor-
ical Society
Page 193 (bottom) Nebraska State Historical
Society
Page 194 Barbara Richardson Collection
Page 195 (top) Barbara Richardson Collec-
tion
Page 195 (bottom) Nebraska State Historical
Society
Page 196 (top) Barbara Richardson Collec-
tion
Page 196 (bottom) William Loren Katz
Collection
Page 197 (top) Denver Public Library
Page 197 (bottom) Denver Public Library
Page 198 (top) Denver Public Library
Page 198 (bottom) Denver Public Library
Page 199 William Loren Katz Collection
Page 200 William Loren Katz Collection
Page 201 (top) William Loren Katz Collection
Page 201 (bottom) William Loren Katz
Collection
Page 202 (top) William Loren Katz Collection
Page 202 (bottom) William Loren Katz
Collection
Page 203 (top) William Loren Katz Collection
Page 203 (bottom) William Loren Katz
Collection
Page 204 (top) William Loren Katz Collection
Page 204 (bottom) William Loren Katz
Collection
Page 205 Library of Congress
Page 206 (top) The National Archives
Page 206 (bottom) The National Archives
Page 207 Library of Congress
Page 208 (top) Library of Congress
Page 208 (bottom) The National Archives
Page 209 Dorothy King Collection
Page 210 The National Archives

Page 211 William Loren Katz Collection
Page 212 (top) Dorothy King Collection
Page 212 (bottom) Library of Congress
Page 213 (top) Dorothy King Collection
Page 213 (bottom) William Loren Katz
Collection
Page 214 (top) Barbara Richardson Collection
Page 214 (bottom) William Loren Katz
Collection
Page 215 (top) Library of Congress
Page 215 (bottom) Library of Congress
Page 217 (top) The National Archives
Page 217 (bottom) The National Archives
Page 218 (top) William Loren Katz Collection
Page 218 (bottom) Library of Congress
Page 220 (top) The National Archives
Page 220 (bottom) The National Archives
Page 221 William Loren Katz Collection
Page 222 William Loren Katz Collection
Page 223 (top) William Loren Katz Collection
Page 223 (bottom) William Loren Katz
Collection
Page 224 (top) William Loren Katz Collection
Page 224 (bottom) William Loren Katz
Collection
Page 225 (top) William Loren Katz Collection
Page 225 (bottom) William Loren Katz
Collection
Page 226 (top) Institute of Texan Cultures
Page 226 (bottom) Institute of Texan Cultures
Page 227 (top) William Loren Katz Collection
Page 227 (bottom) William Loren Katz
Collection
Page 228 (top) William Loren Katz Collection
Page 228 (bottom) Institute of Texan Cultures
Page 229 Institute of Texan Cultures
Page 230 William Loren Katz Collection
Page 231 Barbara Richardson Collection
Page 232 Oklahoma Historical Society
Page 233 Barbara Richardson Collection
Page 234 (top) University of Oklahoma
Library
Page 234 (bottom) University of Oklahoma
Library
Page 235 Barbara Richardson Collection
Page 237 (top) Oklahoma Historical Society
Page 237 (bottom) Oklahoma Historical
Society
Page 238 University of Oklahoma

Page 239 University of Oklahoma Library
Page 240 (top) Oklahoma Historical Society
Page 240 (bottom) Oklahoma Historical Society
Page 241 William Loren Katz Collection
Page 242 (top) University of Oklahoma Library
Page 242 (bottom) Oklahoma Historical Society
Page 243 (top) William Loren Katz Collection
Page 243 (bottom) Oklahoma Historical Society
Page 244 (top) University of Oklahoma Library
Page 244 (bottom) University of Oklahoma Library
Page 245 Oklahoma Historical Society
Page 246 (top) University of Oklahoma
Page 246 (bottom) Oklahoma Historical Society
Page 247 (top) Oklahoma Historical Society
Page 247 (bottom) Oklahoma Historical Society
Page 248 University of Oklahoma
Page 249 Barbara Richardson Collection
Page 250 (top) Library of Congress
Page 250 (bottom) Library of Congress
Page 251 (top) William Loren Katz Collection
Page 251 (bottom) Library of Congress
Page 252 William Loren Katz Collection
Page 253 (top) Barbara Richardson Collection
Page 253 (bottom) Barbara Richardson Collection
Page 254 (left) Barbara Richardson Collection
Page 254 (right) Barbara Richardson Collection
Page 254 (bottom) Barbara Richardson Collection
Page 255 (top) Barbara Richardson Collection
Page 255 (bottom) Barbara Richardson Collection
Page 256 (top) Barbara Richardson Collection
Page 256 (bottom) Barbara Richardson Collection
Page 257 Barbara Richardson Collection
Page 258 (left) Barbara Richardson Collection
Page 258 (right) Barbara Richardson Collection

Page 258 (bottom) William Loren Katz Collection
Page 259 (top) Esther Mumford Collection
Page 259 (bottom) William Loren Katz Collection
Page 260 William Loren Katz Collection
Page 261 (top) Barbara Richardson Collection
Page 261 (center) Barbara Richardson Collection
Page 261 (bottom) Barbara Richardson Collection
Page 262 Barbara Richardson Collection
Page 263 Institute of Texan Cultures
Page 264 Institute of Texan Cultures
Page 265 Barbara Richardson Collection
Page 266 William Loren Katz Collection
Page 268 Carol Storke Collection
Page 269 Barbara Richardson Collection
Page 271 Library of Congress
Page 272 William Loren Katz Collection
Page 273 Library of Congress
Page 275 William Loren Katz Collection
Page 276 Dorothy King Collection
Page 277 William Loren Katz Collection
Page 280 The National Archives
Page 281 Library of Congress
Page 283 Library of Congress
Page 284 William Loren Katz Collection
Page 285 Institute of Texan Cultures
Page 286 Institute of Texan Cultures
Page 287 Institute of Texan Cultures
Page 288 (top) William Loren Katz Collection
Page 288 (bottom) White House Photo
Page 290 William Loren Katz Collection
Page 291 William Loren Katz Collection
Page 292 William Loren Katz Collection
Page 293 Minnesota Historical Society
Page 295 William Loren Katz Collection
Page 297 William Loren Katz Collection

Cover William Loren Katz Collection

Index

abolitionists, abolitionism
    California and, 135–136
    Civil War and, x, 105,
        107, 109, 114
    crisis years and, 90
    and exodus to Kansas,
        190
    going west and, 51
    and slavery on frontier,
        70, 79, 83, 86–87
Adams, Henry, 179–178,
    184–185, 188, 262
Adams, John Q., 288
Adams, Mr. and Mrs.
    John, 193
Africa
    in age of exploration,
        1–2, 6, 23
    buffalo soldiers and, 222
    emigration to, 49, 185,
        233, 240–241, 289
    Oklahoma and, 235
Aguinaldo, Emilio, 275,
    277–280
Alabama, 100, 262, 280
Alaska, 117, 151, 221
Alexander, John, 221–222
Allen, William, 78, 93
Allensworth, Allen and
    Josephine, 194
Alverson, Nan, 73
Amadeus, Mother, 164
American Revolution, 16,
    25, 105
Apaches, xiv, xix, 153, 213,
    217, 224

Aranha, Fliipa Maria,
    14–15
Arizona
    buffalo soldiers and
    cowhands and, 153, 217,
        219, 223–224
    crisis years and, 82, 96
    Estevan and, 23
    women and, 255, 261–262
Arkansas, 19, 32, 109, 126,
    143–144, 161, 169, 241,
    262, 189
Armour, Philip D., 189
Arthur, Chester A., 220
Ashworth, Aaron, 94
Atlanta riot, 290
Atlantic Creoles, 1–2
Austin, Stephen, 55–56
Ayllón, Lucas Vasquez,
    5–6

Bakker, Peter, 1
Barkshire, Arthur and
    Elizabeth Keith, 49–50
"Bar's Fight, The" (Terry),
    24, 25–26
Bartram, John, 15
Bass, Joseph, 289
Bean, Roy, 148, 168
Beaty, Rhoda, 73
Beckwourth, James P., xix,
    29–31, 36–39
Belton, A. G., 233
Benson, Caleb, 205
Berlin, Ira, 1
Beveridge, Albert, 272

Bibb, Henry and Mary
    E., 94
Billy the Kid, 159–160,
    217
Bivins, Horace, 272
Blackburn, Thornton, 83
Black Laws
    California and, 138,
        141–143
    crisis years and, 94,
    going West and, 47–53,
        58–59
Black towns
    Hooks and, 168
    of Kansas, 180–184,
        194–195
    of Oklahoma, 156,
        235–245, 268–269
Bleeding Kansas, 97,
    110–111
Boley, Okla., 156, 238–
    239, 245, 268–269
Bonga (Bonza) family,
    39–41
Boone, Daniel, 31–32,
    36, 38
Booth, Griffith, 82
Boudinot, Elias, 15
Bowles, J., 99
Brackens, Moses, 73
Brant, Joseph, Chief of the
    Mohawks, 10
Brazil, 3, 14
Brazo, John, 29
Broad Ax, The, 275, 279
Broderick, Daniel, 136

Brown, Albert Gallatin, 104
Brown, Benjamin, 219
Brown, Clara, 65–67, 190, 197, 251
Brown, Grafton Tyler, 138, 186
Brown, John, 11, 109
    Civil War and, 109–116
    crisis years and, 98–100
    Kansas and, 179, 186
    and slavery on frontier, 79, 81, 83
Brown, Peter, 124
Brown, William Wells, 82
Buchanan, James, 79–80, 87, 103
Buck, Rufus, 162–163
Buckley, Gail, 276
Bullis, John L., 227–229
Bush, George Washington, 62–64
Butler, Anne, 265
Butler, Luticia Parsons, 254

Cabeza de Vaca, Álvar Núñez, 21
Cain, Richard H., 106
Camp, Abraham, 49
Camp, Charles L., 30
Campbell, Robert L., 277
Canada, Canadians
    cowhands and, 143, 174–175
    crisis years and, 95, 98
California and, 133, 141, 143
    going west and, 63
    Lucy Terry Prince and, 23, 27
    and slavery on frontier, 71–72, 82–85
    and trappers, guides, and mountain men, 37, 39, 40
Capshaw, Mrs. M. L., 73

Captain Dodge's Colored Troopers to the Rescue (Remington), 211
Carolinas
    in age of exploration, 3, 5, 8–9, 16
    buffalo soldiers and, 218–219
    going west and, 42–43, 46, 58
    slavery in, 82
    women and, 250
Carpenter, Louis, 208
Carter, Mr. and Mrs. Henry, 262
Cayton, Horace and Susan Revels, 258
Centralia, Wash., 60
Chapman, Kate, 254
Chase, Salmon P., 79–80
Cherokees
    in age of exploration, 3, 15
    Civil War and, 113
    going west and, 43
    Oklahoma and, 77, 243, 248
Cheyennes, xviii, 38, 152, 211, 223
Chicago
    Ford and, 197–198
    going west and, 58, 60
    and trappers, guides, and mountain men, 32–33
    women and, 266–267
Child, L. Maria, 11
Chippewas, 11–12, 39–40, 59
Chittenden, 30
Chivington, James, xviii, 38
Chocktaws, 10, 15, 77, 238, 243–244
Cibola, 22
City Hotel, 119–120
civil rights
    in California, 130–132,

135–142
    going west and, 53, 59
    Griggs and, 293–294
    women and, 267
    see also voting, voting rights
Clark, Alexander, 52
Clark, Mary, 71
Clark, Peter H., 54
Clarke, Lewis and Milton, 90
Clinch, Duncan L., 17
Clinton, Bill, xix, 288
Coffey, Alvin A., 126–127
Collins, Doris, 260
Colorado
    buffalo soldiers and, 205
    cowhands and, 146–147, 149–151, 154, 159–160
    crisis years and, 94, 96,
    and exodus to Kansas, 190, 194–199
    Ford and, 197–199
    going west and, 65–67
    gold prospecting in, 169, 196–197
    and trappers, guides, and mountain men, 37–38
    women and, 249, 252, 255–256, 258, 160, 264, 265, 289, 292
Columbus, Christopher, xvii, xix, 1, 5, 285
Comanches, xix, 154, 217, 228
Compromise of 1850, 89, 92
Confederacy, 100, 105–106, 115, 179
Congress, U.S.
    buffalo soldiers and, 200, 208
    civil rights and, 292, 294
    Civil War and, 105–106
    crisis years and, 91, 93, 100, 103

and emancipation of
    slaves
and exodus to Kansas,
    176, 187
going west and, 42,
    47–48, 63
imperialism and,
    271–272
Oklahoma and, 233,
    244, 246
and slavery on frontier,
    68, 79, 81
and trappers, guides,
    and mountain men, 38
Conley, Elvira, 269–270
Conners, Mamie, 254
Constitution, U.S.
    going west and, 49
    Fourteenth Amendment
        to, 87
    and slavery on frontier,
        68–69
    Thirteenth Amendment
        to, 59, 179
Conway, Thomas, 187
Cooper, Douglas, 108
Cooper, Gary, 164–165
Costa, Matthieu da, 4
Creeks, 15–19, 69, 77, 107,
    160, 239, 242–243, 251,
    290
Crockett, Davy, 31, 36, 38
Cromwell, R. J., 260
Crows, 36–38
Crumbly, Jess "Flip," 152
Cuba, 7, 103–104,
    271–274, 280
Cummings, Tempie, 74
Custer, George Arm-
    strong, 205, 208, 211

Dakotas, Dakota Territory
    Black towns in, 194
    buffalo soldiers and, 211
    cowhands and, 159
    crisis years and, 97
    women and, 254

Dart, Isom, 169–171
Davis, James, 42
Dawes Commission, 240,
    243
Day, Matthias, 209
De Armond, David A.,
    272
Death of Cleopatra (Lewis),
    12
Debaptiste, George, 55, 83
Declaration of Indepen-
    dence, 7, 10, 227
Deivers, Johnnie, 151
Denison, Elizabeth, 71
Denver, Colo.
    xv, 37, 147
    crisis years and, 94
    and exodus to Kansas,
        191, 194
    Ford and, 197–198
    going west and, 66–67
    women and, 251, 254,
        257, 265,
De Randemie, C. L., 289
Detter, Thomas and Emily
    Brinson, 259
De Voto, Bernard, 30
Dictionary of American
    Biography, 30, 88
Dobie, J. Frank, 172
Dorman, Isaiah, 211
Douglas, Stephen A., 97,
    100
Douglass, Frederick,
    California and, 131
    Civil War and, 107, 114
    in Indiana, 81–82
    Kansas and, 102, 189,
        191, 197
    Oklahoma and, 236
Douglass, H. Ford, 95,
    115–116
Du Bois, W.E.B., xviii, 168,
    293–294
Duesse, De Marge, 256
Duff, Thomas, 140

education, educators
    buffalo soldiers and, 201
    California and, 126–128,
        130–134, 140
    Civil War and, 116
    cowhands and, 173
    Edmonia Lewis and, 11
    and exodus to Kansas,
        178, 182–183, 187, 198
    going west and, 43, 45,
        51–55
    Oklahoma and, 235, 243
    and slavery on frontier
    women and, 248,
        251–252, 256–257,
        260, 263–265, 268
Emancipation Proclama-
    tion, 64, 113–114, 179
Ennis, Charles, 288
Enriquez, Martin, 7
Estevan, 20–23
Exodusters, 188, 289

Factor, Pompey, 228–229
Fagen, David, 277–278
Fields, Mary "Stagecoach,"
    164
Finley, James, 43
Flandreau, Charles E.,
    40–41
Fletcher, Diana, 252
Flipper, Henry O., xix,
    220–221
Florida
    buffalo soldiers and, 227
    imperialism and,
        272–274, 277
    and relations between
        Africans and Native
        Americans, xviii, 1, 13,
        16–21, 23
    slavery and, 83
    and trappers, guides,
        and mountain men, 37
Flowers, Ruth, 249
Ford, Barney, 196–199
Ford, Julia, 197, 199

Ford, Nathaniel, 78–79
Foster, Henrietta Williams
  "Aunt Rittie," 152, 253
Fountain, Sarah, 252
France, xvi, 7, 28, 103,
  122, 282
free people of color
  and California, 125,
    128–131, 134–135
  crisis years and, 92–96,
    102
  going west and, 56
  and relations between
    Africans and Native
    Americans, 5, 16
Frémont, John C., 37, 100,
  119
fugitive slave laws
  California and, 134–135
  crisis years and, 89, 92,
    95
  slavery and, 79, 85

Ganga–Zumba, 14
Garner, Margaret, 72
Georgia
  age of exploration and,
    16
  buffalo soldiers and,
    220, 272
  crisis years and, 100
  murders of African
    Americans in, 288
  slavery and, 82
  women and, 130, 262,
Ghost Dance rebellion,
  214
Gibbs, Mifflin W., 137,
  142–144
Giddings, Joshua, 79
Giddings, Paula, 260, 262
Gillespie, Charles, 127
Goldsby, Cranford "Cher-
  okee Bill," 160–163
Goodnight, Charles, 146
Graham, Anna, 255
Grant, Ulysses S., 101, 128

Gray, Sylvester, 94
Great Britain
  crisis years and, 101, 103
  going west and, 42,
    62–63
  and relations between
    Africans and Native
    Americans, 9, 15–16, 23
  slavery and, 78, 85, 183
  and trappers, guides,
    and mountain men,
    29, 33
Great Exodus, 184–189,
  191, 260, 262
Grey, Eula R. and Emily,
  45
Grierson, Benjamin, 214
Griggs, Sutton E., 292–295
Grose, Sarah, 62, 257

Haiti, 7, 33
Hall, William H., 122
Hamilton, Jeff, 73
Hardin, William, J., 198,
  292
Harper, Francis Ellen
  Watkins, 256, 259
Harpers Ferry, raid on, xv,
  99–100
Harris, Chapman, 82
Harris, Moses "Black
  Squire," 31
Hatch, Edward, 212
Haviland, Laura, 190
Hawaii, 118, 252, 276
Hayes, John B. "Texas
  Kid," 84,
Hayes, Rutherford B., 144,
  187, 162
Haymarket riot, 266
Haywood, Felix, 178
Hendrix, John, 152
Henry, Alexander, 39
Hickman, Robert, 96,
Hickman, Willianna, 181
Hill, Mozell C., 236
Hill, W. R., 180–181

Hinton, Richard J., 105,
  111, 116
History of the Negro Race in
  America (Williams), 203
History of the State of Colo-
  rado, 199
Hodges, Ben, 165–166
Holmes, Reuben, 31
Holmes, Robin and Polly,
  78–79
Hooks, Matthew "Bones,"
  166–168
Horse, John, Chief of the
  Black Seminoles, 19–20,
  226, 229
Houston, Sam, 103, 282
Houston riot, 282
"How the Worm Turned"
  (Remington), 225
Hubbs, Paul K., 133
Hughes, Langston, xv, 99,
  284
Hughes, Robert, 275–276

Ikard, Bose, 146–147
Illinois
  crisis years and, 100,
    112, 115,
  going west and, 42, 44,
    49, 51, 53, 55, 58–59
  and slavery on frontier,
    69–70, 72, 80–82,
    94–96
Imperium in Imperio
  (Griggs), 293
indentured servants, 69,
  71–72
Indiana
  crisis years, 95–96
  going west and, 43–44,
    46, 49–51, 55
  and slavery on frontier,
    69, 71–72, 80–82
Indian Territory, see
  Oklahoma
Inter–Ocean hotels,
  197–198

Iowa, 96, 110, 112
  going west and, 44, 49,
    51, 67, 83
Island Mound, 109

Jackson, Andrew, 17, 62,
    164
Jackson, Oliver T. and
    Minerva, 194–195
Jesup, Thomas Sidney,
    18–19
Jockeys, 156–157
Johnson, Britton, 154–155
Johnson, James Weldon,
    192
Johnson, John H., 187
Johnson, Mary, 141
Jones, John and Mary
    Richardson, 58–60
Jones, Thomas and Bessie
    McCoy, 255
Jordan, George, 210
July, Fay and Mary, 228

Kansas
  buffalo soldiers and,
    207, 213–214, 217, 230
  Civil War and, 105,
    109–116
  cowhands and, 147,
    157–158, 166
  crisis years and, 90,
    93–94, 97–102
  exodus to, 179–199, 289
  and exodus to Oklaho
    ma, 233
  going west and, 44, 46,
    51, 65, 67
  McCabe's life in,
    245–247
  women and, 255, 260,
    262, 269
Keetowowah, 107
Kennard, William, 155
Kentucky
  Civil War and, 109
  cowhands and, 156–157

crisis years and, 96
  and exodus to Kansas,
    179–181
  going west and, 42–43,
    50, 52, 66
  and slavery on frontier,
    72, 81–84
  and trappers, guides,
    and mountain men, 37
  women and, 251
Kentucky Derby, 156–157
Kerr, Howard, 258
Kiowas, 154, 204, 252
Knox, Frank, 274
Ku Klux Klan, 288

Lambert, William, 53,
    83–84
Lane, James H., 93,
    110–116
Langston, Charles, 91
Langston, John Mercer,
    91, 114, 246
Langston City, Okla.,
    233, 233–237, 241, 246,
    268–269
Lanu, 6
Leary, Lewis Sheridan, xv,
    99–100
Leavenworth, Henry, 30
Leckie, William H., xviii,
    209
Lee, Archey, 135–136
Leidesdorff, William,
    118–121
Lemmons, Bob, 171–172
LeMoyne de Bienville,
    Jean–Baptiste, 8
Lester, Sarah, 132–133
Lester, Peter, 135, 137,
    142–143
Lewis, Edmonia (Wild-
    fire), 11–12
Lewis, Jake, 160
Lewis and Clark expedi-
    tion, 34–36
Lincoln, Abraham

Civil War and, 105–107,
    110–111, 114–115
  crisis years and, 95, 100,
    102
  slavery and, 68–69, 87
Lindsay, Robert J., 156
Little Big Horn, Battle of,
    211
Lofton, Victoria C., 74
Logan, Greenbury, 55–57
Long Branch saloon, 150
Los Angeles, Calif.
  buffalo soldiers and, 202
California and, 117, 131,
    141
  civil rights campaigns in
    women and, 251, 257
Louisiana
  buffalo soldiers and, 218
  and exodus to Kansas,
    184
  relations between
    Africans and Native
    Americans in, 7–9
  and trappers, guides,
    and mountain men, 34
  women and, 260, 262
Love, Nat "Deadwood
    Dick," 157–160
Lovejoy, Elijah and Owen,
    80–81
Lowry, Edward, 113
Lynch, Ellen, 160–161
lynchings
  buffalo soldiers and, 279
  and exodus to Kansas,
    191
  Populist movement and,
    292
  women and, 268

McCabe, Edwin P., 182,
    192, 233, 235–236, 240,
    245–248, 289
McGhee, Frederick L.,
    239–295
McGregor, Tom and Rose

Anne, 51
McKinley, William, 168, 271–272, 275, 280
McPherson, James M., 114
mail-order brides, 261
Malvin, John and Harriet Dorsey, 52, 54
Mandans, 35
Manifest Destiny, 103
Mann, Horace, 103
Marchbancks, Vance, 216
Marching in the Desert (Remington), 224
maroons, maroon settlements, 13–14, 20
Martial Spirit, The (Millis), 273
Mathews, William D., 115–116
Mason, Biddy, 130–131, 251
Mason, John, 85
Mason, Lena, 260
Mason, Mary B., 63
Mason, May, 252
Massachusetts, x, 16, 23–26, 80, 101, 122, 131
Masterson, Bat, 158, 160
Mattaponies, 10
Maunder, Sara Elizabeth Heights, 258
Maverick, Mary, 73
Mays, Isaiah, 219
Meachum, John Berry, 55
Meeker, Ezra, 63
Mendoza, Antonia de, 7, 22
Menendez, Francisco, 16
Merritt, Wesley, 213
Mexican War, 117
Mexico, Mexicans
  in age of exploration, 1, 2, 7–8, 19, 21
  buffalo soldiers and, 204–205, 213, 222, 227, 229, 280, 295
  California and, 117–119,

122, 134, 136, 139, 141
  Civil War and, 110
  cowhands and, 145–149, 153, 158–159, 169, 171, 174–175, 291
  crisis years and, 89, 92, 95, 101–104
  going west and, 57, 64
  and slavery on frontier, 72, 74, 82
Michigan
  Black separatism and, 288
  crisis years and, 90, 95–96
  going west and, 44, 49, 53
Miller, Kelley, 274
Miller, Zack, 173–176
Mincy, 170–171
Miner, Sarah, 252
"Miner's Sunday in Coloma, A," 126
Minor, Patrick, 115–116
Minnesota
  buffalo soldiers and, 217
  crisis years and, 96
  going west and, 44–45, 51, 55
  McGhee and, 294–295
  and slavery on frontier, 87
  and trappers, guides, and mountain men, 29–41
  women and, 257
Minton, John, 62, 64
Mirror of the Times, 139–140, 142, 287
Mississippi
  Buffalo soldiers and, 280
  crisis years and, 98, 100, 103–104
  and exodus to Kansas, 186, 191
  McGhee and, 294
  and relations between

Africans and Native Americans, 10
  women and, 253, 260, 262
Missouri
  buffalo soldiers and, 230, 272
  California and, 124, 126–127, 134–135
  Civil War and, 109–112, 114
  crisis years and, 96–99, 109
  and exodus to Kansas, 179
  going west and, 44, 55, 60, 62–64
  and slavery on frontier, 71, 78, 87
  and trappers, guides, and mountain men, 33, 36
  women and, 255
Mitchell, William, 84
Mix, Tom, xix, 173–174
Monroe, George, 128–129
Montana, xv
  buffalo soldiers and, 202, 205, 209, 213, 217–218, 225, 272
  cowhands and, 146, 164, 169
  crisis years and, 96
  newspapers and, 289
  women and, 250, 255, 265
Montgomery, John, 119
Montgomery, Sarah, 253
Mormons, 75–76
Mullins, George C., 202
Murphy, Ike, 156–157

Narváez, Panfilo de, 21
Nebraska
  buffalo soldiers and, 205–206, 208, 213, 221
  crisis years and, 92,

96–97
exodus to Kansas,
190–194
going west and, 51
women and, 257
Negro Abraham, 20
Nevada
crisis years and, 96
and trappers, guides,
and mountain men, 37
women and, 252, 255,
259, 263–264, 268–259
Newby, William H.,
139–140
New Mexico
buffalo soldiers and,
209, 213, 217–218, 230
cowhands and, 145–147,
194
crisis years and, 92, 96
newspapers and, 289
and relations between
Africans and Native
Americans, 23, 32
going west and, 51, 64
women and, 253–255,
270
New Orleans, La.
buffalo soldiers and,
212, 218
going west and, 212
and trappers, guides,
and mountain men, 33
women and, 263
newspapers, xii, xviii, 289
buffalo soldiers and, 284
California and, 130, 139,
142
cowhands and, 173
crisis years and, 98
exodus to Kansas and,
184, 197
Oklahoma and, 235, 241
slavery and, 81
women and, 258
New York
buffalo soldiers and,

223, 278
California and, 122, 142
Civil War and, 105
cowhands and, 156, 176
Oklahoma and, 241
and relations between
Africans and Native
Americans, 4, 9, 12,
14–16
slavery and, 68, 80,
102–103
New York Times, xii, 94,
112, 176, 247
Niagara Movement, 293
Nicodemus, Kans.,
180–184
Nigger Hill, 196–197, 199
Ninth Cavalry
abroad, 272, 275–277,
280
on Western frontier, 204,
206, 210–214, 219, 221
Niza, Marcos de, 22
Norris, Eunice Russell,
195, 260
Northern Pacific Railroad,
61
North Heights, Tex., 168
Northwest Ordinance, 42,
68–69, 87

Ohio, Ohio Valley
buffalo soldiers and, 222
Civil War and, 107, 114
crisis years and, 90–91,
95–96
going west and, 42–45,
48–50, 52, 54
law and, 286–287
slavery and, 68–69,
71–72, 79–82, 84–86
"Old Bill is Dead" (Mill-
er), 176
Olmstead, Frederick Law,
94
One Horse Charley, 146
101 Ranch Wild West

Show, 173–176
Opala, Joseph, 16
Opothleyahola, 107–108
Oregon
crisis years and, 93, 94,
96
going west and, 44–45,
50–51, 60–64
and slavery on frontier,
78–79
and trappers, guides,
and mountain men, 31
women and, 263
Ovando, Nicolas de, 6

Painter, Nell Irvin, 256
Palmares, Republic of, 14
Pamunkeys, 16
Panic of 1893, 61
Parker, Isaac "Hanging
Judge," 161, 163, 240
Parker, John, 85
Parkman, Francis, 29, 37
Parsons, Albert, 266
Parsons, Lucy Gonzales,
266–267
Paul, 32
Paine, Adam, 229
Payne, Isaac, 228–229
Pearson, Richard and
Laura, 250–251
People v. Hall, 137
Pershing John J. "Black
Jack," 205
Philippines, 271, 275–279
Phillips, Joseph, 227
Pickett, Bill, xix, 173–177
Pico, Andreas, 117
Pico, Pio, 117–119
Pierce, Jim, 29
Pike, Albert, 107
Pilcher, Joshua, 30
Pioneer Boot and Shoe
Emporium, 142
Pitkin, Frederick, 67
Pleasant, Mary Ellen,
135–136

Plessy case, 292
poets, poems, 24, xviii, 222, 239, 254–255
Pontiac's War, 10
Pony Beater, 170–171
Pony Express, 128–129
Porter, Kenneth Wiggins, 152, 290
Portugal, 14, 122
Powell, Bill, 225
Powell, Colin, xix
Price, Richard, 6,
Price, W. A., 241
Prince, Lucy and Abijah, 23
Pueblo Revolt, 7
Pullen, Frank W., 272–273

Quarelles, Caroline, 71–72
Quitman, John, 103
Quivers, Emmanuel, 126, 128

railroads
  buffalo soldiers and, 221
  cowhands and, 165, 181, 184
  and exodus to Kansas going west and, 61
  Oklahoma and, 233, 236, 241, 242, 248
  women and, 270
Randolph, Mary, 94
Reeder, Andrew H., 98
Reeder, Mose, 156
Remington, Frederic, 206, 211, 214, 223–225
Reyes, Francisco, 117
Reynolds, John, 70
Richardson, Barbara, xii, 261
Richmond Planet, 273
Ricketts, M. O., 192
Roberts, James "Long," 46
Robinson, Jackie, 142
Robinson, William, 128
rodeos, 146, 154–156, 159,

169, 173–177
Rogers, Daniel, 126
Rogers, Will, 173–174
Roosevelt, Theodore, 244, 273, 278–281
Rose, Edward, 30–31
Rose, Katie, 254
Rothwell, Hattie, 254
Rough Riders, 273
Ruby, Reuben, 122
Rudisell, William and Daisy O'Brien, 255
Ruffin, Josephine St. Pierre, 190
Russell, Bessie and Lucille, 285
Russell, Charles M., xviii, 34–35

Sable, Jean Baptiste Point du, 32–33
Sacajawea, 34–37
Sacramento, Califor.
  civil rights campaigns in, 134–135, 139–140, 143
  education in, 131–134
  mining in, 124, 128–129
St. Clair, Arthur, 69
St. John, John, 67, 183, 188, 190, 260
St. Louis, Mo.,
  buffalo soldiers and, 218, 230–231
  California and, 127
  going west and, 55
  Kansas and, 187, 189
  and slavery on frontier, 71, 80, 87
  and trappers, guides, and mountain men, 36, 40
saloons
  buffalo soldiers and, 206–207, 216, 225
  California and, 130
  cowhands and, 150–154, 157–158, 164–165, 167

Oklahoma and, 247
  women and, 258
Samuels, John and Lee Anne, 181
Sand Creek massacre, xviii, 38
Sanderson, Jeremiah B., 131–132, 138
San Francisco, Calif.
  battles over slavery in, 135
  census, 117
  civil rights campaigns in, 136–142
  cultural and community organization in, 130–131
  education in, 132
  Gibbs and, 142–144
  Leidesdorff and, 118–121
  and trappers, guides, and mountain men, 37
  women and, 251, 264, 270
San Juan Hill, 222, 273, 275, 281
San Miguel de Gualdape, 5–6
Santa Anna, Antonio Lopez de, 19
Saramakas, 6
Saunders, George W., 148
Schubert, Frank, 278
Scott, Dred
  California and, 140
  crisis years and, 94
  exodus to Kansas and, 196
  and slavery on frontier, 86–88
Scott, Eliza and Lizzie, 88–87
Scott, Elizabeth Thorn, 131
Scott, Harriet Robinson, 87–88
Sculptors, 11–12

Seattle, Wash.
    going west and, 62
    women and, 252,
        257–259
Second Seminole War, 17
Sellar–Bullard family, 270
Seminole Negro Indian
    Scouts, 226–230
Seminoles, xviii
    Civil War and, 109
    cowhands and, 161
    Oklahoma and, 239
    relations between Afri
        cans and, 15–21
    slavery and, 77
Seventh Cavalry, 208, 211,
    214
Shadow and Light (Gibbs),
    143–144
Shaver, Dick, 238
Shawnees, 42–43
Sheldon, George, 24
Sherman, William Tecum-
    seh, xvii, 29, 37, 136, 208
Shirk, G. H., 77
Shores family, 192
Shorey, William T., Julia,
    Zenobia, and Victoria,
    141
Shoshones, 34, 146, 170
Siebert, Wilbur, 86
Simmons, Dick, 238
Simmons, Michael T.,
    62–64
Singleton, Benjamin "Pap,"
    185, 187–188
Sioux, xvii, xix, 211, 217
Sitting Bull, 211
Six Killer, 113
Slaughter, John, 153–154
Smallwood, James K., 194
Smaulding family, 249
Smith, James W., xix, 219
Smith, Persifer F., 136
Smith, Robert, 131
Smith, Silas, Melissa Bul-
    ware, and Nolle, 252

Smothers, Samuel, 55
Spain
    in age of exploration,
        6–7, 17, 21
    American imperialism
        and, 270, 275, 279, 294
    California and, 117
    cowhands and, 165, 171
    crisis years and, 103
Spanish–American War,
    222, 293
Sprague, John T., 19
Stahl, Jesse, 154–155
Stance, Emanuel, 210
Stevenson, James, 28–29
Storke, Barbara, 270
Stowe, Harriet Beecher,
    81, 90
Streeter, Floyd, 165
Sullivan, John L., 153
Sumner, Charles, 198, 101
Supreme Court, U.S.
    Dred Scott and, 94, 196
    Edwin P. McCabe and,
        245
    Plessy and, 292
    slavery and, 69, 87–88
Sutton family, 233

Taney, Roger B., 87
Taylor, Quintard, 179
Taylor family, 191
Tennessee
    Civil War and, 109
    cowhands and, 164
    crisis years and, 96, 103
    and exodus to Kansas,
        179, 187
    and relations between
        Africans and Native
        Americans, 16
    women and, 262, 269
Tenth Cavalry
    abroad, 273–274
    cowhands and, 160
    race war and, 280
    Remington on, 223–225

    on western frontier,
        202–206, 214–217,
        220, 222
Terry, Lucy. See Prince,
    Lucy Terry
Tex, 147
Texas
    Black towns in, 194, 283
    buffalo soldiers and, 204,
        206–209, 213,
        215–216, 218, 225–231
    Civil War and, 108, 112
    cultural and community
        organization in, 285,
        287, 290
    cowhands and, 145–148,
        152–156, 158–160,
        165–175, 291
    crisis years and, 94, 96,
        101
    and exodus to Kansas,
        178, 184, 193, 199
    and exodus to Oklaho
        ma, 236
    going west and, 55–57
    Griggs and, 292–295
    race war and, 280–282
    and relations between
        Africans and Native
        Americans, 19
    slavery and, 72–74, 82,
        125
    women in, 253, 262–263,
        265–266
Texas Rangers, 204, 216
They Came Before Colum-
    bus (Van Sertima), xviii
Thomas, James and Mar-
    guerite, 260
Thompson, James, 269
Thompson, Neva, 269
Thurston, Samuel, 93
Ticknor, Isaac, 25
Tickup, 170–171
Tilghman, Mrs., 259
Tillman, Ben "Pitchfork,"
    279

Timboe, 3
Tocqueville, Alexis de, 47
Todd, Edgeley W., 30
Tomahawk (film), 38–39
"To the Great Exodus"
    (Truth), 189
Trail of Blood on Ice,
    107–109
Trail of Tears, 43, 77
"Tribute Paid to Negro
    Cowmen" (Hendrix), 152
Trumbull, Lyman, 94
Truth, Sojourner, 81, 189
Turner, George, 69
Turner, Henry M., 274,
    276
Tuner, James M., 55
Turner, James Milton, 243
Turner, John, 255
Twain, Mark, 276
Twenty–fourth Infantry
    Regiment
    abroad, 272, 277, 280, 282
    on Western frontier,
        201–202, 218–219
Twenty–fifth Infantry
    Regiment
    abroad, 277, 281
    on Western frontier, 202,
        209, 217–218, 272–273
Tyler, Royall, 25

Uncle Jesse, 239
Uncle Mose, 97
Uncle Tom's Cabin (Stowe),
    70, 81, 90, 180
*Under Fire with the Tenth
    U.S. Cavalry* (Bivins),
    272
Underground Railroad
    California and, 142
    Civil War and, 115
    crisis years and
    exodus to Kansas and,
        197
    going West and, 58, 60
    and slavery on frontier,

60, 72, 82, 84–86, 287
Union
    Civil War and, 105–109,
        112–116
    crisis years and, 94,
        100–101, 103
    going west and, 47, 60
    slavery and, 71, 87, 92
Utah
    buffalo soldiers and,
        213, 222, 272, 279–280
    California and, 130
    crisis years and, 92, 96
    going west and, 50
    newspapers and, 289
    slavery in, 75–76
    women and, 250–251
Utes, 171, 204, 211

Valdez, Maria Rita, 117
Vandenburgh, Henry, 69
Van Sertima, Ivan, xvii–
    xviii
Vermont, 24–25
Villa, Pancho, 205, 222
Vince, Allen and Sandy, 74
Virginia   .
    buffalo soldiers and, 222
    crisis years and, 103
    and exodus to Kansas,
        178, 184
    going west and, 43, 60,
        65
    relations between
        Africans and Native
        Americans in, 9, 10, 16
    slavery and, 82
Voice of the Fugitive, 95,
    287
Voltaire, xvi, 11
voting rights
    California and, 137
    crisis years and, 92
    going west and, 50
    women and, 265
    restrictions on, 292, 286

Waggoner, Henry O.,
    197–198
Walker, Arthur L., 149
Walker, William, 103
Wallace, Daniel W., 172
Ward, John, 228
Ward, Mary, 251
War Department, 111,
    113, 211, 282
Warner, Judge, 100
Washington
    crisis years and, 92, 96
    going west and, 44, 50,
        65–66
    women and, 259
Washington, Booker T.,
    194, 222, 294
Washington, D.C., xix, 17,
    19, 20, 106, 110, 185,
    198, 200, 206, 277
Washington, George
    (Centralia founder),
    60–61
Washington, George
    (president), 9, 239
Wattles, August, 43
Wells, Ida B., xii, 236, 268
Western novels, 156
West Point, 205, 219–222
Wham, J. W., 219
Whittaker, Johnson C.,
    xix, 220
Wild Cat, 19, 21
Williams, Cathay, 230–231
Williams, Elijah, 25
Williams, George H., 79
Williams, George Wash-
    ington, xviii, 203
Williams, Moses, 210
Wilmington riot, 279, 290
Wilson, Woodrow, xvi
Winkfield, Jimmie, 157
Wisconsin
    crisis years and, 90, 92,
        94, 96
    going west and, 44, 50

slavery and, 72
and trappers, guides,
    and mountain men, 41
Wise, Henry A., 103
Wood, Fernando, 106
Woods, Peter, 3
Woodson, Carter G., xviii,
    10
Woodson, Sara Jane, 54
World War I, 195, 222, 282
World War II, 245, 272,
    282
Wright, J. Leitch, Jr., xviii,
    3
Wyoming
    buffalo soldiers and,
        206, 222,
    cowhands and, 146, 170
    crisis years and, 96
    exodus to Kansas and,
        198
    newspapers and, 289
    women and, 252,
        255–256

York, 34–36
Young, Brigham, 75
Young, Charles, 222, 280

About the Author

William Loren Katz is the author of 40 books, including such award-winning titles as *Breaking the Chains* and *Black Women of the Old West*. He has been a Scholar in Residence at Teachers College, Columbia University, and he has served as a consultant to the Smithsonian Institution and to school systems from California to Florida and England.